NATURE AND S(

Nature has become increasingly central to social thinking. From the social implications of environmental degradation to the plethora of issues raised by biotechnology, genomics, neuroscience and health, the 'natural' world is increasingly difficult to ignore for sociologists and social scientists. In addition to a wide-ranging treatment of this field, this ground-breaking text presents fresh perspectives that challenge the way we think about the relationship between 'time', 'nature' and 'society'.

Although the natural and social are inevitably intertwined, Tim Newton argues that we should be open to the possibility of difference in our preception of them. In so doing, he contests accepted tenets, such as an overriding need for anti-dualism, and underscores the limitations of current approaches such as social constructionism and critical realism. In addition, he engages with the burgeoning debates on new genetics and neuroscience, takes the material world and human biology seriously, and addresses the issues of interdisciplinarity that are likely to arise in any longer term attempt to work across the social and natural world.

Nature and Sociology will be of great interest to students of a variety of disciplines including Sociology, Psychology, Philosophy and Human Geography, Social and Biological Antropology, and the Life and Physical Sciences.

Tim Newton is Professor of Organisations and Society at the University of Exeter. His current research interests include social theory, sociology and nature, interdisciplinarity, and the historical relationship between commercialisation and the self. He has published widely within sociology, psychology and organisation studies journals.

NATURE
AND
SOCIOLOGY

Tim Newton

Routledge
Taylor & Francis Group

LONDON AND NEW YORK

First published 2007
by Routledge
2 Park Square, Milton Park, Abingdon, Oxon OX14 4RN

Simultaneously published in the USA and Canada
by Routledge
270 Madison Ave, New York, NY 10016

Routledge is an imprint of the Taylor & Francis Group, an informa business

© 2007 Tim Newton

Typeset in Galliard by
Integra Software Services Pvt. Ltd, Pondicherry, India
Printed and bound in Great Britain by
Antony Rowe Ltd, Chippenham, Wiltshire

British Library Cataloguing in Publication Data
A catalogue record for this book is available from the British Library

Library of Congress Cataloging in Publication Data
Newton, Tim.

Nature and sociology / Tim Newton.
p. cm.
ISBN 978-0-415-36684-7 (hard cover)--
ISBN 978-0-415-36683-0 (paper cover)
1. Nature--Social aspects. 2. Geographical perception. 3. Nature and
nurture. 4. Human beings--Effect of environment on 5. Sociology--
Philosophy. 6. Philosophy of nature. 7. Sociobiology.
8. Body, Human--Social aspects. 9. Human genome. I. Title.

HM856.N48 2007

304.2--dc22

2007001560

ISBN 978–041536684–7 (hbk)
ISBN 978–041536683–0 (pbk)
ISBN 978–020301945–0 (ebk)

CONTENTS

ACKNOWLEDGEMENTS

I would like to thank all those who commented on this book, or on earlier related papers, including Phil Sutton, Ian Burkitt, Martin Wood, Chris Drummond, Robin Canniford and Kate Soper. Chapter 2 contains a small amount of material that was previously published as 'Power, subjectivity and British industrial and organizational sociology: The relevance of the work of Norbert Elias', in *Sociology*, 33 (2): 411–440. Similarly, Chapters 2–6 includes occasional passages that were published in 'Crossing the great divide: Time, nature and the social', in *Sociology*, 37 (3): 433–457. In addition, part of Chapter 8 is based on a previously published article, 'Truly embodied sociology: Marrying the social and the biological?', that appeared in *The Sociological Review*, 51 (1): 20–42. My thanks to both journals, and their editors, for permission to reprint material from these articles here.

1

RECOVERING NATURE

In some ways this is a perverse book. Ostensibly it forms part of the growing sociological attention to the relationship between 'nature' and 'society'. Yet its argument swims against the tide of current conjecture in this field. First, contrary to present fashions, it asks whether there remain differences in our perception of the natural and social domain. Second, in spite of sympathising with the desire to interrelate the social and natural sciences, the ensuing argument will continually point to the difficulty of this enterprise.

There are reasons for this perversity. One of these derives from the conventional desire to resist dominant ways of thinking lest they become sufficiently overbearing to deny the possibility of difference. Another hails from the need to underscore the constraints of any exercise if one is to pursue its realisation. In what follows, I wish to explore such differences and constraints through attention to sociological debate concerning the human body, health and the natural environment as well as the 'designs' on our bodies that are represented by new genetics and genomics.

It might be argued that sociologists should still not engage with the natural world. This argument makes sense to the extent that it is difficult to work across the natural and social domain. In addition, there remain reasons to be wary of accounts of ourselves that mix biology and sociology. For instance, sociologists have traditionally been hostile to biological accounts of gender because of the danger that they would legitimate patriarchy and androcentrism as a 'natural and normal' state of affairs (Birke, 1999). Similarly, 'bio-medical' models of health have reproduced accounts of human life which, in spite of a range of reports, still tend to downplay concerns with social inequality and material deprivation (Townsend and Davidson, 1980; Williams and Bendelow, 1998). These anxieties about biologism have been sharpened by projects such as socio-biology and evolutionary psychology. Within the latter, the entire complexity of the social and natural world can be reduced to the desire of a 'gene' or a 'meme' on the basis of formulaic models of natural selection that, at worst, rely on a 'mixture of the stereotypic, the outrageous and the banal' (Dupré, 2001: 54). Concerns about the biological realm have also been buttressed by legacies that have maintained the 'Great Divide' between nature and society. Even where there has been an emphasis on materiality and life, as with Marxism, it can appear that 'with some notable exceptions, . . . "Western Marxism" . . . has been as firmly committed to a dualistic *opposition* between nature and culture as has its "bourgeois" counterpart' (Benton, 1991: 7). The dangers of addressing biology within a social context are also underlined by the difficulty of inventing a term for this terrain which is not already tainted by association, such as 'sociobiology', the 'biosocial' or 'sociological biology' (Shilling, 2003).

With this formidable inheritance, it can seem remarkable that anyone has attempted to erode the partition between sociology and nature. Yet over the past two decades there has been a range of such endeavour. This includes work which has campaigned for the overall project (e.g. Benton, 1991, 2003; Shilling, 1993/2003; Jenkins, 2002), as well as that which has broadened our understanding of the sociology of health and emotion (e.g. Freund, 1990; Williams, 2003a), and that which has strived to reconcile human biology with feminism (e.g. Birke, 1986, 1999; Wilson, 2004). In addition, writers have tried to re-insert a 'biological body' into the sociology of the body by furthering 'a realignment between sociology and biology' (Shilling, 1993: 104), and re-emphasised the material world by treating nature as though 'it did matter' (Murphy, 1994a, 1997; Collins, 1996; Murdoch, 2001), or used the biological frailty of embodiment as a basis to defend a foundational ontology of human rights (Turner and Rojek, 2001). In spite of these varied projects, there still remains more than a grain of truth in Richard Jenkins comment that 'for the moment . . . biology and nature remain almost dirty words within sociology' (2002: 113). Yet a failure to enter the biological terrain represents an implicit acceptance of the 'Great Divide' between nature and society and its assumption that to 'the natural scientist [belong] the things, to the sociologists the remainder, that is, the humans' (Callon and Latour, 1992: 357).

In this book, I shall explore the argument which suggests that 'nature' and its materiality should be incorporated as legitimate aspects of sociological inquiry. Yet at the same time, I will question whether it is possible to construct a 'non-reductionist . . . *theoretical integration* of the human and life-sciences' (Benton, 1991: 21, added emphasis). To put this another way, circling this realm is a range of epistemological debate, of which the most prominent has been that between realists, and critical realists, and 'strict' and 'soft' social constructionists. In approaching this extended, and frequently fractious, debate, I shall be guided by a couple of key thoughts. First, it is still not clear that 'the observer [can] abandon all a priori distinctions between natural and social events' (Callon, 1986: 313). Second, to understand the natural and social domain, it can be helpful to address our *perception* of natural and social temporality.

Forgotten bodies

Human biology can eschew sociological attention because it is such a routine aspect of everyday life. Though we are entirely dependent on our bodies, we tend to forget that 'without this body, with this tongue or these ears, you could neither speak nor hear another's voice' (Abram, 1997: 45). Examining the relation between human biology and sociality therefore requires a re-examination of the taken for granted (Leder, 1990; Shilling, 2003; Gimlin, 2006). For instance, we tend to overlook everyday aspects of our biological selves such as the significance of the human hand. As Bendelow and Williams note:

> the human hand . . . is a remarkable feat of evolutionary engineering: a single tool which manipulates an astonishing variety of objects of different shapes, weights and sizes, each of which needs a precise combination of muscle tensions that mould it into the right shape for the "task in hand".
>
> (1998: 18)

Ian Burkitt argues that tools are also critical to human communication and evolution (Washburn, 1960). They represent 'artifacts with a symbolic significance' (Burkitt, 1999: 40) as reflected in the intricacy of distinctive human activities such as writing, painting, designing, carving, sewing, cooking, and so on. Yet in spite of the social significance of our hands, and the tools they manipulate, they can be so quotidian that we fail to recognise them. Drew Leder reports psychological research which suggests that 90 per cent of people are unable to recognise a picture of their own hands from a small series of such pictures. As Leder observes, the hand represents 'the organ with which I perform my labor, eat my food, caress my loved ones, yet remains a stranger to me' (1990: 1).

Like the hand, the human face allows for considerable complexity and subtlety in communication. Stephen Mennell notes that in comparison to humans 'even the apes have relatively rigid, immobile faces' (1989: 205). Such facial complexity allows for extraordinary characteristics such as the human smile. Except in an evolutionary sense, the smile remains an *extra-discursive* aspect of our biology yet one that is *central* to social discourse (Shilling, 2003). It is a leading actor in our non-verbal repertoire and one that enables considerable communicative subtlety and 'a rich variety of shades of feeling' (Elias, 1987a: 359). As Elias notes, the smile 'can be a hesitant, a withdrawn, a broad, a triumphant, a supercilious and even a hostile smile' (1987a: 359). A more graphic illustration of this subtlety is provided by the musings of a character in one of A.L. Kennedy's short stories. As this character observes:

> You see, there are many types of smile. Everyone is familiar with the insincere *screwyoureally* sort, the *I'mdyingbutkeepingitin*, the *JesusI'mscaredandIhaven'tacluewhatmyfaceisupto* . . . But there is a special smile also, one that can be neither prepared, not simulated, and which convinces me of God's essential benevolence: it has the effect of unquestioning undiluted love and is entirely beautiful.
>
> (2004: 25)

One does not have to share this character's feelings about celestial beneficence in order to relate to this part of our common, and biologically based, humanity. If we follow some life scientists, the distinction between A.L. Kennedy's 'insincere' and 'entirely beautiful' smile also appears closely interwoven with the our brain's neurology. V.S. Ramachandran and Sandra Blakeslee suggest that the sincere 'spontaneous smile is produced by the basal ganglia, clusters of cells found between the brains higher cortex (where thinking and planning take place) and the evolutionary older thalamus' (1998: 13). In contrast, they argue that an insincere smile represents an interaction between the 'higher thinking centers in the brain' and the 'motor cortex . . . which specializes in producing *voluntary* skilled movements' (1998: 14, added emphasis). Yet since smiling 'involves the careful orchestration of dozens of tiny muscles' (1998: 14), it seems that the motor cortex is not up to the job. If we accept such neurological conjecture, an insincere smile can only remain 'forced, tight, unnatural' (1998: 14).

These neurological niceties are also significant to intersubjective machineries of power. This is epitomised by Elias's (1994) study of absolutist royal courts, such as that of Louis XIV. In this work, Elias showed the importance of our human biological make-up to skilled socio-political performance. Drawing on La Bruyére, he noted that the 'accomplished courtier is master of his gestures, his eyes, his face; he is deep and impenetrable; he can dissemble when he is doing an ill turn, *smile on his enemies*' (La Bruyère, 1890: 112, added emphasis, cited, though with a different translation, in Elias, 1994: 476). This oft-cited Eliasian quotation shows how human biology is not just a matter of physiological functioning, or the psychology of interpersonal communication. It is also a means by which we play out power relations. Elias's attention to this machinery of power reminds us how smiling, like other bodily repertoires, forms part of a complex of human emotions that resonate simultaneously through both our bodies and our culture. On the one hand, our emotions are interwoven with our culture, as revealed in the variance of emotional vocabulary across different cultures (Lutz, 1988). On the other hand, emotion is a biologically embodied experience. As William Connolly notes, our affective

> energies find symptomatic expression in the timbre of our voices, the calmness or intensity of our gestures, our facial expressions, the flush of our faces, the rate of our heartbeats, the receptivity, tightness or sweatiness of our skin, and the relaxation or turmoil in our guts.
>
> (2002: 76)

In this manner, our ubiquitous emotions illustrate the intertwining of human biology and culture: emotion represents a biosocial endowment that is central to the expression of human culture (Elias, 1991a).

Yet just as we take our emotional repertoire for granted, so we also tend to forget that our ability to sense anything about our world relies on complex biological interaction, such as that between our sense organs and our brain.

4

A well-known example of this interaction was provided in 1668 by Edme Mariotte's illustration of the perceptual 'blind spot'. The blind spot corresponds to the area where the optic nerve enters the eye. Since we have no photoreceptor cells at this point, there is a blind spot in our eye's perception. However we are not normally aware of this blind spot, or *scotoma*, because our brain appears to 'fill in' the missing detail with information from our other eye. The import of Mariotte's (1668) initial experiment can be easily demonstrated. Take a look at the letters below. Then move this book close to your eyes, cover your right eye and focus the left eye on the 'X'. Keeping your left eye firmly focused on the X, slowly move the book away from you until the O disappears. Following Mariotte (1668), you have discovered your left eye's blind spot.

O   X

Although you may have tried this simple experiment at school, we tend to forget its central implication, namely that our awareness of the world is reliant on intricate biological interaction. It seems that we do not see blind spots because our brain, eye and optic nerve continually interact so as to compensate for our loss of vision. The efficacy of such perceptual processes means that we need rarely stop to question their operations. Nevertheless the ability to see a smile, or to more generally socially interact, appears reliant on the evolution of this complex biology of perception.

According to Nick Crossley, many other aspects of human communication are also deeply social yet are as much a result of our inherited biological capabilities as our social learning. Crossley quotes Meltzoff and Moore's (1983) observation that 'only 42 *minutes* after birth an infant will respond to an adult protrusion of the tongue with a similar gesture – long before they have grasped the concept "tongue" or had time to realize that both they and the parent have one' (Crossley, 1997: 27, original emphasis). This pre-linguistic intercorporeality appears central to the learning of sociality in early childhood development. At the same time, it is part of a more general pre-conscious 'conversation of gestures' between people, as observed when we simultaneously yawn or mirror each other's non-verbal behaviour (Mead, 1934; Merleau-Ponty, 1962, 1968; Goffman, 1971). Such examples are more than just practical consciousness (Giddens, 1984): they suggest that 'a pre-given and primordial "intercorporeality" '(Crossley, 1997: 28) is central to how we both learn and perform human sociality. As with other human characteristics such as the correlation between the human hand and tool use, these facets define the particularities of human social life. In this context, it can seem bizarre that part of the 'sociological faith' is the 'belief that biology and physiology have little or no role to play in explaining the "social" or "cultural" phenomena which interest sociologists' (Jenkins, 2002: 112).

It is also easy to forget how biology informs one of the most distinguishing facets of human beings, namely our capacity for language. Human language and talk 'brings into play various organic elements; not only the larynx, but the mouth and lips, and the overall motricity of the face' (Deleuze and Guattari, 1988:61). In short, the spoken language is a bodily performance (Merleau-Ponty, 1962). It is not just that we need a tongue and larynx, etc, but that we 'taste' words as they 'roll off' our tongues and resonate through our bodies (Abram, 1997: 75). At the same time, this biologically enabled ability has allowed humans to move beyond the limitations of biology and ensure that our evolution is socio-culturally based (Burkitt, 1999). Our biology does not pre-programme our behaviour because our capacity for language means that we can operate well outside of the programmatic. In other words, as with our technological skill, our remarkable linguistic abilities encourage the plasticity which characterises human behaviour. As Gilles Deleuze and Félix Guattari note, this is because the linguistic 'form of expression is independent of substance' (1988: 62). Or as Elias (1991a) stresses, the peculiarities of our biology mean that we are not defined by it. This means that:

> in the case of human societies a great deal of social change can occur such as that from tribe to empire without any biological change . . . Languages enable humans to transmit knowledge from one generation to another and thus make it possible for human knowledge to grow.
>
> (Elias, 1991a: 32)

The remarkable range of symbolisation that occurs in human language is not matched in *quite* the same way in other animal species,[1] and neither is there the same linguistically based capacity for abstract thought and its cumulative development. Together with our extraordinary manipulation of tools, this allows for a distinctive openness in the way we interrelate with our world, as well as the ability to convey the knowledge so gained across generations (Elias, 1991a). In this sense, we can transcend time and space. Nevertheless, this transcendence remains completely interwoven with our biology. Human plasticity arises because 'human beings are *biologically capable* of changing the manner of their social life' (Elias, 1991a: 36, added emphasis). It is this biological capacity that has enabled remarkable social change in human societies, such as the move within a single millennium from tribalism to feudalism, monarchy, urban-industrialism, capitalism and global capitalism.

Together these arguments reinforce the proposition that sociologists should attend to the materiality and biology of the human body, since they suggest that such corporeality is deeply implicated in the social fabric. It is this very close interweaving between our social and biological reality that allows us to take it for granted. Another example of the commonplace nature of this relationship is found in the fact the human race has two genders with a roughly equal divide between them: other things being equal, slightly more boys than girls are born (an androcentrically defined 'sex ratio' of 105, or 5 per cent more boys than girls; Heer, 1975; Goodkind, 1999). Yet the social significance of human gender balance receives *comparatively* little attention. On the one hand, feminist study has enabled a wide range of work on the sociology of gender. On the other hand, there is little concern with the arithmetic of gender balance, except in relation to the politics of female infanticide and prenatal sex selection (see p. 11). However different social relations might pertain if this balance were markedly uneven. In addition, the achievement of an even proportion between the sexes remains a remarkable achievement since it represents a *global* social phenomenon that is somehow produced by *individual* mating. All those 'private' fertilisations of ova by sperm add up to an incredibly balanced 'public' global arithmetic, even though this collective social accounting is dependent on the interaction between 'open' heterosexuality and 'open' biological processes (the meeting of an ova with an XX or XY chromosome). Although there are indications that gender balance in some animals responds to environmental change (e.g. Clutton-Brock and Iason, 1986; West and Sheldon, 2002), or even in relation to human personality (Grant, 1998) and human socio-political context (Cain, 1993),[2] it is extraordinary that a combination of social and biological process achieves such a balance in the first place, especially when it occurs across billions of people. In sum, biological bodies have 'conversations' that are not only independent of the conscious wishes and discourse of individuals, but also produce astonishing collective social arithmetic at a global level. If one were just reliant on human discourse, only a dictatorial control of the sex of unborn children could produce such globally *balanced* arithmetic, and yet it happens 'naturally' through a collective social and biological process. The paradox of this arithmetic is that it is highly socially significant and yet *extra-discursive* in much of its operation.

These quotidian examples of the close relationship between our social and biological selves reinforce Ted Benton's call for a 're-alignment of the human social sciences with the life-sciences' (Benton, 1991: 25) and Michael Bury's call 'to rethink the relationship between sociology and the biological sciences' (1997: 199). If nothing else, they suggest that sociologists should make greater efforts to cross the 'Great Divide' since they imply that to ignore our biology is to circumscribe our understanding of the social.

The politics of nature

'Nature' has long been an ambiguous and dangerous term because of the various ways it has been used to define and enrol us (Soper, 1995). On the one hand, it has been co-opted in order to abuse and exploit, as witnessed in attempts to define the 'natural' superiority of Caucasians, the subjugation of women through their assignment to their 'naturally' subordinate position, or the repression of lower social classes through the erection of a 'natural' social hierarchy or caste system. And lest we think of this as history, there remain numerous contemporary examples of the use of nature in the service of subjugation. For instance, labour market research suggests that ethnicity, gender, sexuality, age, and disability are still routinely used in order to limit access to work. In this manner, it is easy to see nature as an agent of reactionary cultural desire. Yet on the other hand, nature is also increasingly perceived as the subject of cultural abuse through activities such as the degradation of the natural environment, or its subversion through techniques such as prenatal sex selection. Nature can therefore appear Janus-faced, repressed and repressor. It is not surprising therefore that 'the concept of the natural continues to carry enormous moral weight and emotional power' (Sagoff, 2005: 74).

In consequence, 'nature' has strong political connotations, as is witnessed in sociological debate about the body, health and the natural environment (Benton, 1991; Soper, 1995; Yearley, 1996; Dickens, 1996, 2001; Goldblatt, 1996; Murphy, 1997; Adam, 1998; Shilling, 2003). Although much of the discussion of this book will be concerned with understanding the social and natural domain, its argument will periodically reference their political consequence. In order to introduce such political issues to the less informed, three exemplars will now be considered: the politics of environmental degradation; health and the human body; gender and pre-natal sex selection.

Environmental degradation

It is difficult to contemplate nature without considering its current degradation. On the one hand, some writers still question the significance of environmental risks (e.g. Lomborg, 2001). On the other, there are concerns that changes to the environment may be more pronounced than previously anticipated. For instance, the UN's Intergovernmental Panel on Climate Change has raised its forecast for global warming from 3°C to the possibility of almost 6°C by 2100 (Houghton *et al.*, 2001). In addition, environmental threats such as global warming occasion a variety of risk scenarios. These include the flooding of densely populated land, as in Bangladesh and the Nile delta, the 'disappearance' of Pacific islands, and the loss of low-lying land in Western countries such as the Netherlands and the Mississippi delta (Houghton, 2004). There are also concerns that global warming will exacerbate water shortages and falling crop yields in developing countries, and accelerate desertification in areas such as the Southern Mediterranean, North and Southern Africa and the Sahel. More controversial arguments include the suggestion that global warming will raise some surface sea level temperatures beyond 26.5°C, and as a consequence, occasion a rapidity of typhoons, tropical cyclones and hurricanes. In other areas of the world, there is the possibility that the melting of the North polar ice caps will cause sufficient cooling of Atlantic waters to 'turn off' the 'conveyor belt' that brings the warm air and water of the Gulf Stream to North and West Europe. Though considerable hype can surround such doom-laden scenarios, whether through the alarmist briefings of green pressure groups or Hollywood blockbusters such as *The Day After Tomorrow*, this does not detract from their significance. As Peter Dickens argues, 'While the apocalyptic visions of irreversible environmental degradation may still turn out to be over-stated there is still plenty of evidence of widespread environmental destruction' (1996: 27). In particular, the heavily mediatised debate about global warming can detract from other environmental concerns such as species extinction and loss of bio-diversity, soil degradation and depletion of the ozone layer, air and water pollution, toxic waste, nuclear radiation, and so on. In addition, there are concerns relating to nitrogen emissions caused by fertilisers and fossil fuels, with some environmental scientists suggesting that nitrogen emissions are more important than carbon emissions (because high emissions can occasion de-oxygenation of rivers and lakes).

Surrounding all these debates are anxieties about the geopolitics of energy. For example, there are predictions that we will experience short-falls in oil production at some time between 2007 and 2025 from organisations as various as the Peak Oil Association, Greenpeace and Shell. Although there is considerable debate and contestation in this area (e.g. see Odell, 2004), there remains concern that 'the tip over point' – where oil demand exceeds supply and prices accelerate – will be reached before alternative supplies of energy will be on stream. Such predictions arouse 'Doomsday' fears that have as much to do with the possibility of an entrenched global recession as the pursuit of a green agenda.

Whether these risks should be seen as underplayed or unnecessarily cautious (Furedi, 2005), they point to the way in which the relationship between human beings and nature remains both contentious and central to human society. At the same time, they illustrate the difficulty of regulating the relationship between human beings and the natural environment. For example, the ability to reach global ecological agreements has had a chequered career, most notably in the difficulties experienced in getting the USA to ratify the Kyoto protocol. In addition, some of those who are signatories to Kyoto are pursuing environmental policies that are at odds with their supposed commitments. For instance, the recent UK government's White Paper, *The Future of Aviation*, envisages increases in British aviation carbon dioxide emissions which 'even by 2010 . . . would entirely negate the reductions achieved by the Government under the Kyoto Protocol . . . ' (House of Commons Environmental Audit Committee, 2003: 9; see Newton, 2005). Such observations raise doubts as to whether global environmental agreements can be adequately policed, whether in the 'North' or the 'South' (Yearley, 1996; Gray, 1999).

The history of environmental degradation illustrates the continuing significance of nature for all life forms on this planet (Goldblatt, 1996). It reminds us that human beings appear closely dependent on, and interdependent with, the natural world (Elias, 1991a). In addition, it points to the gross inequalities between people in their access to the world's resources since, for many people, the need to degrade the natural environment is interrelated with the threat of famine, disease and poverty (Dryzek, 1997; Banerjee, 2003). Yet the sociology of the natural environment is not the only arena in which human biosociality is interwoven with social inequality. As a now lengthy tradition in sociology reminds us, human bodies are an expression of a variety of power relations (Bourdieu, 1989; Elias, 1994).

Health and the body

There is an unusual level of agreement that health inequalities persist in western countries such as Britain, 'whether measured in terms of mortality, life expectancy or health status' (Acheson, 1998: 10). Put bluntly, it would appear that if you are from a lower social class in the UK, you are more likely to die in infancy, and if you survive, you will probably have a significantly shorter life, and suffer greater physical and mental ill-health during that life (Acheson, 1998; Shaw *et al.*, 1999, 2002). As Shaw *et al.*, note, social class differences in health have 'real, lethal meaning for large groups of people living in Britain today' (1999: 107, cited in Williams, 2003a: 47). There is also evidence that indicates that countries which have lower income inequality exhibit lower class-related differences in health, such as in Sweden and Japan (Wilkinson, 1996; Williams, 2003a). In addition, there are suggestions that 'health class' differences have been exacerbated by neo-liberalist economics and the decline of the welfare state (Coburn, 2000).

In sum, health remains a fiercely political issue. It is therefore not surprising that sociologists have examined its politics by attending to issues of class, as well of those of gender, ethnicity and sexuality, and the broader ideology of 'medicalization'. Early commentators suggested that the latter ideology provided a convenient means of social control (Zola, 1972; Illich, 1975), although this thesis was subject to later critique on the grounds that it overplayed the passivity of patients (Taussig, 1980) and the complex processes through which health is managed (Conrad, 1992). Foucauldian analyses furthered such critique to the extent that they questioned simple images of medicalised social control and emphasised the ways in which people bought into new health-related subjectivities, such as those relating to the 'management' of 'psychological stress' (Newton, 1995) or the need for fitness and diet regimes and the self-management of health (Lupton, 1995). At the same time, some writers feared that the net effect of this sociological critique, particularly in its latter Foucauldian and post-structural form, was to lose sight of biology (Bury, 1995) and the significant role which medicine has played in 'improvements in the quality of life of the Western population over the past century' (Williams, 2003a: 20). In addition, there remain concerns that sociological critique ignores the complexity and open-endedness of medical practice (Kelly and Field, 1994, 1996) and the fact that 'medicine itself is not composed of a body of like-minded individuals' (Williams, 2003a: 20).

Some writers have suggested that the politics of health is also mediated by psychosocial processes. For instance, Wilkinson suggests that:

> The poor suffer psychosocial effects of deprivation as well as its direct material effects. Indeed it is important to recognise that as well as the greatest material deprivation, those at the bottom of the social hierarchy also suffer the greatest social, psychological and emotional deprivation,

and this may well have a greater impact than the more direct effects of material deprivation.

(1996: 176, cited in Williams, 2003a: 48)

Though the 'psychosocial' refers to a multitude of processes (Elstad, 1998) whose influence is contested (Carroll *et al.*, 1996), there is nevertheless growing interest in the socio-political pathways through which the social context of people's lives becomes translated into health outcomes. For instance, Peter Freund (1990) draws on Arlie Hochschild (1983) in order to argue that the social status of individuals affects their physiological functioning, which in turn influences their health (see Chapter 8). As Williams comments on Freund, 'the implications of his argument seem to suggest . . . that society affects physiological reactivity deep within the recesses of the human body . . . ' (2003a: 51).

These claims provide further support for the argument that our social under-standing is foreshortened if it ignores biological issues. If we follow Freund, we can only understand the politics of health by attending to the biological path-ways through which social inequality becomes translated into health inequality. In effect, such argument reinforces the position of those who stress that 'for far too long, the biological has been dismissed as irrelevant to the sociological enterprise' (Williams and Bendelow, 1998: 211).

Gender and prenatal sex selection

Gender forms a central part of any politics of nature since discourses about nature have long been deployed as a means to define gender, especially as this relates to the confinement and repression of women (e.g. Soper, 1995, Birke; 1999; Wilson, 2004). A dramatic illustration of this argument is provided by biological techniques that provide a means to eliminate rather than just confine or repress. Prenatal sex selection (PSS) provides the technological ability to determine the sex of the unborn child. It provides further illustration of the significance of 'nature' for our social and political lives since the predominant fear with PSS is that it will be used to deny girls a right to life through 'female "foeticide" ' (Brown and Webster, 2004: 59). In addition, the politics of PSS also demon-strate tensions between the rhetoric of 'consumer choice' and the ethical concern for human rights. On the one hand, there are clinicians and life scientists who are argue in favour of the parents' right to choose the sex of their children. On the other hand, other commentators suggest that PSS further enables prenatal female infanticide, particularly in patriarchal societies. Authors such as Kusum argue that PSS in India enforces discrimination against women not just from the 'cradle to the grave' but 'now from womb to the grave' because it is used to favour the birth of boys over girls (1993: 163). Others suggest that PSS has been part of 'massive societal change' in countries such as Korea and China (Stephen, 2000: 301). Daniel Goodkind argues that 'recent evidence from East Asia suggests that parents use prenatal sex testing to selectively abort female foetuses, a practice manifested in rising sex ratios (males per females)' (1996: 111; cf. the House of Commons Select Committee on International Development, 1999). He further argues that sex ratios ordinarily total about 105–106 males per 100 females, but they have recently reached 113 in Korea and China and 110 in Taiwan (Goodkind, 1999). Even though countries such as India and China have enacted legislation outlawing PSS, Sudha and Rajan note that such legislation has 'had little impact' in India (1999: 585). These concerns are qualified by those who suggest that the 'real magnitude' of sex-selective abortion 'has been exaggerated' in China due to 'the under-counting of female births' (Peng and Huang, 1999: 487). In addition, other commentators suggest that PSS may actually be preferable to the use of backstreet abortion. Yet what remains alarming is the apparent attitude of medical professionals whose work impacts on PSS. In a study of 2903 medical geneticists and genetic counsellors located in 37 countries, Dorothy Wertz and John Fletcher reported that 'few, except for geneticists in India, mentioned the societal implications of sex selection' (1998: 257). Even though PSS decisions determine who has the right to life, Wertz and Fletcher indicated that 'the typical response' of medical geneticists was 'as follows: I don't approve of sex selection, but *they have the right to make their own decisions*' (1998: 269, added emphasis). This acceptance of the ideology of consumption leads some to fear that prenatal intervention may lead to the surrender of medical genetics to 'free-market eugenics' as 'free' consumers choose not just the sex of their child but a range of other cosmetic 'enhancements'. In other words, pre-implantation diagnosis will be used to select human embryos with 'desirable' characteristics. Wolfram Henn, a human geneticist at Saarland University (Germany), argues that the advent of large-scale DNA sequencing and DNA chips may mean that genetic research will be able to locate such complex properties 'as longevity, body shape or intelligence' (2000: 445). He poses the following question: 'Could there be any reasonable doubt that a DNA chip or other testing device that promised parents-to-be a better chance – although no guarantee – of a tall, slim, bright child would be excellently marketable?' (Henn, 2000: 445)

Drawing on this kind of highly futuristic scenario, fears have been raised over the possibility of 'reproductive tourism' as parental consumers 'choose' countries which allow the use of pre-implantation diagnosis to facilitate the selection of boys rather than girls, or even babies with desired 'cosmetic' enhancements. Whether or not one agrees with these futurist scenarios (see Chapter 7), PSS and pre-implantation diagnosis pose problems for international regulation. As the head of the UK Human Fertilisation and Embryology Authority stated in a surprising aside, 'I think we will see a competitive moral disarmament' (Leather, 2004) – as reproductive tourists travel to the markets with the least restrictive regimes. According to an article in *Fortune* magazine, PSS already represents 'big business' (Wadman, 2001: 174). This article reports the case of the *Genetics and IVF Institute* at Fairfax, Virginia which offers a PSS service. The clinic is reported to be receiving 'between 250 and 500 calls a month from interested parents' from around the world (Wadman, 2001: 175) and *Fortune* estimates that the business is worth in excess of $200 million in the USA. The Fortune article reports that one former employee at *Genetics and IVF Institute* noted that 'a lot of what [its founder] does is motivated by the business of medicine, not the beneficence of medicine' (Wadman, 2001: 175). Though one should be very cautious as to the reliability of such reports, they are illustrative of the concerns associated with reproductive tourism. As we shall see in Chapter 7, this is but one of a range of ethical and political concerns that relate to the wider issues posed by new genetics and genomics.

A cause celebré

Sociological interest in nature is partly stimulated by the way in which the relationship between the natural and social domain represents one of change. This is particularly so in the case of the fears and fantasies that are aroused by genomics. Every project needs its cause celebré, and it may be that the desire to realign biology and sociology has found its realisation in the 'genomic imagination' (Franklin, 2000; Fujimura, 2003). On the one hand, there is nothing particularly new about this imagination which, technically, is at least three decades old and bio-ethically has correlates at least as far back as Plato and Aristotle (Baillie, 2005; Sagoff, 2005). On the other hand, genomics may be proving effective as an enrolling device if only because of the phenomenal level of attention to the subject and the range of social science funding support it has received.[3]

The genomic imagination has aroused interest because it seems to place biology centre-stage in our understanding of the social world, and yet simultaneously threaten to reformulate the relationship between the natural and social world through a 'radical reformulation of all its ethological and imaginary references' (Guattari, 1992: 29) and a 'reshaping [of] society and life' (Rabinow, 1992: 241). Not surprisingly, genomic visions hold interesting ontological and epistemological implications, and this alone may explain their efficacy as an enrolling tactic. In consequence, it is worth giving them a little introductory attention.

In one sense, genomic discourse appears as another twist in the age-old marriage of biology and technology: for centuries human beings have used biotechnology in plant and animal breeding or in the development of products such as bread or beer. In another, it typifies the technological panoplies of modernity and their futurist promise of progress and advance. As Giorgio Agamben and Zygmunt Bauman argued, it was particularly in the modern era that biological technique fundamentally refashioned our world. Indeed, Agamben suggested that the remoulding of biological identity 'constitutes the decisive event of modernity' (Agamben, 1998: 4; cf. Bauman, 1989), as witnessed in the emergence of a biopolitics of health and governmentality (Foucault, 1979; Rabinow, 1992; Fujimura, 1999; Rabinow and Rose, 2006). Alongside such projects came the development of the modern pharmaceutical industry and the industrialisation of 'nature' by 'agribusiness'. The twentieth century witnessed further 'remaking' of nature, particularly the remarkable biotechnological interventions in human identity represented by developments such as the contraceptive 'Pill' or hormone replacement therapy. In this context, genomic dreams represent a modernist acceleration of our 'bio-plasticizing' possibilities. They state that nature will, 'at last', be 'ours' – the final realisation of a Christian Enlightenment promise.

This promise evokes images of nature as *rewritable* text, ever open to human cultural desire. To put this another way, life science has become infused with the language of IT:

> [Biology] has dropped the vocabulary and concepts of classical mechanics, physics and chemistry . . . in favour of the vocabulary of linguistics and communications theory. Messages, information, programmes, codes, instructions, decoding: these are the new concepts of the life sciences.
>
> (Canguillhem, 1994: 316; cf. Keller, 1995: 117–118)

Through informational metaphors, nature appears as a script which can be edited or erased (Franklin, 2000) and a range of research work has furthered this spectacle of 'nature as text'. For instance, life scientists have worked on the possibilities that flow from creating an additional human chromosome, chromosome '47' (e.g. Pagán, 2004). For some, such bioinformatic development presents another opportunity to rewrite our 'tired old bodies' and, as with any other item of human manufacture, create 'new model' human beings. Such 'germline engineering' can envisage extraordinary changes to human biology because it promises to rewrite the 'bio-script' that is passed on through sexual reproduction to our children. Futurist accounts of this potential have become increasingly common, not only amongst science fiction writers, but also in the work of life scientists. As Jürgen Habermas notes, these futurist scenarios 'step out of 'science-fiction literature and invade the scientific features page' (2003: 41). In marrying biology to information technology, some life scientists see the human genome as being as plastic as any other piece of programmable text. The following quotation from a 'biophysicist', though lengthy, graphically encapsulates this vision of a plastic, infinitely manipulable, biology:

> Imagine that a future father gives his baby daughter chromosome 47, version 2.0, a top-of-the-line model with a dozen therapeutic gene modules. By the time she grows up and has a child of her own, she finds 2.0 downright primitive. Her three-gene anticancer module pales beside the eight-gene cluster of the new version 5.9 . . . 5.9 features a whopping nineteen antivirus modules instead of the four she has and an anti-aging module that can maintain juvenile hormone levels for an extra decade

and retain immune function longer. The daughter . . . cannot imagine giving him her antique chromosome and forcing him to take the drugs she uses to compensate for its shortcomings. As far as reverting to the pre-therapy, natural state of 23 chromosome pairs, well, only Luddites would do that to their kids'.

(Stock, 2002: 76)

Gregory Stock, Director of the 'Program on Medicine, Technology and Society' at the School of Medicine, UCLA, is an unapologetic evangelist for the 'redesign' of the human race. In the above quotation, he suggests that the 'improvement' of our genetic legacy will soon be no more complicated for parental 'consumers' than updating our computer software. In spite of the 'bads' associated with twentieth century scientific development such as biological warfare, the atomic bomb, rapid environmental degradation, etc. (Beck, 1992), or the strong eugenicist associations of genomic research (Nelkin and Lindee, 1995), life scientists such as Stock believe that, so long as sufficient 'precautions' are included, only 'goods' will flow from genomics. Stock is not alone in his thesis: other life scientists such as the former editor of *Science* magazine, Daniel Koshland, suggest that genomic interventions should be used to 'improve' the human 'gene pool' and thereby 'bring us smarter people and better leaders who are more responsible in their lives' (2000: 29). Koshland further argues that the consumer 'demand for gene enhancement therapy . . . will probably be very large' (2000: 27). As Langdon Winner comments, it 'appears that a number of scientists . . . are willing to own up to the godlike implications of their proposals for human bioengineering' (2005: 388).

Such genomic fantasy seems to threaten a radical attack on the ability to defend ontological foundations for our world. Biological nature no longer appears as the stable 'bedrock', a permanent backdrop and constraint upon human creation. Instead it is potentially as capable of being as rewritten as any other work of fiction. Within some unrestrained genomic scenarios, there is no longer any certainty as to who we are, and the biological universe became slippery and subject to as much reconstruction as the social, 'inherently manipulable and re-formable' (Rabinow, 1999: 13). In these fantasies nature can appear 'after' culture, the plaything of our cultural sensibilities.

Yet alongside this vision of plastic heaven, genomic discourse also re-invokes eugenic nightmares where race, gender and sexuality are policed, and the enchantment of the deviant and the abnormal are biologically obliterated. If the biological future of the human race were to shift 'from chance to conscious design' (Stock, 2002: 75), then the inevitable sociological questions occurred: who are the designers, and what vision and imagination informs their technology and their desire? For some, fears of a genomic return to eugenics seem overplayed, a triumph of 'hype' over feasibility (Brown, 2003; Hedgecoe, 2004; Rose, 2005). For others, they present a current possibility.

Book structure

This book is roughly divided into two parts. Chapters 1–6 are principally concerned with how we understand the relationship between the natural and the social domain. For example, Chapter 2 examines the 'contest' between realist and constructionist prescriptions for social science engagement with nature, as well as programmatic attempts to circumnavigate this terrain (such as that of the Strong Programme and actor-network theory (ANT)). Though this involves revisiting 'old' debates, it remains difficult to avoid the parameters of their contestation.

Chapter 3 then addresses an important characteristic of much sociological debate about nature, namely its anti-dualist prescription. Some writers declare that they have 'an anti-dualist "axe to grind" ' (Williams and Bendelow, 1998: 4) whilst others are strongly opposed to Cartesian and Newtonian thought. Although Chapter 3 will not countenance a return to dualist contention, it shall nevertheless seek to question aspects of anti-dualist argument. In addition, it will suggest that we need to remain open to the possibility of difference in our *perception* of the natural and the social terrain. In pursuing this argument, detailed attention will be paid to Ian Hacking's (1999) distinction between 'interactive' social kinds and 'indifferent' natural kinds (and its similarity to the earlier proposition of R.G. Collingwood). It will be suggested that, although Hacking (1999) produces interesting and provocative argument, difficulties arise in maintaining his distinction between the natural and the social. As a means to begin to address these issues, and as prelude to later discussion, critical consideration will be given to writers who have examined temporality in nature and society. Contrary to existing assumption, it will be argued that it is difficult to 'collapse' the 'times' that surround natural and social process.

Chapters 4 and 5 draws on and extends the work of Norbert Elias. The advantage of Elias is that he combines anti-dualist sympathy with attention to differences in our perception of natural and social temporality, along with an account of why these differences may occur. Chapter 4 illustrates Elias's distinction between natural and social time, while Chapter 5 considers Elias's explanation of this distinction, namely the exceptional qualities of human language and symbolisation. Chapter 5 also addresses the chief omission in Elias's account: the significance of human technology. A common theme of both these chapters is the need to attend to the perceived temporality of natural and social process. In particular, it will be argued that although the natural and the social can both be seen as characterised by 'flux', the 'dynamically constituted' longevity and relative constancy of many natural processes do not seem to be similarly mirrored in the social domain. To put this another way, the social still appears to be distinguished by a stronger, and more thorough-going, historical specificity *of process* than that which we tend to see in the natural realm (Collingwood, 1946).

Chapter 6 presents what might be described as a 'case study' illustration of some of the foregoing argument. It addresses the epistemological difficulties that historical specificity presents for critical realists, particularly when they attempt to draw temporal parallels between 'nature' and 'society'. Critical realists are confronted with the problem of how they maintain their attachment to notions of social stability and endurance, especially where there are perceptions of 'accelerating' social change. At the same time, critical realism illustrates the difficulties that can result from trying to apply similar temporal concepts between the natural and social domain. This is particularly so with concepts that assume some temporal stability of process, such as references to 'regularity' (Cartwright, 1999), or to natural/social 'laws', 'patterns', 'recipes' or 'tendencies'. These problems of temporality are given further illustration by considering the implications of temporality for the politics of nature, such as that observed in the sociology of the body and the natural environment.

The last three chapters focus on recent sociological 'adventures' within the natural domain. These include sociological attention to new genetics and genomics (Chapter 7); the body, emotion, health and sexuality (Chapter 8); and neurology and the brain (Chapter 9). As illustrated in Chapter 7, genomic futurism presents us with a fantastic and novelistic spectacle, albeit one that can be quite at variance with current 'technical' possibility. Although I shall concur with those who remain sceptical about such spectacle, I remain wary of entirely dismissing its implications. Nonetheless, part of the problem with genomic futurism is its tendency to base its *expansive* imagination on the assumption that life can be *reduced* to a 'gene machine'. The difficulties consequent upon reductionism receive further treatment in Chapter 8. Reductionism is still a problem, if not the 'bête noire', for sociological engagement with life science, and Chapter 8 explores two strategies for dealing with reductionism, one based on its tactical co-option, the other on its avowed avoidance. There have long been proclamations that it is possible to engage with a non-reductionist, or 'holistic', life science (Benton, 1991; Harrington *et al.*, 2006), and hopes of meaningful interdisciplinary encounter have been furthered by neurological study that points to the complexity of brain and neural processes. Nevertheless, Chapter 8 uses two 'cautionary tales' to illustrate the difficulties that may occur in trying to conjoin sociological concern to reductive *or* (seemingly) non-reductive life science. These difficulties suggest that interdisciplinary concord remains a precarious achievement.

Issues of interdisciplinarity receive further attention in Chapter 9. The chapter starts by addressing the programmatic implications of Chapters 2–6. In particular, if one assumes that the way we look at the natural and social realm is influenced by a perception of differing temporalities, the questions remains as to how we arrive at programmes that meaningfully connect the natural to the social domain. To take a variant of a very old question, how do we marry the complex neurology of the brain with our sense of human consciousness? One answer, following Spinoza and Hampshire, is to apply a 'perspectival parallelism' (Connolly, 2002: 88) that uses a movement 'back and forth' between the biological and the social/phenomenological. Instead of trying to collapse all differences between the biological body and the 'mind', parallelism provides a strategy to work across difference whilst accepting a Spinozist 'unity of substance'. Yet such parallel manoeuvres are not without their limitations, as will be illustrated through comparison of the Spinozist sympathies of William Connolly and Antonio Damasio. These difficulties point once more to the issue of interdisciplinarity. In consequence, the book closes with a critical examination of interdisciplinarity, applying its prescriptions to an earnest conversation between the phenomenologist, Paul Ricoeur and the neuroscientist, Jean-Pierre Changeux (Changeux and Ricoeur, 2000).

Lastly, the reader should be forewarned that this book will not provide the comforts that derive from proselytised prescriptions or neat conclusions. Even though Chapter 9 alludes to 'ways forward', the present writer has not encountered any that can be described as free of complication.

2

KNOWING NATURE

Nature, and its scientific understanding, has provided a fertile ground for contestation within the social sciences. This chapter will be concerned with some of the parameters of this contestation. It will focus on the question of how we deal with the materiality of nature and whether we can treat 'nature' and 'society' in equivalent terms. These issues have proved difficult to resolve. Some writers refer to the 'communication impasse' (Soper, 1995: 7) between different 'combatants'. Others bemoan the way in which debates have become 'rigidified, not to say fossilised' (Dickens, 1996: 71). Furthermore nature in its various guises has been the subject of controversy since antiquity, possibly because 'nature' is a strong cultural symbol and yet also 'beyond culture'. According to the anthropologist, Jean Marie Benoist, the 'opposition between culture and nature is the very basis of western metaphysics' (1978: 59). It is perhaps not surprising therefore that our knowledge of nature remains subject to dispute, and that more modest writers on nature commence their discussion with the caveat that they can only offer the 'sketchiest account of its convolutions' (Soper, 1995: 28). Similar restrictions apply here, and my discussion must necessarily focus on the concerns that are particular to this book.

In what follows, I shall explore a key site for the contestation of nature, namely the dispute between constructionists and realists (especially critical realists). Contrary to the desire of writers as divergent as Peter Dickens (1996) and Alan Irwin (2001), it has proved difficult to progress beyond the parameters of this debate. As a point of comparison, I shall also explore discussion amongst anthropologists over the treatment of nature and culture. The chapter will close by considering the attempt by actor-network theorists to circumnavigate the 'abyss between words and world' (Latour, 1999a: 121), and contrast their position with that of writers associated with the Strong Programme in the sociology of science.

Taking nature seriously: the realist critique

A number of writers have asked whether one can construct a sociology of the environment that operated 'as if nature did not matter' (Murphy, 1997: 6), or a sociology of health without attending to the physiology of ill-health (e.g. Freund, 1988), or a sociology of the body that does not explore the biological body (Shilling, 2003), or a sociology of gender or reproduction that refuses to address the ways in which biology informs gender (Birke, 1986, 1999, 2003; Parisi, 2004; Wilson, 2004). Underpinning much of this argument is a concern that unless sociologists engage with life science debate, it will remain difficult to counter biosocial accounts which are reductionist, determinist or reactionary. This is not a recent argument. As Steven Rose *et al.*, noted some time ago:

> The post-1968 New Left in Britain and the United States has shown a tendency to see human nature as *almost infinitely plastic*, to deny biology and acknowledge only social construction. The helplessness of childhood, the existential pain of madness, the frailties of old age were all transmuted to mere labels reflecting disparities in power. But this denial of biology is so contrary to actual lived experience that it has rendered people the more ideologically vulnerable to the 'common-sense' appeal of reemerging biological determinism.
>
> (1984: 10, added emphasis)

Experience over the past two decades furthers this argument. Biologically determinist accounts of social life are no longer 'emergent' but instead represent a mainstream narrative that appears almost omnipresent in popular media, especially in relation to new genetics and genomics (see Chapter 7). Relatedly, a range of projects reduce social life to 'genetic' or evolutionary imperative and thereby extend the biological reductionism witnessed in socio-biology and evolutionary psychology (Dupré, 2001; Shilling, 2003). The prevalence of such 'Genes R Us' stories suggests that it is all the more important to engage with biological argument even if 'new biologists' such as Rose or Lewontin have tended to 'discourage sociologists from appropriating the fruits of their fields' (Fuller, 2000: 178).

In spite of the commonality of biologically determinist accounts, there remains a general acceptance amongst most sociologists that our understanding of nature is socially constructed. A lengthy tradition in the sociology of science suggests that we have no unmediated access to the natural world and that science proceeds by conventions that are, at least in part, socially determined. Yet though most sociologists accept the 'softer' elements of this constructionist inheritance, there are also those who remain concerned that the natural domain is downplayed or repressed within social constructionist analysis. In particular, there is a sense that 'the social shapes the material to a far greater degree than the material shapes the social' within 'strong' social constructionism (Williams and Bendelow, 1998: 128). These anxieties are often informed by realist, or critical realist, critique (e.g. Williams, 1999), and realist projects are partly constituted through their opposition to the perceived constructionist tendency to reduce nature to culture, and the 'trading [of] biological reductionism for social reductionism' (Williams and Bendelow, 2003: 135). Realists acknowledge that aspects of nature such as the human body or the 'natural landscape' are strongly culturally influenced, but emphasise that they are not a product of culture alone. For instance, the natural landscape is shaped through its composition by elements such as carbon, oxygen and water which remain 'beyond talk'. Similarly, we cannot as yet talk our way out of the constraints of nature. As Kate Soper notes, 'human biology is such that we cannot fly unaided, exist on a diet of grass, survive for more than limited periods without air or water, emit or detect certain sounds or smells, and so on' (1995: 139). Or as the horror of the Asian Tsunami reminds us, we cannot control nature's 'plagues' such as earthquakes, flooding, drought, meteors, etc. In other words, we cannot 'afford to suppose that the exceptional characteristics of our species *exempt* us from ecological principles and from environmental influences and constraints' (Catton and Dunlap, 1980: 25, original emphasis).

Realists argue that these facets of nature have frequently been downplayed in feminist and sociological analysis due to an 'over-determination by cultural modes and conventions' (Soper, 1995: 139). For example, Soper argues that human sexuality cannot be reduced to cultural preference alone. In particular, contrary to 'contemporary feminist and gay writing', heterosexuality is not just 'an arbitrary and coercive "norm" of human sexual conduct' (Soper, 1995: 142). Instead, Soper suggests that 'heterosexual relations . . . are a prescription of nature in the sense that they have been essential to the reproduction, and thus the history, of the species' (1995: 142). Such observations do not imply that heterosexuality should be prescribed as 'nature's norm', but neither does it mean that we can 'escape the determination of biology' (Soper, 1995: 143). For instance, even human reproduction that avoids heterosexual relations through the use of sperm banks and IVF remains reliant on 'the most extensive knowledge of biological . . . process' (Soper, 1995: 143).

We do not have to agree with Soper's realism in order to see the logic of her overall argument. Her central proposition is that there remains a biological 'otherness' to nature than cannot be captured by constructionism. As she further suggests, 'If the body is viewed as entirely the historical effect of cultural powers, then no plausible explanation can be given of why it is that all human bodies are subject to processes of growth, reproduction, illness and mortality' (Soper, 1995: 133). No human being has yet been asked if they want to be born, and no one has been able to talk their way out of an eventual death. Such biological and maturational processes appear beyond talk. Given their extradiscursivity, Soper argues that we must make some epistemological and ontological appeal beyond constructionism and cultural analysis.

Many realists also argue that, for all the imperfections of natural science, it still remains the principal method through which we 'know' nature. In consequence, they react against what they see as the constructionist tendency to circumscribe, or dismiss, scientific knowledge about nature. They contend that although science presents partial accounts of nature, they 'are not just *arbitrary* social constructions' (Murphy, 1994a: 196, added emphasis). Soper argues in favour of 'the possibility of an objective knowledge of natural process' whilst noting that this does not imply 'an uncritical acceptance of the "authority" of [natural] science' (Soper, 1995: 32). Similarly, Murphy suggests that although sociologists cannot countenance certain natural science predilections (e.g. toward reductionism or determinism), scientific understanding remains capable of being reoriented 'in a beneficent direction' (Murphy, 1994a: 220; cf. Benton, 1991). Others, particularly critical realists, are more adventurous in their defence of scientific reasoning, arguing that 'science is about "digging deeper", establishing further structures and causal powers behind the layer of mechanism already established' (Dickens, 1996: 74; cf. Dickens, 1992). Dickens acknowledges that biology is socially constructed, yet he stresses that it is 'more than *just* a social construction. It refers to real causal powers and mechanisms . . . [which] exist independently of discourse and lie behind the growth and development of organisms' (1996: 82, original emphasis).

Whether they promote scientific understanding or not, realist critics fear that constructionism represents a colonizing project which detracts from understanding the biological realm. As Simon Williams opines:

> Constructionists, of course, may reasonably object that the 'extra-discursive' features of body and world are not denied. They can only be known, however, . . . through particular frames of reference or configurations of power/knowledge . . . All too often, however, the slide from this perfectly reasonable, weaker claim to stronger endorsements of the constructionist line proves tempting if not irresistible: one in which the discursive and the extra-discursive are collapsed anew with no attempt to theorize these issues *both ways*, so to speak. What this amounts to, in the final analysis, is not so much the overcoming of biological reductionism as its *inversion* through a new form of reductionism or 'discourse determinism' in which all is reduced to the social *qua* power/knowledge. In doing so, the biological is itself written out or rendered unimportant, except as yet another ('rival') body of power/knowledge. An infinite regress it seems.
>
> (2003a: 22, original emphasis)

Others suggest that this denial of biology means that constructionism also hinders political engagement. They suggest that if pain and pleasure just reflect cultural preferences, we have no basis to object to practices such as foot-binding, clitoridectomy, child abuse or torture (Soper, 1995; Turner and Rojek, 2001). According to Soper (1995), it is only by acknowledging the materiality of nature that we can address the politics of nature. She stresses that we must acknowledge this materiality because 'it is not language that has put a hole in its ozone layer' (Soper, 1995: 151) – at least not directly. In consequence, unless we adopt an epistemology which accepts the materiality of nature, its otherness and extradiscursivity, we will limit our ability to challenge environmental degradation, health and reproductive inequalities, or even gender politics. From this perspective, questioning strong constructionism combines an epistemological and political project where the aim is to question, if not reverse, the perceived dominance of constructionism. Realists also suggest that the constructionist 'slide' toward believing that 'all is talk' represents an egocentric anthropocentrism that denies the otherness of nature. Similarly, the constructionist reluctance 'to "concede" the undeniability of . . . "materiality" ' (Butler, 1993: 10) represents an arrogance that is conditioned by a privileged western experience sheltered from the more intrusive effects of nature, whether poverty, pain and hunger, or earthquakes, flooding and tsunamis.

Retort and counter-retort

Constructionists have reacted against this critique by arguing that construc-tionism is not antagonistic to the otherness of nature or to political engage-ment (e.g. Burningham and Cooper, 1999; Irwin, 2001). For instance, Kate Burningham and Geoff Cooper suggest that it is incorrect to claim that construc-tionists deny nature since 'the vast majority of social constructionist analyses of environmental issues . . . do not cast any doubt on the reality of environmental problems' (1999: 305). Constructionists merely emphasise that this 'reality . . . is socially constructed' (Burningham and Cooper, 1999: 308). For example, Laclau comments that 'a stone exists independently of any system of social relations, but it is, for instance, either a projectile or an object of aesthetic contemplation only within a specific discursive configuration' (1990: 101, cited in Burningham and Cooper, 1999: 308). To such retort, a realist might however object that such argument is insufficient because it fails to address *why* a stone 'exists inde-pendently'. Since our (social) world is full of such seemingly independent natural objects as stones, the sociology of nature must address their independence and extradiscursivity (Soper, 1995). It is insufficient to 'bracket out' this issue because it is central to how we experience nature. For instance, many of the problems of the environment, or human health, occur because nature appears to have an inde-pendent 'life of its own'. We cannot deal with nuclear waste because nuclear radi-ation is 'beyond' human time, affecting 'people yet to be born . . . [and] . . . future generations without means of redress' (Adam, 1998: 111). Similarly, it is the 'independence' and intractability of diseases such as cancer which result in their candidature as a major human health problem. For realists, the problem is that nature remains independent and we therefore need an epistemological account that can account for this independence.

Nevertheless, Burningham and Cooper maintain that constructionists can 'bracket out' the reality of nature and still engage 'in political debate, or make political interventions' (1999: 310). They reinforce the argument that 'the soci-ologist should remain *agnostic* about the existence and extent of the conditions [of nature] and simply consider the claims made about them' (Burningham and Cooper, 1999: 308, added emphasis). They further imply that this 'agnostic' position advantages political engagement because it 'will not justify itself in objectivist terms by . . . claiming knowledge of an assumed incontestable reality' (1999: 210). For instance, they suggest that social scientists should *not* attempt to adjudicate between the rival claims that surround genetically modified (GM) crops, such as that between the biotechnology industry and environmental groups such as Greenpeace and Friends of the Earth. Yet a realist might again object that it is impossible to take any serious political position unless one actively engages in the 'independence' and 'reality' of nature: otherwise, how do we evaluate the competing claims of the biotech industry and environmental groups? Unless we impute some measure of validity to the scientific claims of rival groups, how do we compare their argument? Are competing scientific arguments about the materiality of nature to have no meaningful role in their adjudication? If so, how can we make a thorough assessment of whether, say, GM crops are a good or a bad thing, or make any other statement relating to the politics of nature? This realist critique argues that constructionist 'agnosticism' remains a 'cop-out' that prevents meaningful political engagement, and such argument reinforces the perception that 'constructionism . . . does not in fact have a politics' (Abbott, 2001: 87).

In reply, constructionists maintain that a reliance on scientific accounts may limit understanding of the complex character of debates such as that of GM (Irwin, 2001: 182). Furthermore, constructionist agnosticism has the advantage of furthering a 'relatively detached perspective' since it lays bare the claims-making process and can thereby 'bring more "reality" to the debate rather than less' (Sutton, 2004: 64; cf. Irwin, 2001: 167). In addition, Burningham and Cooper suggest that the realist critique is misguided because it fails to adequately distinguish between 'strict' and 'mild' constructionism. They argue that in targeting criticism at strict constructionism, realist critics ignore the fact that a 'majority [of constructionist studies] employ a mild or contextual construc-tionism' (Burningham and Cooper, 1999: 303). But this retort is unlikely to satisfy critics of constructionism because it is often the very ambiguity of construc-tionist positions to which they object. For instance, Murphy argues that:

> The social constructivist is a magician, suspending nature and evading and concealing its relationship to accounts of nature not with smoke and mirrors, but by shifting between the true mediative and the constitutive positions . . . This results in an internally contradictory formulation.
>
> (1994b: 969)

Like Williams (2003a), Murphy contends that constructionists often slide between a *mediated* account of nature which acknowledges its otherness and facticity, and a *constitutive* approach which argues that 'there is no reality beyond the constructs we imply when we talk of "reality" ' (Woolgar, 1983, 245, cited in Murphy, 1994b: 958). To put this another way, constructionists stand accused of 'ontological oscillation' (Burrell and Morgan, 1979: 266). As Burningham and Cooper note, most social constructionists 'adopt a mild perspective' (1999: 305) since they accept the 'reality' of nature. Yet in acknowledging this 'real' materiality, soft social constructionists can be accused of admitting 'a more realist form of ontology by the back door' (Burrell and Morgan, 1979: 266). In addition, while soft constructionists make explicit or implicit ontological statements about the 'reality' of nature, their 'bracketing policy' means they fail to theorise them. In sum, the charge is that there is an inherent contradiction in the soft constructionist stance.

Adrian Franklin (2002) provides an example of this contradiction by maintaining a moderate constructionism alongside an emphasis on the materiality of nature. Franklin argues that 'social constructionists of nature *do not and should not* obliterate the value of conceptualising nature . . . as an *objective reality, a real materiality that exists prior* to any social constructions that people may put on it' (2002: 51, added emphasis). He further observes that nature represents 'an extra-discursive entity' (Franklin, 2002: 43) which has 'true natural properties' (2002: 44). Yet in spite of this surprisingly strong acceptance of elements of realist ontology, Franklin 'oscillates back' to a stress on the primacy of social construction. Specifically, he suggests that 'ultimately it is our *constructions of nature* in terms of what 'it' is, what it means and its instability in relation to competing claims that is of *most importance*' (Franklin, 2002: 51, added emphasis). In other words, Franklin adopts the conventional constructionist line that language and culture come first because they mediate our understanding of nature. Yet in combining this constructionist stance with an affirmation of the 'objective reality' of nature, Franklin's stance is reminiscent of Burrell and Morgan's (1979) reference to ontological oscillation. In effect, Franklin acknowledges the 'real materiality' of nature but then sidesteps the import of this affirmation. For realists, this position remains problematic because they expect an explicit acknowledgement of realist ontology to be accompanied by an attempt to address it. In other words, is it sufficient for constructionists to stress the 'reality' of nature but then effectively dismiss the latter's ontological significance?

Given this prolonged dispute between realists and constructionists, it is not surprising that some writers have sought to move beyond it. For instance, Phil Macnaghten and John Urry confess to finding this lengthy quarrel a 'rather dull debate' (1998: 2), and they set about trying to transcend it by focusing on the ways in which social practice is embedded in nature. With a similar aim, though drawing on a sociology of scientific knowledge (SSK) tradition, Alan Irwin endeavours to 'move beyond the natural–social dichotomy' (2001: 172). Though both these projects can be seen as noble endeavours, the question remains as to their success in transcending existing conflicts between realists and constructionists especially when, as Irwin notes with respect to his own account, they proceed from 'a broadly constructivist perspective' (2001: 185). As Phil Sutton observes, elements of constructionist philosophy are common to the argument of Urry, Macnaghten and Irwin. In consequence, their argument becomes a target for the usual complaint that constructionism emphasises social concerns at the expense of nature. According to Sutton, the net effect of their combined argument is that it is 'very difficult to see how "nature" plays any significant role' (2004: 73). Rather than transcendence, the alternate programmes of Irwin (2001), and Macnaghten and Urry (1998) could therefore be accused of representing 'business as usual'.

To sum up, there remains a continuing debate between constructionists and realists over the interpretation of 'nature and society'. Yet it is difficult to avoid for anyone concerned with the sociology of nature. As Sutton suggests, 'rather than being a "dull debate", [it] . . . was and is an absolutely necessary one for sociologists to engage in if the discipline is to have useful things to say about environmental issues' (2004: 75). Related comments have been made in science studies, as in David Stump's argument that these kind of 'issues will not go away until we have understood completely why the old debate flourished and have provided a new means to frame science studies that will overcome both the realist/constructivist dichotomy and the rationalist/relativist one' (1996a: 447). The 'necessity' of this debate may also explain the length of its contestation. For instance, the conflicts examined above partly represent a continuation of earlier disputes, particularly those witnessed within SSK (e.g. Knorr-Cetina and Mulkay, 1983; Pickering, 1983, 1992; Collins, 1992; Lynch, 1993). Indeed, it might be argued that they were better addressed in earlier SSK and science studies debates, particularly in SSK approaches such as the Strong Programme (see p. 28). However continuing skirmishes and contestations over nature are far from unique to sociological argument. Many elements of these can also be found in other social science discourse about 'nature and culture'. In what follows, I shall now examine related work within anthropology which, like its 'sister' sociological dispute, has been strongly informed by feminist debate.

Nature and culture

In the 1970s and 1980s, feminist anthropologists highlighted the association between two binary contrasts, namely nature/culture and women/men. On the one hand, there were increasing attacks within anthropology against the dualist treatment of nature and culture (Howell, 1996). On the other hand, as with sociological commentary, there was a concern that 'women' and 'nature' had been combined in a pejorative manner where women were seen as dominated by their emotional 'instincts' and 'doomed by their biology to be natural' (MacCormack, 1980: 17). As Elizabeth Grosz later put it, 'by implication, women's bodies are presumed to be incapable of men's achievements, being weaker, more prone to (hormonal) irregularities, intrusions, and unpredictabilities' (1994: 14). In Western thought, this association has been used in a highly repressive manner, as with the pathologisation of women as 'neurotic' and 'hysterical' in nineteenth century medical thought (Foucault, 1979; McNay, 1992). The Christian Enlightenment association between men and cultural ideals of reason and intellect, and of women with nature, legitimised 'the insidious manner in which men's control over women is built into a notion of culture's control over nature, reason over emotion, and so on' (Strathern, 1980: 180; cf. Lutz, 1988). Feminist writers challenged the woman/nature couplet through illustrating its cultural relativity and by questioning our understanding of nature (MacCormack, 1980; Strathern, 1980).

This questioning of nature was also interrelated with debates about kinship in anthropological study. Anthropologists had variously criticised 'biologistic' kinship studies which assumed that the biological is *prior* to the social. They argued that kinship reflected cultural relations (Schneider, 1972), or constituted a fluid connection between nature and culture (Strathern, 1992), or represented the use of biological discourse to rationalise social inequality and hierarchy (Yanagisako and Delaney, 1995). These reconceptualisations of kinship were later combined with anthropological attention to new genetics and genomics. Since kinship had previously been conceived as a genealogical grid based on a 'well-defined system of blood-ties' (McLennan, 1886: 270, cited in Schneider, 1972: 35), and that for earlier anthropologists 'blood . . . meant . . . genetics and biology' (Schneider, 1972: 32), it is not entirely surprising that 'new' kinship studies have addressed biology and genomics (e.g. Franklin and McKinnon, 2001).

At first sight, the trajectory of this reconceived kinship study, and that of other feminist anthropological research, appears to privilege culture over nature (and thereby invert early work on kinship). In other words, it implies that there is no such thing as human nature since its meaning is always dependent upon how nature is socially constructed within particular cultural settings. Yet it is misleading to assume that this simply replaces a biologistic supremacy with a cultural one. For instance, although MacCormack stressed the strong significance of social and cultural construction, she fought shy of siding with those such as David Schneider (1972) for whom 'nature is entirely a cultural concept' (MacCormack, 1980: 4). In spite of strong arguments in favour of social and cultural construction, this resistance to total cultural supremacy has continued within elements of feminist anthropological thought. For example, Sarah Franklin *et al.*, declare that 'while nature and culture are increasingly isomorphic, in that they are acquiring each other's powers, their distinctiveness continues also to be crucial' (2000: 9).

Nevertheless there can be a tendency to privilege culture over nature through an acceptance that much of nature, and gender, is performative and socially constructed. In consequence, realists might well make the same criticism of such social anthropology as they make of constructionist sociology. In other words, just as they see a slide from a soft constructionism to a strict version in sociology, so they might well interpret similar trends amongst social and feminist anthropologists. Whether or not this is the case, anthropologists do evince some similar proclivities to their cousins in sociology. For example, there can be a reluctance to fully accept what might be termed a 'strict' constructionism position and yet an equal detraction from embracing a 'mild' position for fear it might endorse biological determinism. This kind of equivocation has led some writers to argue that nature and biology have long been downplayed within feminist thought in much of the social sciences. For instance, Lynda Birke asserts that feminist analysis of the human body has often presented it as 'a passive recipient of cultural practices, denied even the agency of experience' (1999: 34). Birke (1986, 1999, 2003) emphasises the materiality of the body and women's experience of this materiality. In this respect, her argument bears some resemblance to that of realists such as Soper or Williams. It suggests that we need epistemological approaches which can align constructionist and culturalist logic with the 'unavoidability' of biology and nature (Shilling, 1993).

Yet the question remains as to whether such alignment is possible, either within sociological or anthropological debate? Given the continuing difficulties of reconciling nature with culture, can we arrive at a position where the 'boundary between the two domains [are]... in some sense, *dissolved*' (Murdoch, 2001: 112, added emphasis). The longevity of the disputes within anthropology and sociology suggest that such 'dissolution' may be difficult. Nevertheless there is one well-known attempt to circumnavigate this terrain, namely actor-network theory. In consequence, the remainder of the chapter will consider its argument and the cantankerous exchange between its representatives and those of the Strong Programme.

Crossing the great divide

Latour has endorsed, and encouraged, a wholly false stereotype of the Strong Program.

(Bloor, 1999: 110)

There is no reason to stick out of loyalty to an absurd position just because it is attacked by even more stupid enemies.

(Latour, 1999a: 117)

Can we cross the divide between nature and society? Or is this distinction incapable of dissolution? One way to begin to examine these issues is to explore the rather bitter exchange between advocates of the Strong Programme, or the 'Edinburgh School', and those allied to ANT. ANT tends to be seen as an attempt to erode, or at least 'bypass', the barriers between the natural and the social arena. In contrast, through its maintenance of a subject–object distinction, the Strong Programme is sometimes portrayed as protecting those barriers, especially by ANT writers.

A number of elements of the Strong Programme appear in keeping with (what might now be described as) a constructionist perspective. Its advocates argue that the scientific interpretation of nature is constructed within the 'local cultural tradition' of particular generations of scientists (Barnes *et al.*, 1996: 31). They suggest that natural scientists do not have unmediated access to knowledge about nature since such knowledge is historically contingent and dependent upon socially determined rules of interpretation and classification, 'the local, contingent, causes of belief' (Bloor, 1999: 84). Contrary to predominant beliefs, natural science theories do not succeed simply because they are the 'right' and 'true' analysis of the natural world. Instead, their success is 'dependent on the interpretive traditions' in which their work is embedded (Barnes *et al.*, 1996: 31), and scientific findings which fit with an existing tradition will be more readily accepted than those that do not (Kuhn, 1962). Science does not proceed by showing that there is a better probability that theory X is correct than theory Y. Instead, the probability that theory X will succeed is situated within socially determined 'prior probabilities', namely the existing beliefs of a particular scientific sub-culture (in probabilistic terms, Strong Programme writers resemble Bayes theorem advocates who set their prior probabilities by scrutinising the expectations of the 'local scientific culture').

Though the Strong Programme has sometimes been seen 'as an idealist sociological account which denies the existence of an external world' (Barnes *et al.*, 1996: 202), its constructionism is perhaps more appropriately seen as 'soft' rather than strong/strict. In part, this is because its advocates endorse the materiality of nature, and acknowledge the way in which 'the material world around us makes its presence felt' (Barnes *et al.*, 1996: 1). Based on this sort of contention, Michael Lynch goes as far as to suggest that the Strong Programme expresses 'a strong commitment to sociological realism and scientism' (1993: 73). While this may be an overstatement, Strong Programme writers do nevertheless explicitly address materiality and accept ' "there is something out there", independent of our minds' (Haddock, 2004: 30). Yet as Adrian Haddock (2004) notes, Barry Barnes 'wants to remain silent on the question of what the nature of this "something" is' (2004: 30). Furthermore, although Barnes (2001) claims to be an 'external realist' his argument remains at a considerable distance from most realist conjecture. On the one hand, both Barnes and Bloor acknowledge 'external reality'. On the other, this reality remains bracketed out to the extent that they distrust scientific attempts to define materiality and do not accept that science provides any kind of privileged or truthful account of nature. In this manner, the Strong Programme encapsulates what Mike Fortun calls 'an ethics of oppositional critique and an ethics of suspicion' (2005: 161) that continually emphasises the social determination of 'science'. This emphasis has led some to suggest that the Strong Programme is radically relativist because 'truth' appears solely dependent 'on the sanction of the [scientific] community (Haddock, 2004: 37). Yet such relativism is no more radical than much subsequent constructionism.

However it is not the constructionist sympathy of the Strong Programme that has led to the most antipathetic and acrimonious exchange with ANT writers. Instead it is the Strong Programme's maintenance of a subject–object distinction. In particular, Strong Programme advocates argue that sociologists must study how scientists interpret nature rather than nature itself: 'For the scientist the world is the object of study; for the sociologist it is the scientist-studying-the-world that is the object' (Barnes *et al.*, 1996: 30). It is this distinction between the object of knowledge and its interpretation by a knowing subject with which

ANT writers were to take exception. ANT adherents challenged the need of Strong Programme writers to 'separate the world from the actor's description of the world' (Bloor, 1999: 93) and their desire to create 'a wedge between nature itself and the description of it provided by the knowing subject' (Bloor, 1999: 94). Instead of this disparaged subject–object separation, they sought to illustrate how the natural and social are 'co-produced'. For actor-network writers, this strategy was necessary in order to bypass the traditional differentiation between nature and society. From this perspective, the problem with the Strong Programme subject–object distinction was that it simultaneously privileged the human actor and obscured the co-production of our world. Perhaps the best-known example of this co-production remains Latour's (1988) analysis of the discovery of the anthrax vaccine by Louis Pasteur. Latour stressed that the anthrax bacillus was not just an object that sat passively by whilst natural scientists competed to explain anthrax. Instead, it was active in the unfolding drama, an equal player in determining scientific accounts. As Murdoch comments, 'we should not imagine that the bacillus is simply a thing "out there" waiting to be discovered by the intrepid human "in here" ' (2001: 118–119). Instead Pasteur's science involved a co-production that allowed both the bacillus and the 'great scientist' to emerge. ANT language such as enrolment, inscription, visualisation, translation, interessement, black-boxing, etc. is concerned to describe this co-productive emergence between natural things and humans, to make 'the transition visible' (Latour, 1999a: 121). Similarly, inventing terms such as 'actants [that] . . . are not in nature, nor in society' (Latour, 1999a: 125) was designed to problematise traditional notions of agency by stressing that agency is a co-production of nature and society rather than a principal property of one or the other. From this ANT perspective, the problem with the Edinburgh school was that 'the idea that the very definition of the *agency of matter* could be one of the concepts to topicalize has not even crossed their minds' (Latour, 1999a: 125, added emphasis). Furthermore, since the Strong Programme professed agnosticism over the validity of any particular scientific account, this meant nature, in effect, '*makes no difference*' (Latour, 1999a: 117).

This critique, and its emphasis on co-production, appeared to some to be a radically new approach to tackling the natural and social domain. Not surprisingly it occasioned its own research traditions, even though they did not become quite the orthodoxy that Latour (1999b) professed to fear. Instead, ANT has been subject to continuing contestation and dispute. First, ANT writers have been accused of presenting a caricature of earlier approaches. In particular, associates of the Strong Programme have questioned Latour's claim that they deny natural objects any agency. As Bloor notes, 'followers of the Strong Program would recommend treating nature and society symmetrically by saying that *both* have causal efficacy in bring about [social] belief' (1999: 96, added emphasis). In consequence, it is not the case that natural things 'don't do very much' in the work of the Edinburgh School (Latour, 1999a: 117). In addition, Bloor asserts that we still need to make a distinction between 'nature and beliefs about, or accounts of, nature' (1999: 87). Although natural things may be actors, they are not the kind of actors that can simply tell us whether to believe one scientific account in preference to another. Nature can be as ambiguous as any other actor whose lines convey several, or contradictory, meanings, and slight alterations in research design or apparatus can occasion quite different research 'outcomes'. According to Bloor, 'nature will always have to be filtered, simplified, selectively sampled, and cleverly interpreted to bring it within our grasp' (1999: 90). In consequence, a subject–object distinction remains necessary since our social knowledge about nature is 'not dictated by . . . nature itself' (Bloor, 1999: 90). This means that we must attend to the 'normative principles' and 'social institutions' (Bloor, 1999: 109) which influence the way we 'filter' and 'interpret' nature.

Yet the question remains as to whether the subject–object distinction allows Strong Programme advocates to sidestep the need to address the agency of nature. Though not as guilty of the ontological oscillation of some later constructionists, the emphasis on social mediation still carries the danger that nature appears secondary. For actor-network theorists, it is this 'imbalanced' asymmetry which they have sought to avoid. However ANT writers can also be questioned as to their strategy. In particular, the ANT desire for a 'generalized symmetry' has resulted in asymmetrical analyses which often downplay the social side of the 'co-production' equation (Newton, 1999). Or as Hacking puts it, 'this branch of social studies of science seems to me to assign too much agency to nature' (2002: 17).

One way to illustrate this is to compare ANT with the perspective of Norbert Elias. Both approaches share an emphasis on what Elias called *Homines aperti*, or the image of 'people in the plural, . . . of . . . relatively open, interdependent processes' (Elias, 1970: 121). This shared emphasis led John Law to comment that 'the explanatory attitude of [actor-network] writers is not so different from that of Norbert Elias' (1994: 113). Yet there are differences in their treatment of the social. Whereas Elias (e.g. 1983, 1994) undertook detailed analysis of the historical development of the modern sense of self, ANT writers tend to leave this arena under-theorised. The consequence is rather asymmetrical analysis. For example, whereas ANT writers exhibit meticulous attention to the historical networks that surround the development of, say, the Kodak automatic camera (e.g. Latour, 1987, 1991), they do not show a similar concern with the interdependency networks that condition human action. In other words, if we imagine an individual holding a Kodak camera, ANT writers tend to tell us a lot about how the camera was constructed, but not the individual holding it. There is little attention to the lengthy historical interdependency networks that condition the practical and discursive consciousness of human beings – such as that which Elias details in his studies of court society (Elias, 1983, 1994). To use ANT terminology, human beings are often 'black-boxed' within ANT analysis.

In effect, ANT studies tend to represent people as *predictable* parts of the network, whose actions can be taken for granted within a particular network configuration. This black-boxing of the human is epitomised by Latour's (1991) story of the hotel manager who ensures that his hotel door keys are returned by making them heavy and unwieldy to carry. In this analysis, Latour's principal interest lies with the agency of the hotel key. There is little concern with human agency except where it becomes unpredictable, as is the case with 'exceptionally distracted professors' who refuse to return their heavy hotel keys (Latour, 1991: 108). Humans are treated much like a Kodak camera since they can be assumed to act in a certain way given a certain actor-network configuration. At the same time, the significance of the social is downplayed through being, in ANT terms, 'punctualised' (Callon, 1991). For example, there is no concern with the historical development which has led to the hotel key being seen as the *property* of the hotel manager, or the *social etiquette* which deems it 'polite' to return hotel keys (Elias, 1994). Even though some ANT studies pay greater attention to the social processes surrounding actor networks, there often remains a limited exploration of both human agency and its historical construction. For instance, Callon's (1986) study of the fisherman and scientists at St Brieuc Bay represents human actors as largely following a clearly intelligible 'script', determined 'logically' by the characteristics of the actor-network architecture.

Yet it is not that ANT exhibits total ahistoricism in its treatment of the human self. Not surprisingly given their emphasis on *Homines aperti* and networked agency, Callon and Latour show sensitivity to the 'false' sense which many people have of themselves as *independent*, 'sovereign', actors – or *Homo clausus*, in Elias's terms. For example, cash money allows us as consumers to feel independent of the production and trading networks on which we depend (Newton, 2003b). Put bluntly, I need not care whether my clothes were manufactured in sweatshop conditions even though interdependency chains connect me to the low-paid, and possibly ill-treated, workers who produced them (War on Want, 2006). In this manner, I can remain blissfully ignorant of the complex socio-natural interdependencies in which I am situated, and this ignorance feeds my sense of 'independence'. ANT, like the work of Elias, is therefore situated within sociological critique which suggests that 'this is an independence which is at bottom merely an illusion' (Marx, 1973: 163). Yet ANT writers do not deconstruct such aspects of the human 'black-box' in the same way which they do with the non-human. In particular, although Latour and Callon question the independence of human actors, they do not examine the actor networks through which that sense of independence has been achieved. In consequence, asymmetry could be said to be built into ANT analyses because they often provide a history of technology without a corresponding history of the self or the social terrain. In Elias's (1970) terms, they fail to study, (1) how a human actor achieves a sense of being an independent *Homo clausus* partly because interdependency networks are historically obscured and in consequence seem part of our intimate subjectivity, and (2) the historical development of figurational patterns such as complex global market independencies which encourage the feeling of being an independent sovereign self (Newton, 2002, 2003b).

These observations question whether ANT represents an effective alternative to the subject–object distinction associated with the Strong Programme. On the one hand, ANT can be seen as a creative attempt to avoid the relegation of nature to a secondary category. On the other, the question remains as to whether treating 'nature' or 'society' in equivalent terms represents an avoidance strategy rather than a 'bypassing strategy' (Latour, 1999b: 17), particularly where their analyses appear asymmetrical. In addition, is it possible to explore the 'coproduction of society and nature' (Callon and Latour, 1992: 349) without engaging in a more detailed examination of whether differences remain between the natural and the social arena? As Murdoch notes, we 'need to ask whether a *single* perspective should attempt to embrace interdisciplinary thinking (the apparent ambition of ANT)' (2001: 129, original emphasis). In other words, can we treat natural and social 'objects' as ontologically equivalent, or accept that the 'only viable position is for the analyst not to take any ontological position' (Callon and Latour, 1992: 352)? What if the natural and the social arena are not ontologically equivalent? If so, is it meaningful to treat their co-production as unproblematic?

Conclusion

As argued in Chapter 1, our social lives are interrelated with our biology and the physical world. From this perspective, it does not make sense to erect barriers between our understanding of nature and society. Yet as illustrated above, attempts to 'cross the great divide' have proved a fraught endeavour. Nevertheless, it is possible to imagine new variants on current thought that might transcend some of its existing limitations. For example, actor-network theorists might pay as much attention to the history of social selves as natural 'actants' by adopting an Eliasian perspective that interwove our social and natural history. In this fashion, a more comprehensive 'bypassing strategy' might be achieved. However questions would still remain. In particular, it could be argued that such bypassing strategies would remain ineffective if there are differences in our perception of the natural and social domain. Can one treat these domains as equivalent if we 'see' them differently? Can we 'bypass' differences in the way in which we understand their operations?

Circling around these issues is the contestation between advocates of constructionism and realism. As noted, this contestation has a lengthy lineage (Abbott, 2001). It will be argued in Chapters 4–6 that the length and obstinacy of this debate derive in part from continuing differences in our perception of natural and social temporality. For now, it seems fair to say that, *contra* some realist critique, social constructionism has revealed a range of insights into the operation of natural science and the sociology of nature (Sutton, 2004). Yet the question remains as to whether it is sufficient to remain agnostic about the claims of scientists or to acknowledge the materiality and 'reality' of nature, but then refuse to address the latter's epistemological and ontological implication. At the same time, it is uncertain as to whether realists have all the answers. As will be argued in Chapter 6, realists can also be accused of too strong a desire to apply a uniform epistemology across the natural and social terrain. Can we, for instance, assume that talk of regularities can be applied to both nature and society?

The difficulties of interrelating the natural and the social are not unique to sociology, as reference to anthropological debates and divisions reveals (Holden, 1993; Goodman and Leatherman, 1998). Transcendence appears problematic in many social sciences. In this context, it is not surprising that a working philosophy has evolved which questions the divide between the social and natural arena, namely 'anti-dualism'. Yet although anti-dualism represents an understandable strategy, it carries the danger that it may also obscure the possibility of difference. In order to further explore such possibilities, the next chapter will critically address the adequacy of current anti-dualist contention.

3

BEYOND ANTI-DUALISM?

Any discussion of the relation of nature to society has to consider *the* bête noire of the politics of nature, namely the 'sin' of dualism. For many writers, the social science treatment of nature has been too wedded to the legacies of Cartesian dualism. In this context, asserting the possibility of difference between the social and natural domain can look like heresy. Yet it is this kind of heresy which I now wish to explore. I will first consider limitations in current anti-dualist argument, drawing on the work of John Meyer (1999). In so doing, my intention is to explore the possibility of difference rather than re-invoke dualism. As a means to address difference, I shall focus on Ian Hacking's (1999) distinction between 'interactive and indifferent kinds'. This distinction is interesting because it challenges strong anti-dualism by asserting that there are differences in our understanding of the natural and social terrain.

The metanarrative of anti-dualism?

Dualism is frequently presented as the evil 'sin' to which any right-minded social thinker should object. To a reasonable extent, Callon and Latour adopt this position (e.g. Latour, 1999a: 122). It underpins their argument that 'the observer must abandon all a priori distinctions between natural and social events' (Callon, 1986: 313) and their concern to illustrate how 'Society and Nature are intertwined' (Callon, 1986: 201). Anti-dualist desires are common elsewhere, particularly in work on the natural environment and on the body and corporeality. For example, Grosz asserts that:

> Dualism . . . is . . . at least indirectly responsible for the historical separation of the natural sciences from the social sciences and humanities, the separation of physiology from psychology, of quantitative analysis from qualitative analysis, and the privileging of mathematics and physics as ideal models of the goals and aspirations of knowledges of all types. Dualism, in short, is responsible for the modern forms of elevation of consciousness . . . above corporeality.
>
> (1994: 7)

In such formulations dualism carries a heavy load, being responsible for many of the ills of knowledge construction since the Enlightenment. Though some of these ills are rightly proclaimed, a too dominant anti-dualism carries the danger that we will circumscribe our understanding of the natural and social arena.

As John Meyer (1999) notes, critique of dualism has represented a common tactic in the social science treatment of nature where Western thought is frequently portrayed as co-extensive with the 'cleavage between humanity and nature' (Meyer, 1999: 7). Culprits in this critique are many and varied, from Descartes backward to Christianity and the beginnings of Western philosophy. As an exemplar of this anti-dualistic critique, Meyer cites the work of the ecological writers, Val Plumwood and Peter Marshall, both of whom decry the supposed imbalance within Western philosophy. Such imbalance seemingly leads to human life being divorced from nature by 'a rationalist tradition from Plato onwards [that] . . . separated the mind from the body, the observer from the observed, and humanity from nature' (Marshall, 1992: 5, cited in Meyer, 1999: 6). Similarly, Plumwood argues that 'the Platonic, Aristotelian, Christian rationalist and Cartesian rational traditions' have occasioned 'a total break or discontinuity between humans and nature' (Plumwood, 1993: 70, cited in Meyer, 1999: 6).

Within such critique, dualism appears as the philosophical root of all evil. Yet as John Meyer (1999) observes, it is naïve to assert this dualistic tradition if only because of the commonality of *anti-dualist* sentiment within Western thought. According to Meyer, this has included the likes of 'St Francis of Assisi, Spinoza, Emerson, Thoreau, Kropotkin and Heidegger' (Meyer, 1999: 10). Meyer asserts that such writers cannot be discounted as a 'minority tradition', and in consequence, we need 'call into question . . . the very existence of a dominant dualistic paradigm in the first place' (1999: 10). As Meyer further argues:

> If Western thought were truly so dualistic, after all, then presumably most of us (those influenced by the history of Western thought) should find the view that humans are constituted by nature to be ultimately *incomprehensible*, rather than more or less incontrovertible. That this position is comprehensible and even compelling suggests that it is not as novel or as threatening to extant thought as many imagine'.
>
> (1999: 11, original emphasis)

Following Meyer, it seems ironic that writers on nature frequently decry the one-sidedness of dualist treatment of nature and yet simultaneously exhibit a remarkable ability to erect their own rigid barriers between 'the heroes and villains among Western thinkers' (Meyer, 1999: 19).

Yet against Meyer, it might be argued that Western thought is still dominated by inappropriate, and unecologically friendly, conceptions of nature. However Meyer also questions this argument. He suggests that the 'dominant conception' thesis – that is the view that Western thought is predominantly antithetical to nature – is another common feature of environmental discourse. Prime culprits within the dominant conception thesis are Descartes, Hobbes, and Newton and their supposed legacy of mechanistic and atomist thought. Meyer cites Freya Mathews' (1991) *The Ecological Self* as an example of the dominant conception thesis. According to Mathews, the supremacy of Newtonian thinking remains a serious obstacle to ecological reform. True to dominant conception form, Mathews argues that we need to replace Newtonian assumptions with a 'post-Newtonian model of reality' (1991: 57) that is informed by twentieth century physics such as quantum mechanics, general relativity theory and geometro-dynamics (Misner *et al.*, 1973; cf. Capra, 1975, 1983).

As Meyer notes, the tactic here is straightforward. By associating particular epochs with certain dominant conceptions of nature, writers such as Mathews believe that ecological change will follow from *a change in the dominant concep-tion*. For instance, if we replace the atomism, stasis and mechanism of the 'Newtonian World Machine' (Capra, 1983: 37) with the stress upon flux, inter-dependence and complexity of quantum mechanics and complexity theory, we can appear to arrive at a model of nature which is more sympathetic to concerns that are 'organic, holistic and ecological' (Capra, 1983: 66). At the same time, the assumption that Western thought denies nature enables ecological programmes to seem radical simply by reasserting human interdependence with nature, as is frequently observed among advocates of programmes such as ecocentrism and ecofeminism (Dryzek, 1997). Yet as Meyer notes, for such critique to work, it is important to assume that 'only one conception of nature [is] . . . dominant in any particular era' (Meyer, 1999: 16). For example, if Newtonianism is merely 'an interpretation of some particular thinkers within the West, rather than the . . . dominant model' (Meyer, 1999: 15), it cannot be seen as the evil culprit which every right-minded thinker must reject. In other words, derivative critique tends to assume that its evil targets, such as Newtonian or Cartesian thought, have hitherto represented relatively all encompassing and pervasive philosophies which are therefore in need of urgent replacement by more 'eco-friendly' accounts of nature.

This argument has a number of limitations. First, the argument that an epoch is dominated by a single, or singular, model of nature is too simplistic since any particular historical period tends to be characterised by competing philosophies. Second, it too easily accepts the naturalist fallacy that nature can provide a model for our politic or ethic (Moore, 1903). As Meyer asserts, why should any norm-ative position follow from a particular reading of nature, such as that of complexity theory or quantum mechanics? Third, the outright rejection of models of nature, such as those of Newtonian and Cartesian thought, is too draconian. This is most obviously illustrated in the work of Spinoza, whose metaphysics draws on that of Descartes, yet simultaneously furthers an ontological monism (see Chapter 9). More recently, Emmanuel Levinas employs elements of Cartesian argument on the grounds that Descartes provides a vehicle to explore how the subject is consti-tuted in 'the Other' (since the Cartesian idea of God provides a sense of the

Other that cannot be presumed by, or reduced to, the subject – an 'alterity irreducible to interiority'; Levinas, 1994a: 211). Although we may question Levinas's use of Descartes, his argument illustrates the intellectual vandalism that may result if we reject certain writers outright. Finally, anti-dualist critique tends to downplay possible differences between nature and human society. Yet as Meyer argues, we can accept human difference and exceptionalism without rejecting 'nature's evident role in constituting who we are' (1999: 19; Catton and Dunlap, 1980). In other words, the desire to break down the barriers between nature and culture, mind and body, the social body and the biological body, 'natural time' and 'social time', psychology and physiology, etc. manoeuvres our attention away from entertaining thoughts of difference between the natural and social terrain. At its most fervent, it implies that having demolished the barriers, we can move beyond 'bypassing strategies' and build a common ontology and epistemology across the natural and social sciences. Yet can we defend such a single and singular perspective, a theory to encompass everything, if not 'of everything'? Is it really the case that 'the difference between "nature" and "culture" . . . glides into a zone of indiscernibility' (Connolly, 2002: 62)? What if differences remain in our understanding of natural and social process?

It is precisely this last question that is posed by Ian Hacking (1999). Hacking declares that he has 'deliberately avoided the lazy terminology of social construction' (1998: 101) although he plays with its logic. Controversially, he argues that there is a difference between our understanding of natural and social 'kinds', and in consequence his thesis is worth exploring because of its challenge to an exclusive anti-dualism. In what follows, I shall outline Hacking's argument, explore its resonance with the earlier contention of R.G. Collingwood (1946), and consider its counter-argument (drawing especially on Roger Smith, 2005).

Different kinds

In *The Social Construction of What?* Hacking suggests that much of the controversy within the sociology of science has arisen from a failure to distinguish two 'kinds' of object, namely 'interactive kinds' and 'indifferent kinds'. This use of the philosophical term, 'kind', is perhaps a little surprising when, as Hacking notes, 'too much philosophy has been built into the epithet, "natural kind"' (1999: 105). In addition, Hacking's deployment of the term is chiefly taxonomic, referring to 'principles of classification' (1999: 104) rather than its more traditional sense of essentialism and 'laws of nature' (Dupré, 2002: 33). Notwithstanding this caveat, John Dupré seems right to conclude that Hacking's (1999) thesis provides a 'real richness . . . in the variety and depth of the examples . . . which . . . are illustrated' (Dupré, 2000: 676).

Hacking uses these illustrations in order to argue that social scientists are generally exploring 'interactive kinds'. The latter refer to objects which are affected by our knowledge of them since they 'become *aware* of the how they are classified and change their behavior accordingly' (1999: 32, added emphasis). Hacking provides the example of the 'child viewer of television'. Not only has the 'child viewer' been variously constructed, as either too passive or too (hyper) active, but these very classifications inform parent's perception of their children such that they become concerned about how much television their children watch, and their children may then react against this concern. These processes may then further affect social science knowledge about child television viewing. In sum, we have an interactive, complex, and iterative process of social construction. Hacking argues that most of the objects of the social sciences are of this 'interactive kind' because people are aware of, and respond to, social classifications. In this respect, Hacking's argument may be seen to draw on a range of argument that suggests that human beings are both responsive and reflexive to the knowledge they construct of their social world. This part of Hacking's thesis is conventional. As Bernstein observed, 'fundamental changes in the concepts, ideas and language used by men [*sic*] necessarily entail fundamental changes in their social relations' (Bernstein, 1979: 67, cited in Smith, 2005: 6). What distinguishes Hacking from other social science attention to reflexivity is his assertion that many of the objects that concern natural scientists are, unlike those of the social sciences, indifferent to their classification. To illustrate this indifference, Hacking draws on Pickering's (1983) *Constructing Quarks*. He suggests that Pickering's account is typically constructionist in its argument that 'discovery' of quarks was strongly contingent upon the particular historical evolution of physics. In other words, things could have been otherwise given a different history. In contrast, Hacking suggests that 'most physicists . . . think the quark solution was inevitable' (1999: 31) and he expresses sympathy for this position to the extent that he agrees that 'quarks, the objects themselves, are not constructs, are not social, and are not historical' (1999: 30; cf. 1999: 99). Contrary to first impressions however, this argument is not based on a rejection of constructionist logic. Within his own terms, Hacking appears to strongly accept the tenet that reality is socially and historically constructed – which is not surprising in a writer who declares that his 'own debts to Michel Foucault are great' (1998: 85). Yet Hacking is far from a straightforward Foucauldian and he is disparaging of those who ossify Foucault[1]. With regard to quarks, Hacking argues that we understand such natural objects differently to those found in the social realm. As he puts its:

> Quarks . . . do not form an interactive kind; the idea of the quark does not interact with quarks. Quarks are not aware that they are quarks and are not altered simply by being classified as quarks. There are plenty of questions about this distinction, but it is basic. *Some version of it forms a fundamental difference between the natural and the social sciences. The classifications of the social sciences are interactive. The classifications and concepts of the natural sciences are not.*
>
> (Hacking, 1999: 32, added emphasis)

Such comments are reminiscent of earlier argument. For instance, writing in 1935, R.G. Collingwood distinguished between the social arena, the understanding of which he saw as necessarily historical, and the analysis of nature.

> This at least is certain: that, so far as our scientific and historical knowledge goes, the process of events which constitute the world of nature *are altogether different in kind* from the processes of thought which constitute the world of history.
>
> (Collingwood, 1946: 217, added emphasis)

Collingwood's separation of our understanding of nature and society derived from the argument that we cannot get 'inside' nature and think or feel as nature might. For example, we cannot understand what it means to be 'a blade of grass' (Collingwood, 1946: 200; commenting on Croce, 1921). In contrast, by virtue of being humans, we can get inside the social arena and understand its history: we have a privileged 'insider' access to such historical analysis which does not apply to our knowledge of the natural world. In understanding social life, we are not only able to describe the actions of social agents as an 'outside' observer but also can try to get inside in order to 're-enact' and 'discern the thought of [the] agent' (Collingwood, 1946: 213; cf. Dray, 1995)[2].

Although Hacking's contention is reminiscent of Collingwood, it differs through a stronger emphasis on the double, rather than the single, hermeneutic of social life (Giddens, 1984). It is not just that we have a privileged access to the social arena but that such access 'interacts' with its object, and in so doing, redefines it. Following Hacking, it is this *interactivity* that differentiates social from natural knowledge rather than our privileged access to the social arena per se. In contrast, although Collingwood does note the possibility of a double hermeneutic (see Collingwood, 1946: 84), this observation is not as central to his argument as his single hermeneutic, 'insider' knowledge.

To sum up, Hacking suggests that there is a 'fundamental difference' between the natural and the social sciences that results from differences in our understanding of interactive and indifferent kinds of object (1999: 32). This argument is interesting if only because it presents a counter to the dominant fashion within constructionism and much of the sociology and history of science. In contrast to Hacking, writers within the latter fields have tended to argue that nature represents a province that is not 'indifferent' to social construction. A particular strong example of this counter-thesis is provided by Roger Smith who argues that we need to:

> question the separation [of the natural and social sciences] by looking again at *the view that knowledge of humans changes the object of knowledge while knowledge of the physical world does not. It is not obviously true.* Once, for analytic purposes, we put the question of differences of practice aside, we can see that the very arguments which suggest that

the human world changes along with our knowledge of it *apply also to the physical world and our knowledge of it*. If knowledge of the physical world is knowledge framed by one set of concepts rather than another, then it is in principle possible to change the framing concepts. And for all practical intents and purposes, except perhaps for people who believe that they have access to the noumenal, to the 'really real', beyond the reach of language, this amounts to the claim *that the world changes along with our knowledge of it*.

(Smith, 2005: 13, added emphasis)

Given that Smith's proposition presents a direct challenge to that of Hacking, it is worth exploring further. In one respect, Smith adopts an uncontroversial position which suggests that science is historically contingent and that understanding of nature changes as different sets of knowledge emerge, as is classically illustrated by the shift from Ptolemaic to Copernican astronomy or Newtonian to Einsteinian physics (Kuhn, 1962). Yet Smith goes significantly further in arguing that knowledge of nature changes nature, and in this respect, his argument is more contentious. For instance, it is one thing to suggest that science can occasion technology that 'manifestly changes the world' (Smith, 2005: 13). However it is quite another to imply, as Smith (2005) does, that knowledge and scientific technique frequently change nature. If we accept this premise, then it should follow that if I train a telescope on a distant astronomical galaxy in the aim of some scientific inquiry, that galaxy will change in some significant way. But why should this distant galaxy change? Why should it be other than indifferent to my observation? According to Smith, the answer is that the human knowledge gained from the use of my telescope will still potentially change the natural world even if the galaxy does *not* actually appear to change:

> If telescopic observation of galaxies does not alter those galaxies, in the ordinary sense of the word 'to alter', this is a matter of contingent limitations of power not of theoretical principle. Knowledge makes a difference in the world wherever it has the power to do so.
>
> (2005: 14)

From Hacking's perspective, the problem with this 'catch 22' argument is that it implies too great a correspondence between natural science knowledge and its object. It might of course be objected that wave-particle duality, Heisenberg's uncertainty principle, and 'Schrödinger's cat' illustrate how human observation can effect natural process. Yet these oft-cited examples are principally concerned with measurement effects, rather than those of human observation *per se*. In any case, we would need a remarkable sense of our own omnipotence in order to believe that our observations routinely change nature. For example, natural science may give us technologies as various as the iPod, synthetic hearts, or nuclear power, but this does not change the nature of silicon, heart tissue, or the

41

longevity of nuclear radiation. In addition, many of the 'bads' associated with science (Beck, 1992), and of environmental degradation, arise precisely because human knowledge is incapable of changing nature to suit its own ends. Furthermore, it remains difficult to assert that science has changed natural forms. People are still composed of blood and bones, neurons, complex cellular processes, etc. In spite of several centuries of natural science research, the physical world still seems to be formed of water, air, carbon, and so on. In other words, there remain numerous instances where we do not have 'the power' to change nature, and in Hacking's terms, it therefore appears 'indifferent'.

In addition, following realist critique such as that of Soper (1995), it could be argued that Smith's position represents a rather anthropocentric view of the world. To put this another way, why should the natural world change just because our knowledge of it alters? In Hacking's terms, why should a quark care? It can seem arrogant to assume that our knowledge of nature will tend to change 'its nature' – which, at times, almost seems to be Smith's charge[3]. Just because we 'change [our] framing concepts' (Smith, 2005: 13), why should nature adjust accordingly? At worst, such an assumption tends towards the 'geocentric' conception of the world that Elias saw as characterising pre-Copernican European society. The latter 'represented the primary impulse of human beings, still observable in little children, to consider themselves as the *central frame of reference* for everything they experience'. (Elias, 1987: xxxvii, added emphasis). Smith's argument that nature 'changes along with our knowledge of it' (2005: 13) could be accused of making human experience the 'central frame of reference', particularly as it appears to deny nature autonomy from human beings and the whim of our variable perception. Following Smith, it can almost seem that if we have the power to change things, nature will follow suit. But one has to ask why this human omnipotence should occur unless one subscribes to a geocentric and anthropocentric view of the universe, or believes that nature really is about to become an artefact of culture (Soper, 1995). Furthermore, *contra* Smith, we do not need access to 'the "really real" ' to argue that nature can be 'beyond the reach of language' (Smith, 2005: 13). For instance, in proposing that natural kinds are indifferent, Hacking is not claiming access to some noumenal realm. Instead, he is suggesting that our senses suggest that there is something beyond us, an extra-discursive other, and that the operation of this other is not necessarily affected by what we think or say about it.

Nevertheless, shortcomings in Smith's argument do not mean that Hacking's thesis is without limitation. Indeed, Hacking's binary distinction becomes most interesting where it begins to break down. Hacking appears aware that his distinction becomes stretched where it is applied to processes that combine *social and biological* elements, such as autism or schizophrenia. Commenting on such behaviours, Hacking notes that 'in the constructionist camp, these disorders are interactive kinds of illness. In the biological camp, they are thought of as indifferent kinds. Here is a very sharp instance of the fundamental tension between the "real" and the "constructed" ' (1999: 109).

As Hacking observes, this tension arises in part because biological processes are not immune to how we think about them. We 'can learn how to control our nervous tension, or our heartbeat' and 'changes in our ideas may change our physiological states' (1999: 109). Nevertheless Hacking argues that this phenomenon, which he terms 'biolooping' is distinct from his concept of social interactivity (1999: 109; cf. Lynch, 2001; Hacking, 2002). In effect, he suggests that there is a difference between the interactions that occur biologically and those that happen socially. It is only the latter that can be termed an 'interactive kind'. In contrast, 'biological kinds, . . . like all indifferent kinds, *are unaffected, by what we know about them*' (1999: 123, added emphasis). At first sight this argument conflicts with Hacking's acknowledgement of 'biolooping'. In other words, if our ideas 'may change our physiological states' (1999: 109), it is surely the case that biological kinds are affected by 'what we know about them' (1999: 123). Hacking manages to combine these seemingly contradictory arguments by stressing that it is human awareness that differentiates social kinds from natural kinds. On the one hand, he acknowledges that biological kinds such as microbes interact with human knowledge and behaviour. For instance, their behaviour may be characterised by 'quickly evolving strains that resist our antibacterial medications' (1999: 106). On the other hand, Hacking emphasises that 'the classification microbe is indifferent, not interactive, although we are certainly not indifferent to microbes, and they do interact with us. But not because *they know* what they are doing' (1999: 106, original and added emphasis).

In sum, the difference between interactive and indifferent kinds, and social and physical/biological kinds appears to boil down to the issue of human awareness. But can we defend this distinction? One could easily argue that, say, microbes are as aware as humans in this sense that they react and respond to human interventions such as penicillin (Latour, 1987). In consequence, it might be suggested that there are no meaningful differences between social and biological kinds. Both exhibit a form of awareness and both interact and are changed by their environment. To put this another way, Hacking's (1999) argument is inadequate to the extent that he does not specify what it is about our understanding of human awareness that differentiates it from physical or biological awareness. Without some explication of the processes that make human awareness distinctive, it is difficult to defend it as being a different 'kind', or one that is somehow more 'interactive' than those of 'nature'.

A very similar problem applies to Hacking's other central argument that social kinds exhibit lesser stability than natural kinds. For example, he shows how our perception of child television viewing, or autism, or schizophrenia can rapidly change, partly as a consequence of the way in which knowledge about these issues interacts with experience of them. As Hacking observes, views about schizophrenia have variously been seen as a neurophysiological disorder, a 'scientific delusion' (following R. D. Laing's anti-psychiatry movement), and a 'genetic' issue. At the same time, Hacking stresses how even people's experience as 'schizophrenics' has changed as the nature of 'delusions' and hallucinations alter over time. In its social sense, schizophrenia is therefore interactive and unstable. It constitutes 'a moving target' (1999: 114).

In contrast, Hacking suggests that natural kinds are stable in relation to human knowledge. Quarks remain quarks since they are not affected by our knowledge of them, and in consequence, 'the targets of the natural sciences are stationary' (1999: 108). In making this argument, Hacking's explanation is again reminiscent of that of Collingwood, especially the latter's assertion that 'nature stays put, and is the same whether we understand it or not' (Collingwood, 1946: 84)[4]. Yet Hacking's contention represents a refinement of that of Collingwood, partly because of his attention to the conflict between realist and constructionist proposition. In distinguishing natural stability from social instability, Hacking is trying to move beyond such conflict. On the one hand, the tendency of realists, and most natural scientists, is to see stable scientific knowledge as a consequence of the 'real' stability that exists in the natural world. On the other, constructionists tend to see such stability as a performative 'achievement' of the way in which science has been socially constructed. Hacking responds to this dispute by arguing that 'the "form" our knowledge takes is [socially and historically] contingent, but once we have asked the questions, they get answered in a fairly predetermined way' (1999: 233). In other words, Hacking accepts much of the import of science and technology studies (STS) that suggests that 'science is ' "socially shaped" and could have been otherwise' (Brown and Webster, 2004: 32). But he also asserts that given a certain sociotechnical history, the outcomes of science cannot be seen as arbitrary. At first sight, this appears equivalent to saying that although natural scientific knowledge evolves according to the social and political context (most notably, the experience of war), it nevertheless interacts with something out there which is both 'real' and stable. To this extent, Hacking looks like a realist, at least about nature (see Chapter 2). Yet elsewhere Hacking describes the stability of natural science as performative to the extent that it depends on certain styles of reasoning (e.g. see Hacking, 1998: 159–199).

Drawing on the historian of science, A. C. Crombie (1994), Hacking argues that notions of scientific objectivity are dependent on certain historically contingent styles of reasoning such as the scientific methods which we associate with taxonomy and experimentation, or statistics and probability. Rather than a 'unity' of science, we therefore have different, historically situated styles of reasoning (Hacking, 1996). Assertions of the truth or falsity of scientific statements only make sense within a certain style of reasoning such as laboratory experimentation. In other words, though Hacking goes considerably further than, say, the Strong Programme's acknowledgement of materialism and realism, he still seems to fight shy of nailing down reality in the manner of committed realists. To put this another way, Hacking does not repeat the realist line that 'the world "out there" determines the results of scientific inquiry' (Stump, 1996b; cf. Dupré, 1996), or provide unqualified support for Collingwood's (1946) thesis that nature is simply stable. Instead nature appears stable to us because scientific methods such as experimentation are 'stable, enduring, accumulating over the long haul'

(Hacking, 1998: 192). The stability of nature is therefore partly a consequence of the social construction of scientific method: 'overall the laboratory stabilizes itself by a mutual adjustment of ideas (which includes theories of different levels), material (which we revise as much as theories) and marks (including data and data analysis)' (Hacking, 1996: 73). Yet at the same time, Hacking suggests that there is also something different about our understanding of nature. In particular, unlike the 'moving targets' of the social arena (Hacking, 1999: 113), the objects of natural science do not change just because of our knowledge about them.

Yet as with Hacking's other distinctions, questions arise as to the ease with which stability and instability can be associated with the natural and social realm. The problem is that not all natural kinds are unaffected by human knowledge of them. For instance, microbial viruses are aware of human knowledge in the sense that they quickly evolve to evade human attempts to use knowledge to control them. As with autism, childhood television viewing, or schizophrenia, microbial viruses may rapidly respond to, and interact with, our knowledge about them and therefore also constitute a 'moving target'. *Contra* Hacking (1999), such natural kinds can appear both interactive and unstable. In consequence, Hacking needs something more to defend his distinction. In recognition of this point, Hacking again alludes to the significance of human awareness. It is human awareness which underlies his concept of interactive kinds, and it is interactivity which informs his differentiation of social instability from natural stability. Yet this still remains problematic if only because biological kinds can also be said to be aware, if indirectly, of our knowledge about them. As noted, the problem with Hacking's account is that it does not answer the question of how the awareness of natural kinds differs from human awareness. Moreover, in spite of Hacking's continued interest in language (e.g. Hacking, 1975, 1995, 1998, 2002), he provides little explication of this sense of human awareness even though it appears central to his thesis[5].

In sum, Hacking (1999) provides a refreshing and challenging thesis but one that ultimately fails to adequately interrelate human sociality, awareness and temporality and explain why they differ from that of other natural domains. The questions that are left unanswered in Hacking's analysis will be further explored in Chapters 4 and 5 by addressing differences in our perception of natural and social temporality as well as the significance of language and technology for human social 'plasticity'. Yet before we can engage with these issues further, we need to consider one other matter that can inform our understanding of stability, namely the significance of time and temporality. If as Hacking (1999) suggests, natural kinds are stable and social kinds are unstable in relation to human knowledge, we need to examine why we perceive such *differing* temporalities in the natural and the social world. But as we shall see, most current sociological accounts of temporality proceed in the opposite direction. That is to say, they follow the anti-dualist desire to collapse, rather than differentiate, the times of nature and society.

Time and nature

It is hard to think of nature without thinking about time. Whether we attend to the 'big bang' that supposedly heralded the creation of our galaxy, or the Darwinian evolution through which life forms evolve, or nature's changing seasons, or our own diurnal rhythms, nature appears interwoven with our experience of temporality. In addition, temporal issues are of direct relevance to the politics of nature. For example, issues such as environmental degradation represent very long term changes which may be difficult to 'reverse' in a human lifetime: species extinction, global warming and nuclear radiation appear either irreversible or very slow to 'repair'. The problem is that we are not as yet such overseers of time that we can 'turn off' nuclear radiation or quickly reverse global warming or species extinction.

Temporality is also interesting because it illustrates the close interrelation between the natural and the social arena. On the one hand, our sense of time 'bears the *historically social* features of the society creating it' (Nowotny, 1994: 101, added emphasis). For instance, the '9 to 5' of 'clock time' is a product of industrialisation and our contemporary sense of time is interwoven with work, markets and capital (Adam, 1995). Similarly, our social sense of time has varied according to historical era, from sixth century Benedictine 'timetables', to Protestant 'punctuality' and time-saving, to the clock time of industrialisation and the instantaneous 'electronic time' of contemporary global capitalism (Adam, 1995; Urry, 2000). Such 'social' senses of time also remain deeply interwoven with the natural world (Nowotny, 1994). For example, when a contemporary individual looks at her watch, she can be forgiven for forgetting that clock time is defined by the position of the earth in relation to the sun. Yet as Barbara Adam notes, clock time is not just 'an artefact of the number system' (1990: 54) since this 'system' is a human representation directly linked to the earth's rotation. As Adam suggests, ' "our" social time as it emerges from common usage is inseparable from the rhythms of the earth' (1995: 24)[6].

The observation that the times of nature and biology are closely interwoven with those of society is supportive of anti-dualist contention (see p. 35). Following such thinking, Adam and John Urry argue that we should attack, if not dissolve, the borders between time, nature and society. For instance, they both contend that a dualist separation between the times of nature and society is inappropriate because our social life remains deeply patterned by 'natural time', such as the changing seasons or the 'glacial' timescapes of human evolution (Macnaghten and Urry, 1998; Urry, 2000). They also suggest that social scientists have inherited an artificial distinction between our social sense of time and the way in which we see time operating in nature. Urry asserts that 'most social scientists have operated with a conception of "social time" that is separate from, and opposed to, the sense of time employed by the natural sciences' (2000: 107). As a result, 'social scientists have generally held that natural and social times are quite different from each other' (2000: 107). In tracing the influences on this distinction, Adam places particular blame against Pitirim Sorokin and Robert Merton, especially a paper which the latter authors published in 1937. Adam argues that:

> From the publication of this paper onwards, physical time has become understood to come in fixed and infinitely divisible units that can be measured. Human time, on the other hand, may include the latter but cannot be fully explained by it.
>
> (1988: 202)

Adam suggests that the problem with this analysis is that it divides the world between a decontextualised Newtonian natural time and a social time which, by contrast, is described as context dependent, historical and reflective of the 'rhythm of collective life' (Sorokin and Merton, 1937: 619). She argues that this dualist sense of time is outdated because of developments in twentieth century science. In these newer natural science conceptions (within quantum mechanics, chrono-biology, thermodynamics, complexity theory, etc.), time appears as historical, irreversible, rhythmic and 'context dependent' (Adam, 1988: 215). In consequence, contemporary science collapses Sorokin and Merton's distinction between natural and social time because *both* appear as characterised by complexity, irreversibility, rhythm, and context dependency.

In sum, following Adam and Urry, the problem with the social sciences is that they have not caught up with the newer notions of time found in natural science. As Adam argues, 'when we use time in social science it is likely to be Newtonian time' (1988: 207). Moreover, she contends that the Newtonian ideal of 'independence of time and space' (Adam, 1998: 40) has some pretty dire consequences. Not only does Newtonian time 'exclude life . . . knowledge . . . any kind of human activity, emotion, interest and frailty' (Adam, 1998: 40) but it is also 'dominated by Cartesian dualism' (Adam, 1990: 152). The task for social scientists is to replace this deleterious and outdated Newtonian sense of natural time with the insights of contemporary science. Furthermore, Urry suggests that post-Newtonian models of temporality are relevant across the natural and social sciences (Macnaghten and Urry, 1998; Urry, 2000). For example, the post-Newtonian natural science stress on impermanence, turbulence and instability appears mirrored in the growing social science emphasis on mobility, 'flows' and fluidity, rather than social stability and social structure. Urry argues that these parallels remain insufficiently stressed in social science which is too reliant on Newtonian and Cartesian legacies.

Taken together, the work of Adam and Urry therefore presents an attack on nature–society dualism and the supposedly outmoded conceptions of time found in social science thought. Yet several questions can be raised in relation to their analysis. In particular it contains many of the elements which Meyer (1999) highlights in his critique of anti-dualist contention. As noted above, Meyer questions whether dualism has ever been as uniform and pervasive as its critics suggest. In the present context, it can be argued that Adam and Urry overplay the influence of Newtonian and Cartesian thought and underplay the extent to which social scientists have drawn on more wide ranging influences when addressing issues of temporality. Just as environmental critics such as Freya Mathews argue that 'Newtonianism does not reflect the world as it really is' (1991: 29, cited in Meyer, 1999: 14), so Urry, and especially Adam, have argued that Newtonianism has dominated the social science conception of temporality. Similarly, Adam and Urry repeat exactly the same prescription as Mathews in their argument that Newtonianism must be replaced by the sense of historicity and interdependence contained in new natural science conceptions such as those found in quantum mechanics and complexity theory.

Given this similarity, it is not surprising that Meyer's (1999) analysis provides critical commentary on Adam and Urry's thesis. First, Newtonian time has not been as dominant as Adam and Urry suggest. Social scientists have not generally clung to Newtonian arguments such as that of temporal reversibility. In any case, as Meyer (1999) argues, it would be very surprising if any era was solely dominated by one conception of nature. Such argument downplays the probability that any historical period, including our own, is characterised by *multiple* characterisations of nature rather than a singular dominant paradigm. Second, there has been a widespread rejection of the 'apeing' of the natural sciences, whether Newtonian or post-Newtonian, as well as sweeping attacks on the Cartesian dualism, 'objectivity' and decontextualisation which Adam (1990) associates with Newtonian thinking. Third, the early arguments of writers such as Sorokin and Merton were explicitly based on a rejection of Newtonian conceptions of time. In their introduction, Sorokin and Merton use the argument of Kant, James and Bergson precisely in order to question Newtonian argument. For instance, they note that '[William] James . . . sees the concept of an "objective" time as a useful fiction' (1937: 616) while 'Bergson holds that "imaginary homogeneous time is an idol of language, a fiction" ' (Bergson, 1911: 274, cited in Sorokin and Merton, 1937: 616). Though Sorokin and Merton use such critique to differentiate social time from natural time, their central concern is to question the Newtonian image of time as 'uniform, homogeneous . . . purely quantitative' (1937: 621). Given that Sorokin and Merton's thesis was based on an *explicit rejection* of Newtonian time in the social arena, and *that Adam credits Sorokin and Merton as a central influence on the social sciences*, it remains difficult for Adam to then assert that 'when we use time in social science it is likely to be Newtonian time' (Adam, 1988: 207). If we are so influenced by Sorokin and Merton's anti-Newtonian legacy, how do we remain such loyal Newtonians?

Fourth, dualism has not been as all pervasive as its critics suggest, whether in relation to environmentalism or temporality. As Meyer (1999) observed, the questioning of dualist contention has been far more than a 'minority tradition' (see p. 36). Fifth, Meyer's review suggests that staunch opposition to dualism may result in perspectives which deny the possibility of difference between humans and the rest of nature. With respect to temporal issues, the danger with Adam and

Urry's anti-dualist desire is that it results in perspectives which ignore possible differences between our experience of time in nature and society. An illustration of these dangers can be found in Urry's attempt to illustrate the close correspondence between natural time and social time[7]. For instance, together with Phil Macnaghten, Urry argues that the similarity between social and natural time is reflected in the way in which identical metaphors can be used to be describe them (Macnaghten and Urry, 1998). Macnaghten and Urry provide the example of 'glacial time', by which they mean time that is experienced as 'extremely slow and ponderous' (Urry, 2000: 157). In the natural arena, glacial time is witnessed in 'the thousands of years it takes soil to regenerate, for radioactive contamination to dissipate, or for the impact of genetically modified organisms to be clearly evident' (Urry, 2000: 158). At a social level, it is seen in concern about the past and in people's identification with a particular place and location. It seems that 'people feel the weight of history, of those memories and practices within that very particular place, and to believe that it can and will still be there in its essence in many generations' time' (Urry, 2000: 35).

Glacial time thus denotes the intergenerational and inter-millennial sense of natural *and* social timescapes. Yet the question remains as whether we can apply such parallels between the times of nature and society. In particular, do these parallels reveal how the 'the temporalities of culture and nature interpenetrate and implicate each other . . . [and therefore] cannot be separated into social and natural time' (Adam 1995: 144)? The answer is that such parallels tend to feel 'stretched' since it is very difficult to draw convincing comparisons between, say, the millennial sense of radioactive decontamination and our social experience of time. Though some humans may desire a feeling of stability, it is difficult to locate social parallels to the apparent *inter-millennial* stability which we associate with natural elements such as carbon or oxygen[8]. Furthermore, 'social glaciality' may often reflect a short-term and revisable perception. For example, people's 'timeless' sense of place and location may represent nothing more than a short-term mourning for the 'loss of the past'. In addition, as Lash and Urry (1994: 246–247) themselves note, our nostalgia for the past may be conditioned by a perception of an accelerating speed of social change (Virilio, 1991, see Chapter 4). In consequence, the question remains as to what is 'glacial' about our social lives beyond a nostalgic desire for stability in a world of seemingly 'accelerating change'. Yet once one doubts this example of glacial social time, Urry and Macnaghten's argument about the metaphorical similarity of social and natural temporality starts to unravel. Instead of illustrating strong nature–social parallels, metaphors such as glacial time point to the difficulties of collapsing social and natural time.

None of the above argument is meant to suggest that the tempo of our social lives is not closely interrelated with those of nature. Yet this does not mean that we can necessarily equate natural time and social time or dissolve all distinction between them. As the work of Hacking (1999) and Meyer (1999) implies, the danger with an overbearing anti-dualism is that it may detract from the possibility of difference between our perception of the natural and social domain. As will be further discussed in Chapter 4, in spite of the current fashion for anti-dualism and 'anti-Newtonianism', we should not assume that we can collapse *all* differences between our understanding of 'nature' and 'society'.

Conclusion

Many of the writers reviewed above have made major contributions to the philosophical and sociological understanding of nature and temporality. Yet some of their work contains what might be termed 'an excess of anti-dualism'. On the one hand, anti-dualism represents a necessary challenge to dualist argument. On the other, its over zealous application can obscure the multitudinous currents of thought that occur at any one time, as well as the possibility that there are differences in our understanding of the natural and social world. As Meyer (1999) suggests, we can accept human difference and exceptionalism without reverting to the assumption that humans are 'separate' from nature. Equally, we can remain open to difference in our perception of nature and society without re-invoking dualism.

Furthermore, it can be difficult to apply a uniformity of thinking across the natural and the social arena, even if it is only to use similar 'metaphors' in each terrain. As the above discussion of natural and social time suggests, such uniformity can appear 'forced' or inappropriate. In this context, Hacking's (1999) thesis presents a refreshing challenge to 'strong' anti-dualism by underscoring the difficulties of trying to collapse our interpretation of nature and society. In effect, Hacking accepts that reality is socially constructed, yet within the terms of that construction, he suggests that we see differences in the operation of the natural and social realm. In particular, we see different degrees of correspondence in natural and social science between knowledge and its object. Central to such difference appears to be the issue of human awareness. Yet Hacking's argument appears incomplete because it fails to differentiate human from other forms of animal and material awareness. In other words, if humans are exceptional, what are the characteristics of our exceptionality (Catton and Dunlap, 1980)? In addition, why should our exceptionality impact on our perception of nature and society? I shall return to these questions in Chapter 5. Before that however, it's necessary to delve further in into issues of temporality, especially the ways in which we implicitly differentiate between the temporal attributes that are applied to the natural and social domain. The next chapter will argue that it is difficult to discount seeming differences in our perception of natural and social temporality, and that these perceived differences are likely to condition the performance of natural and social science.

4

TIME

In this and the next two chapters, I wish to argue the following:

1. That our perception of temporality is significant to how we see the natural and the social world.
2. That this perception is significant to differences between the natural and social sciences and to different understandings of the natural and social arena.
3. That perceived temporality may condition epistemological debate, such as that between constructionism and critical realism.

Following from the arguments developed in previous chapters, I shall address possible *differences* in our perception of natural and social temporality. In so doing, my intention is *not* to re-invoke a dualistic position. Nature encompasses all of the diverse connections between that which we label the physical, biological and social arenas (Elias, 1992). Yet sensitivity to dualism does not mean that we have to deny that there are *any* differences between our perception of the natural and the social domain. I wish to maintain an anti-dualistic stance but remain open to difference (Newton, 2003c). Stating this position is important if only because there has been a tendency to decry or downplay the human 'obsession' with differentiation. The distinctions which we make are seen as questionable, or unfortunate, projections on to a world which is fundamentally 'one', an *undivided whole* (Bohm, 1980: 11). Yet an *uncritical* commitment to 'narratives of wholeness' may be equally problematic. In particular there is a danger that such a commitment will blind us to the relative differences which appear to exist in our understanding of the natural and social terrain. It is to the possibility of such difference that I wish to attend, and to the ways in which it may condition epistemological debate.

The arguments that follow may cause some displeasure to both realists and constructionists. Critical realists may not like the critique of their argument that appears in Chapter 6 and constructionists may bristle at the assumptions that are employed in the present chapter. In particular, I shall make certain statements about nature that are partly reliant on natural science knowledge. In consequence, the impression may be created that science can provide an impartial and definitive account. Yet it is not my intention to suggest that knowledge is other than contingent and partial. In part, the problem is one of language. In making statements that rely on current natural science knowledge, it can appear that one endorses such knowledge as a true, unmediated, account of the world. Even if arguments are couched in a tentative language (e.g. natural science knowledge *appears to suggest* such and such), the overall effect may look like an endorsement of the truth of natural science. In addition, my use of such tentative language may appear like weasel words to some constructionists because I shall cross the line between treating natural science as conjecture and taking it seriously. Yet so long as we treat natural science knowledge as no more than a social construction, or avoid adjudication as to its legitimacy, we are in danger of preventing such knowledge from being meaningfully deployed (see Chapter 2). In other words, it is not simply that 'all is reduced to the social' (Williams, 2003a: 22) in strong constructionist proposition, but that we will limit debate if, *in effect*, we remain agnostic or 'bracket off' natural science knowledge.

In sum, the ensuing argument is based on the supposition that scientific knowledge is a particular and codified representation of our universe. To put this another way, it remains the case that objects such as carbon or a neutron only exist in the sense that human beings name them and study them. Yet at the same time, it requires a 'primitive egotism, and anthropocentrism' (Hampshire, 1971: 222) to assume that such natural objects, once named, only exist because we do, or that they would cease to exist if humans were to disappear. Furthermore, as Hacking (1999) notes, once humans applied certain 'styles of reasoning' to studying the natural world, it does appear that there was some stability in the kinds of observation that could be made (see Chapter 3). Such stability further challenges anthropocentric views of the world that assume that nature only exists because we are capable of naming it.

In what follows, comparison will be made below between the social and the natural domain, wherein the latter includes that which is conventionally defined by the 'biological' and the 'physical'. Although these broad categories contain considerable heterogeneity, it will nevertheless be argued that there is some commonality in our perception of their temporal process. Specifically, natural processes seem to evoke a different sense of temporality to those of the social terrain. In other words, contrary to some existing proposition, 'natural time' does not appear to be entirely synonymous with 'social time' (see Chapter 3). Most notably, the longevity that we associate with many natural processes does not appear to find its correspondence within the social arena. In making this distinction, there is no intention to resurrect a metaphysical sense of 'natural kind' that would firmly distinguish between the natural and the social, or make unqualified recourse to essentialism or 'laws of nature' (Dupré, 2002). Instead, in referring to social and natural processes, I shall assume that they are dependent on, and modifiable within, the particularities of context.

In exploring the argument that social and natural temporality are differentiated, I shall draw on the work of Norbert Elias. In addition, I will focus attention on the contrast between the relative flux and constancy of natural and social processes. In considering this contrast, my arguments in this and the next chapter will partly represent an attempt to move beyond some of the shortcomings identified in Hacking's (1999) account (see Chapter 3).

Differentiating natural and social time

Using Elias to emphasise temporal differentiation may seem a strange choice given that he is generally portrayed as a theorist who stresses the close interweaving of time, nature and the social. Thus Adam argues that Elias 'transcends the dualisms of. . . natural–social time' (1990: 18) and Urry approvingly cites Elias's argument that 'nature, society and individuals are embedded in each other and are interdependent (1992: 16)' (quoted in Urry, 2000: 119). Furthermore, Elias does express a strong anti-dualist stance which is antagonistic to the use of 'bipolar antithesis such as "nature and culture", "body and mind" or "subject and object" (1991a: 5). He also attacks those who 'treat. . . "social time" and "physical time" – time in society and time in nature – as if they existed. . . independently of each other' since 'this cannot be done' (1992: 88). Yet this antipathy to divorcing natural time and social time is not equivalent to the desire, expressed by Adam and Urry, to *collapse* the distinction between the two (see Chapter 3). To put this another way, Elias's anti-dualism is complex and not only admits, but encourages, certain distinctions between the natural and social arena. In particular, Elias does not treat natural and social time in the same terms since he distinguishes between them through regard to their *relative pace of change*. These differences in pace, Elias asserts, are central to how we understand the natural and the social sciences. First he stresses that the 'physical arena' exhibits an extremely slow pace of change with the consequence that current analyses of it may have validity in thousands of years time. As Elias observes of experiments in physics:

> One can legitimately expect [physics] experiments done in one's own present time to have the same results as they would have had 2000, 20 000 or 200 000 years in the past or the future and, who knows, at any point in the universe.
>
> (1991b: 172)

This is possible because 'the tempo of *physical* evolution, compared to the development of human societies, is *extraordinarily slow*' (Elias, 1991b: 173, added emphasis). Elias comes to a similar conclusion when comparing social and biological processes. For Elias, our bodies have natural scripts such as 'blood and bones' which are 'biological universals' (Elias, 1992: 149), and which are often so slow to change and evolve that it almost appears as if they 'do not change over time' (Elias, 1992: 149). Yet these same bodies 'respond' to a *relatively* quickly changing social arena. As Elias notes:

> Blood circulation and brain structure, birth and death are shared by all people. But this can no longer be said of the structure and dynamics of the groups formed by human beings, nor, therefore, of language. *These can change relatively quickly. They are different at different times and in different places.*
>
> (1991b: 174, added emphasis)

Elias suggests that our bodies contain very slowly evolving natural processes, yet interact with a rapidly changing social arena.

Elias thus argues that physical and biological processes are often far slower to change that those of the social. One might however moderate this argument, and Elias partly does so,[1] to note that, (1) it is within *current representation* of the natural and social sciences that natural processes *appear* slower and, (2) natural science remains historically contingent. Yet these qualifications do not detract from Elias's argument that social and natural processes can appear to us to be characterised by differing temporal paces. What is more contentious is Elias's suggestion that epistemological position is determined by temporality. Elias argues that different epistemologies apply to biology and physics because they seem to have greater longevity and a slower pace of change. Elias suggests that one *cannot*:

> on the plane of relations between people ... proceed with the aid of concepts ... of the same kind as those used on the level of atoms or molecules ... [since we lack] the assumption that the same *regularities* that can be observed in the present are to be observed in *all places and times, past, present and future, in exactly the same way.*
>
> (Elias, 1991b: 173–174, added emphasis)

In other words, it is the longevity of process in the natural world which means that we can talk of regularity or predictability. According to Elias, natural processes are repetitive, universal, and tend toward ahistoricism since they occur 'in all places and times ... in exactly the same way' (see above quotation). In contrast, the rapidity of change in the social arena means that we cannot work with the same epistemological assumptions. Nature and society are thus seen as being differentiated by the temporality of their processes, respectively longer term and shorter term, and these temporal distinctions inform the kind of epistemological assumptions which can be made in the natural and social sciences.

These arguments are of course open to critique. First they might be criticised for appearing to denote a Newtonian sense of time, but as Elias makes clear elsewhere, this is not his intention (Elias, 1970: 360–361; 1974: 21–24; 1992: 39–44, 121–130). Though not guilty of this supposed 'sin', it could be argued that Elias employs a dated conception of natural science temporality that has been overtaken by developments such as 'quantum reality' or chaos and complexity theory which have resonance across the physical, social and biological sciences (see Chapter 3). Such work questions the assumptions of natural science regularity, replicability and predictability implicit or explicit in the quotations from Elias (1991b) above. As Prigogine argues, 'classical science emphasised order and stability; now, in contrast, we see fluctuations, instability, multiple choices, and limited predictability at all levels of observations' (1997: 4). When all is a complex flow and flux, can we speak of endurance, regularity and predictability, even conditionally?

It is certainly the case that notions of endurance and predictability have been challenged. Yet Derek Lovejoy argues that a lack of predictability does not necessarily mean an absence of determinism. As he notes, complexity theory has given rise to 'a fundamental confusion between *determinism* and *predictability*. Nobody doubts that the phenomena underlying the weather are deterministic, but the weather itself is, nevertheless, not entirely predictable' (1999: 445, added emphasis; cf. Bird, 1997: 144).

In addition, chaos and complexity theory does not even negate predictability. As Raymond Eve notes:

> When I drive my car to work each day, many chaotic dynamics occur within the inner workings of the vehicle. However, contrary to post-modernist proposition that chaos means nothing is predictable, I seem to arrive each day at the same office.
>
> (1997: 274)

In addition to this conceptual confusion regarding determinism and predictability, there remains the danger that the current sociological emphasis on fluidity, flow and flux will obscure *longevities* which are apparent 'under normal circumstances' within natural processes (e.g. Bachelard, 1983; Lash and Urry, 1994; Mol and Law, 1994; Castells, 1996; Luke, 1998; Urry, 2000). For instance, as Elias (1991b) implies, physical elements such as carbon appear to us to have highly enduring physical properties throughout the universe. Similarly, though physical processes can exhibit rapid change such as that of weather patterns, it remains the case that some of the physical relations underlying such phenomena seem remarkably enduring. For instance, consider the following statement:

> Make water hot and it will tend to expand, evaporate and boil.
>
> (Collier, 1994: 65)

This is a statement that speaks to both popular experience and to natural science. Following the latter, it denotes a physical relation that appears central to the 'complexity' and 'flux' of weather patterns, yet looks likely to hold over past and future millennia. To put this another way, though complexity and flux problematise linear predictability (Byrne, 1998), they do not seem to imply *a lack of longevity within 'nature'* since the complexity and flux of, say, weather patterns appear to rely on remarkably enduring natural processes such as the expansion and evaporation of heated water. Even quantum physicists assume some longevity in quantum mechanics. On the one hand, the processes that they observe may be random and extraordinarily fast. Yet on the other hand, the relations within such processes seem to endure. A commonly used illustration of this endurance comes from the use of hi-fi equipment such as CD players. The latter rely on the application of quantum mechanics and on the observation that these mechanics endure and are repeatable again and again. Otherwise, it is argued, our hi-fis would not work on more than one occasion. In other words, although natural processes are characterised by flux, they also appear to exhibit a considerable degree of constancy.

Such observations support Elias's contention that the natural world is associated with greater regularity and longevity of process, at least as it appears in the physical sciences. This perception of regularity is of course conditional and may be dependent on '*just so*' laboratory settings (Cartwright, 1999: 2, original emphasis). Yet following Elias (1991b), this does not alter the conjecture that the probability of obtaining similar 'results' should be the same within the physical sciences in another century or millennia, given the same set of experimental conditions. Nevertheless, the question remains as to whether similar conjectures can be entertained with respect to biology and the life sciences. On the one hand, evolutionary biology suggests that there are aspects of our biology that seem very slow to change. For instance, fossil records suggest that the human 'brain of 100 000 years ago is the same brain that is now able to design computers' (Mayr, 1997: 74). On the other hand, we should not treat such assertions of stability as a blanket endorsement of evolutionary biological argument since, like physical science, it is historically contingent and influenced by the values and desires of its practitioners (Keller, 1991). Neither should we assume that human biological processes are necessarily very slow in their 'operation'. On the contrary, much of the living world appears subject to constant and very fast change, *and to this extent*, seems to be in flux. As François Jacob argued, a bacterial cell can contain 'some two thousand distinct reactions' which 'diverge and converge at top speed' (1976: 272). Or as John Dupré observes, 'in a typical cell in a human body many thousands of chemical reactions are taking place every second' (2006a: 3). In other words, cellular metabolism seems extremely rapid and cellular 'life' may be very short. Yet the reproduction of the bacterial cell, like other cells, also appears dependent on processes which look as though they have great longevity, namely the complex interactions which surround DNA, RNA, mRNA, RNAi, etc. Evolutionary biologists and bioanthropologists appear to have observed DNA in skeletal remains that date back several millennia, and such research produces the stereotypic illustration of nucleotide sequence. Although researchers in these fields note that 'there are still many difficulties and methodological problems in analysing DNA obtained from archaeological specimens' (Filon *et al.*, 1995: 366), their work nevertheless suggests that DNA has long been part of human and animal biology. Evolutionary biology also indicates that other aspects of cells, such as the existence of a membrane and cytosol, represent a biological ordering of considerable duration (Davey *et al.*, 2001). On the one hand, in spite of the traditional depiction of evolutionary as gradual (e.g. Futuyma, 1983: 84–85) or 'punctuated' (Eldredge and Gould, 1972),[2] certain common evolutionary changes can be very fast, as with bacteriology and virology.[3] On the other hand, the *processes* involved in rapid evolutionary change seem to show a notable longevity. For example, in spite of their 'almost unlimited mutation mechanisms' (Dupré, 2006b: 13), viruses appear to be composed of either double- or single-stranded DNA or RNA, elements which, as noted, seem to be characterised by a remarkable duration. Similarly, this argument is not negated if one accepts 'neo-Lamarckian' arguments that evolution proceeds partly through epigenetic inheritance since the latter still appears reliant on processes that are probably of considerable duration, such as those surrounding DNA methylation or 'genomic imprinting' (Jablonka and Lamb, 1999: 96–112). Indeed, the debate about epigenetic inheritance partly involves a quest for 'mechanisms' of epigenetic inheritance, or an '*epigenetic inheritance system*' (Jablonka and Lamb, 1999: 80, original emphasis) that would explain the *long-term* operation of neo-Lamarckian processes *across time*. It might of course be objected that the relationship between nucleotide sequences, cells and proteins has become far more confusing, ambiguous and uncertain. Yet there still seems to be agreement that there are such things are RNA 'ribbons' or strands of DNA, even though the 'gene' represents a concept that has long been 'in trouble' (Keller, 2000: 66) due to its increasingly 'fuzzy' and uncertain nature (Keller, 2006). In other words, although there are significant doubts concerning key molecular biology concepts, and their sometimes cavalier application, it still appears that the processes surrounding DNA, RNA, mRNA, RNAi, etc. are significant to cellular reproduction and genetic and epigenetic inheritance. In addition, in spite of the instability of genomic processes, there remains remarkable closure in many of their 'outcomes'. Otherwise, it would not be the case that almost all of us have two hands and two eyes, and two eyebrows, ears, lips, feet, legs, arms, etc. and that all of these are of an identifiably human form. As Keller observes, 'in each generation the fertilized egg grows, with astonishing dependability, into an adult that is still clearly recognizable as a member of that species' (2000: 105). Although this process may be as much 'developmental' as 'genetic', there remains an extraordinary fidelity in our processes of inheritance, and fossil remains suggests that this fidelity has been maintained over several millennia (for instance, early humans appear to have had features more or less identical to our own).

I shall return to this argument later in considering images of biological 'flux and constancy', but the key argument for now is that, although biology is considerably more complex that Elias's references to 'blood and bones', many biological processes seem to exhibit the kind of longevity which Elias (1991b, 1992) suggested. In sum, though many biological forms, such as cellular metabolism and sexual conception, are very fast, they appear to rely for their reproduction on biological processes that can show considerable longevity, such as the genomic, cellular and developmental 'interactions' that produce sexual fertilisation, and cellular reproduction and differentiation. In contrast, it is difficult to locate a similar constancy and longevity of processes in the social arena. Supposedly enduring social processes, such as those linked to capitalism, look fleeting when viewed from the geological timescale that seem to be observed with natural forms such as carbon or DNA. To take another example, our attitude towards violence against the body has changed rapidly in the West (Elias, 1994), a change which enabled Foucault to achieve his dramatic 'opener' in *Discipline and Punish* (Foucault, 1977). In comparison to the inter-millennial stability which we associate with many physical and biological processes, human configurational shifts appear remarkably fast, as witnessed in the moves *within a single millennium* from tribalism to feudalism, monarchy, urban-industrialism, capitalism and global capitalism.

In spite of the association of quantum reality with complexity, choice and uncertainty, the natural world does not seem to be characterised by the same sense of changeability and flux. If nothing else, there remain the 'essential constants... of current physics' (Virilio, 1991: 45), namely gravity, Planck's constant and the speed of light. Though there is now debate as to whether the last of these was the same when the universe was very young (Albrecht and Magueijo, 1999), this does not detract from the present consensus that the speed of light has remained constant for numerous millennia. Similar constancy is hard to locate within social processes. Given their endurance, the most likely candidates are language and technology. Yet such human social attributes are characterised by images of remarkable plasticity and flexibility, in contrast to the millennial stability which we associate with natural constants such as the speed of light.

None of the above argument is meant to imply that the physical, biological and social are other than intertwined. For instance, it seems probably that human evolution represents an interweaving of human sociality and biology wherein, say, human technology was as much a cause of human evolution as its outcome (Washburn, 1960; Li, 2003). As Ian Burkitt suggests, our hands may have biologically evolved to greater refinement and dexterity partly *as a consequence* of pre-existent socio-cultural skills of tool use (1999: 39). In this manner, the biosocial arena appears as an interwoven complex. Yet this does not mean that the biological and the social are governed by an identical temporality *of process*.

Equally, none of the above argument is meant to imply that biology lacks plasticity. For example, our brain's neurology may be capable of rapid change through the development of new neural networks, such as may take place in childhood development or following brain injury (Poldrack, 2000). Yet such 'brain plasticity' relies on complex neurochemical processes that may have occurred for several millennia, such as those surrounding the 'firing' of a synapse. Although synaptic processes appear subject to variation in terms of the 'excitatory' or 'inhibitory' effects of our neurochemistry, and a considerable degree of 'synaptic plasticity' (Abbott and Nelson, 2000: 1178), it seems likely that synaptic processes have formed a key element of our cognition for some considerable time (Davey *et al.*, 2001). In contrast, the social world which thought both enters, and reflects, is one where such longevity of process is difficult to locate. Technolinguistic plasticity has allowed us to move within just a few centuries to seeing the sun rather than the earth as the centre of the universe, and from periods of celebrating human violence to a stress on its containment (Foucault, 1977; Elias, 1994).

Finally, none of the above argument is meant to suggest that natural science knowledge is other than partial and contingent. In particular, the appearance of regularity and longevity in natural processes represents a performative achievement. In other words, natural scientists have gradually constructed a technological repertoire which enables the performance of temporal feats such as replicability and regularity in environments such as laboratory settings. In this sense, natural science remains dependent on historically contingent modes of human reasoning and remains, in part, a social construction. Yet once natural science techniques have been reliably assembled, they do appear capable of performing remarkable temporal 'tricks', such as the demonstration of conditional replicability and regularity across time and space (Hacking, 1999). On the one hand, the results of any natural science research are open to interpretation and social (re)construction and, in consequence, the *social 'significance* of experimental results are not stable and unchanging' (Wray, 2005: 52, original emphasis). On the other hand, given a certain historically situated style of reasoning (Crombie, 1994; Hacking, 1999), it remains possible to achieve certain temporal performances, such as replicability and regularity. In contrast, it remains very difficult to 'bring off' the same temporal feats in social science.

The ability to perform regularities in natural science does however raise the old question of *how much* their observation is a function of human social construction (Hacking, 1999). In other words, does nature exhibit a good measure of independence? As K. Brad Wray notes, 'even though the significance of experimental results are subject to change as theories change, the features of the world that our theories in the *natural sciences* aim to model may be what they are independent of what our theories say' (2005: 53, original emphasis). The preceding argument provides some partial support for the thesis of independence (even though this does not equate with support for realism – see Chapter 6). In particular, if one assumes longevity to many natural processes, and a short-term temporality in the human social domain, it seems likely that the human understanding of nature often represents a temporary, and revisable, understanding of natural processes that may exhibit much greater stability. For example, the human observation that the heating of water leads to its evaporation has probably been subject to varying human interpretation. When humans first learnt how to control fire (Goudsblom, 1992), the boiling of water may have seemed to contain certain magical properties and an alchemical potency (Elias, 1987b). Much later, we came to see this process as reflecting water's composition of two seemingly contradictory elements, one highly flammable (hydrogen) and one highly resistant to fire (water). Later still, quantum mechanics suggested that the processes surrounding the boiling of water contained elements of indeterminacy. Yet these historically varying, partial and contingent human interpretations do not detract from the likely longevity of the processes surrounding the evaporation of water, or their significance to the earth's climate. In sum, it seems reasonable to suggest that, even though humans have dramatically shaped the natural world (Macnaghten and Urry, 1998), many natural processes appear to contain a longevity that is not a mere consequence of human interpretation. To put this another way, unless we adopt a position of human egocentrism (see Chapter 3), we can assume that natural life goes on without us.

In addition, it is interesting to note that the longevity of natural processes has made it more likely that a moderately intelligent, linguistically communicative, animal such as humans would discover natural stabilities such as fire, the boiling of water, or the sprouting of seeds. If natural processes were short-term and unstable, it would make it difficult to discern their 'operation' or build any cumulative knowledge about the natural world. It is their apparent longevity that makes them open to scientific and technological 'capture' (see Chapter 5). On the one hand, our 'discoveries' about nature are historically contingent. On the other, the seeming longevity and stability of natural processes makes it more likely that a reasonably intelligent 'technolinguistic' animal would, sooner or later, be able to detect some of their 'method' (Hacking, 1999).

Relative specificity

And surely everyone must have been struck by the incongruity of the fact that humankind can solve abstruse problems of theoretical physics so elegantly and so empoweringly, yet flounders in the dark when it comes to running an economy, or even a love affair.

(Collier, 1994: 248)

In spite of the above argument, it might still be suggested that the social sciences can accomplish similar temporal achievements to those of the natural sciences. For example, Nancy Cartwright (1999) suggests that the situation is essentially the same within the disciplines of physics and economics. She contends that regularities in both these spheres remain deeply conditional since 'economics and physics equally employ *ceteris paribus* laws' (Cartwright, 1999: 151). In addition, she argues that regularities are scarce because 'most situations do not give rise to regular behaviour' (1999: 89). Given these shared constraints, Cartwright suggests that physics and economics are presented with equivalent difficulties in defending assumptions of regularity. In other words, natural and social time are similar, if not identical.

Yet there are tensions in Cartwright's thesis. Central to her argument is the assumption of a presumed scarcity of regularity since it allows her to draw similarities between physics and economics. Cartwright maintains that 'outside the supervision of a laboratory or the closed casement of a factory-made module, what happens in one instance is rarely a guide to what will happen in others' (1999: 86). However it is not difficult to think of numerous situations in the natural arena where an occurrence at one moment in time is a guide to what will occur at a later date. For instance, our human experience tells us that the sun will rise every day, water will boil when heated, apples will rot when exposed to air, and so on. Furthermore these regularities are not dependent on the 'just so' conditions of laboratory experimentations and are not a particularly 'contrived' experience of life.

It is true that there are some regularities in the social arena but they differ through their much greater historical specificity (Collingwood, 1946). For instance, Cartwright refers to an example drawn from economics, namely the writing of a bank cheque. She argues that the organisation surrounding such financial credit provides an example of 'a *law-like regular association* . . . that . . . is a consequence of a causal capacity generated by an elaborating banking and legal code' (1999: 117, added emphasis). This example of financial credit is worth pursuing further because, *contra* Cartwright (1999), it is illustrative of the difficulty of defending conditional regularity in the social domain. As Geoffrey Ingham suggests, systems of financial credit are directly '*constitutive* of capitalism' (1999: 79, original emphasis). But this does not mean that we can impute 'law-like regularities' to them. The problem is that financial systems remain too historically specific. For instance, *contra* Fukuyama (1993), it is unlikely that capitalist 'machinery' constitutes the 'end of history'. Similarly, it is specious to accept the argument that current variants of economic liberalism can be universally exported, whether through persuasion or terror. Socio-economic relations remain temporally and spatially specific and this precludes an ability to make 'law-like' statements. They have developed and varied across differing settings such as the pre-feudal, feudal, monarchic, mercantile, urban-industrialist, capitalist and global capitalist, and there is little reason why any particular economic machinery should acquire a temporal transcendence. For instance, it is reasonably clear that there have been significant shifts in financial credit arrangements, most notably that between 'credit' and 'cash' money (Newton, 2003b). In particular, credit in sixteenth century England invoked Cartwright's 'law-like regular association' (1999: 117) to the extent that lengthening credit networks seemed to occasion increased social discipline (Brewer, 1982; Muldrew, 1993, 1998). Yet by the nineteenth century, this supposed law-like regularity appeared meaningless because cash money was more likely to encourage social 'indifference' than social discipline (Newton, 2003b). Although it involves another detour, it is worth examining this example of early 'credit society' a little further since it illustrates the relatively fast shifts that can occur in the social domain, and the consequent difficulties of establishing conditional regularities. In so doing, it points once more to differences in our perception of natural and social time.

In early modernity, 'credit' money had been associated with increased social discipline because 'households were linked by trust in chains of credit' (Muldrew, 1998: 10). According to Craig Muldrew (1993, 1998), 'the [early modern] market was something which linked strangers through hundreds of thousands of different transactions in *increasingly lengthy chains of [credit] obligation, and this affected people's behaviour*' (1998: 10, added emphasis). Most significantly, within these interdependency networks, 'the collapse of one businessman could bring down many others like a line of dominoes toppling over' (Hoppit, 1986: 67). In consequence, those embroiled in such credit networks remained at risk of penury, imprisonment and financial ruin.[4] It is therefore not surprising that the 'mannerly conduct necessary to improve business and *secure credit* was as much a form of *social discipline* as those values connected with work itself' (Brewer, 1982: 215, added emphasis). As I have argued elsewhere, with the development of more complex bank networks and 'cash' money, a critical shift in these credit relations occurred through their increasing time–space distanciation (Newton, 2003b). The consequence was that the social discipline of 'credit' money was replaced by the social indifference of 'cash' money. In other words, the development toward cash money represented a major shift in the form of interdependency, an inversion in the relations of trust. Instead of the localised, personal, and often face-to-face trust between creditor and debtor of Muldrew's early modernity, those using cash money need have little concern as to the financial or moral probity of other parties to an exchange. On the one hand, cash money always connects people since it 'constitutes the buyer and seller' (Callon, 1991: 138). Yet on the other, it enables the possibility of detachment since buyer and seller need 'never physically meet one another' (Giddens, 1991: 18) and a buyer can often abandon a seller in favour of another. Instead of social discipline, we have the 'growing indifference of [cash] money' (Simmel, 1990: 441). Applying Bauman (1989), such indifference furthers economic 'barbarity' because cash money allows us to forget about the 'producers' of our goods and the conditions under which they labour (Newton, 2003b).

In sum, instead of the increased social discipline associated with 'credit' money in early modernity, the transition to cash money provided an ability to both simultaneously connect and disconnect, to 'bind and loose all bonds' (Marx, 1973: 377). Creditors no longer had to be directly concerned with the creditworthiness and social discipline of debtors or others in their financial 'community'. Complex interdependencies might now matter little to the mass-market consumer. Rather than feeling disciplined by the market, the emergent consumer of Wedgwood china, tea, coffee, spices, etc. could remain blissfully unconcerned as to the predicaments of their production (Bermingham and Brewer, 1995). Applying Marx, this is because cash money helped to facilitate the development of a global market which allowed 'the *connection of the individual* with all, but at the same time also the *independence of the connection from the* individual' (Marx, 1973: 161, original emphasis). In effect, in a relatively short space in time, the shift from credit to cash money stimulated very different kinds of social relations. The 'discipline' of 'face to face' credit was replaced by the seeming freedom and independence of cash money. It is therefore illustrative of the difficulties of postulating social regularities, laws, patterns or 'recipes' given the historical specificity of human social relations. In consequence, Cartwright's (1999) attempt to build 'law-like' regularities around financial credit is disabled by the very specificity of such credit systems.

This specificity is not *similarly* mirrored in the natural arena because of the longevity which seems to surround many natural processes. It appears likely that water will continue to boil, apples to rot, and the sun to rise. It is of course the case that the natural domain contains historical specificity. For example, biological evolution is historically specific in the sense that, following Darwinian thought, it is the product of particular places and periods of time. Yet it also relies on biological process, such as cellular mechanisms, that appear to have considerable longevity. In sum, the difficulty with Cartwright's argument is that insufficient emphasis is placed on the *relative* specificity of the social and natural domains, especially in relation to their historicity. On the one hand, Cartwright does point to the specificity of the social, and how 'what happens in the economy is a consequence of a mix of factors with different tendencies operating in a particular environment' (1999: 141). On the other hand, in drawing parallels between disciplines such as economics and physics, Cartwright does not stress the significance of their differing historical specificities.[5] In particular, her analysis lacks a strong sense of the longer term, intergenerational, temporal perspective that pervades Elias's analysis. Yet from such a perspective, natural regularities, whether 'just so' or minimally contrived, often appear far less historically specific than those of the social arena.

In sum, it remains difficult to collapse social and natural time because of the far greater historical specificity of the social arena and the remarkable longevity *of process* which appears to characterise many aspects of the domain of nature. The consequence for the natural and social sciences is that the temporal 'tricks' of the former are difficult to apply to the latter. In this context, the advantage of Elias's (1991) work is that it underlines the significance of perceived temporal differences between natural and social processes and the differences in longevity seemingly apparent within each arena. It suggests that although it is mistaken to resurrect divisions based on these perceived disparities, it is equally suspect to assume a totalising position that states that all is 'flux', 'unstable' or lacks regularity. As shall be argued below, images of flux and complexity do not cancel out the longevity and constancy that appear to characterise many natural processes. In what follows, I shall explore the seeming flux and constancy of natural processes and contrast these conjoint characteristics with the social arena. In attending to these two temporal opposites, flux and constancy, I do not intend to deny the considerable variation in speed of natural processes (Adam, 1995; Connolly, 2002). Yet the distinction between flux and constancy can be helpful in pointing to differences in our perception of 'nature' and 'society'.

Flux and constancy

It might be objected that I have relied too much on natural science knowledge in the above argument. For instance, constructionists might question this reliance given that such knowledge can only remain historically contingent and bound by the parameters of human discourse. Realists might counter such critique on the grounds that it tends to 'neuter' scientific knowledge. In addition, they might re-assert their argument that such knowledge is not 'arbitrary' (see Chapter 2). Yet whatever one's position, it is possible to make points similar to those that I have made above by relying only on the lay experience of nature. Take my earlier example:

Make water hot and it will tend to expand, evaporate and boil.

It states that, as lay persons, we experience water as evaporating and boiling when it is heated. Intersubjectively, we may 'live' this differently at different times – the kettle may seem slower or faster to boil according to our impatience – yet we still know that this natural process has a constancy and a replicability. If water behaved like language, it might say, 'Sorry, I'm not boiling today' or 'I'm busy, try me later' – but our intersubjective experience tells us that it cannot do that. There is a constancy to its process that is unlike our human social arena: water will boil when heated again and again however variously we experience this process. There remain few social processes that are quite like this, and in this sense, we do not see the natural and the social in equivalent temporal terms – whether we define this perception through our intersubjective 'lived' experience, or through the more contrived trappings of natural science. Phenomenologically, we experience the temporality of natural processes in a manner that is not mirrored in human social experience.

Yet there is a further problem with the arguments that I have made above since they run against the grain of those who have questioned images of fixity and order in natural science (Byrne, 1998). In other words, my encouragement of Eliasian notions of longevity and constancy in natural process might be subject to the standard critique that I am invoking a Newtonian image of an ordered and static natural world. For instance, Lynda Birke argues that traditional images in biology promote a sense of fixity that downplays the vitality of biological processes. At the same time, such fixity is politically conservative to the extent that it suggests that biology determines and constrains our lives – for example, 'fixing' the possibilities of our gender or sexuality. Birke maintains that images of fixity and constancy need to be challenged precisely because they are still common in the life sciences.[6] She uses the example of the thyroid gland to illustrate the stress on control and constancy in homeostatic depictions of biological process:

consider the control of the parts of the endocrine system; the thyroid gland, for instance, secretes a hormone (thyroxine) that affects subsequent output of thyroxine, so that output is relatively stable. It does this by means of its effects on the pituitary, which in turn affects the thyroid. *This control is moment to moment*, as soon as the thyroid responds and reduces thyroxine secretion, the pituitary will detect the falling levels and so increase its stimulation of the thyroid – and so on.

(1999: 89, added emphasis)

Although Birke does not deny the constancy of such processes, she seeks to question the broader sense of fixity and control which these images engender. In so doing, she attempts to further a new biology which connects with feminist desires for socio-political transformation through its emphasis on dynamism and change. As Birke stresses, 'our bodies are constantly being made and remade; bones, muscle and connective tissue – all are constantly in flux' (1999: 151). In a similar fashion, Steven Rose stresses that the 'moment-to-moment stability of the organism is maintained not statically but dynamically' (1997: 157). Moreover, the development of the organism is also subject to chance events and a 'combination of predictability and unpredictability' (Rose, 1997: 154). In addition, it is also the case that our biological processes can seem remarkably fast in relation to our cognitive or social capacities. As Antonio Damasio notes, brain 'neurons get excited and fire themselves away in just a few milliseconds . . . By the time you get "delivery" of consciousness for a given object, things have been ticking away in the machinery of your brain for what would seem like an eternity to a molecule' (2000: 126–127).

None of the arguments that I have made above are intended to question the conjecture of writers such as Birke, Rose or Damasio. Instead, my concern is to illustrate how the natural arena appears characterised by a mix of temporalities, some of which resemble a situation of (varying degrees of) 'flux' whilst others exhibit extraordinary longevity. As Birke notes, processes of biological control are 'moment to moment' and yet they also exhibit constancy. For instance, if a constant process of interaction between our pituitary and our thyroid does not occur, biological knowledge suggests that we are likely to end up with a thyroid which does not work, and individuals with a deficient thyroid may report how it 'wreaks havoc' with their body. Similarly, if we lose the constancy of the millions of interactions that daily occur within our bodies, we are likely to experience some other kind of serious health problem. As Birke puts it, we cannot 'escape the meat' (1999: 145) and constancy of biological process appears central to our ability to take our health 'for granted'. At the same time, it is extraordinary how this constancy seems to be maintained in spite of the speed, dynamism, complexity, and error-proneness, of biological process. For example, on the one hand it is remarkable that 'the union of egg and sperm ultimately produce[s] an organism which may consist of a hundred million . . . cells, differentiated into tissues and organs, *precisely located in space in relation to one another*' (Rose, 1997: 105, added emphasis). On the other hand, such constancy and precision is reliant on cellular processes which are far from stable as is illustrated by the complex interactions which surround DNA. As Keller notes, 'DNA is not intrinsically stable: its integrity is maintained by a panoply of proteins involved in forestalling or repairing copying mistakes, spontaneous breakage, and other kinds of damage in the process of replication' (2000: 26–27). What we think of as 'tireless' genomic replication depends on complex cellular interactions. This system appears remarkable in the fidelity of its replication, but as Keller observes, 'the genetic machinery of the cell provides the most striking example known of a highly reliable, dynamic system built from vulnerable and unreliable parts' (2000: 31). As Keith Baverstock comments,

> in every cell of our bodies the bases in the DNA are being replaced at the rate of about 100 every minute because they have become damaged. The genetic code for our very existence is constantly falling apart and being rebuilt. Here is stability based on dynamics'.
>
> (2006: 1)

In other words, constancy seems to be the *product* of extraordinary biological dynamism. On the one hand, 'our bodies are made of extraordinary unstable material' (Cannon, 1932: 37, cited in Birke, 1999: 96), and yet on the other, except when we experience ill-health, we *consistently* reproduce them. We do not just continually 'shed our skin' but consistently recreate all our organs and our 'blood and bones'. Biologically we appear to be characterised by images of constancy and flux.

This characteristic also seems to apply to many of the natural processes observed in the physical sciences. An illustration is provided by Baverstock (2006) where he draws on the British physicist, Michael Faraday, and his lecture on the *Chemical History of the Candle* (Faraday, 1860/1962). As Baverstock argues, the 'humble candle' (2006: 12) shows how stability and dynamism are common conjoint features in nature:

> A lighted candle shows an extraordinary stability (*in terms of the constant output of light*) *which relies on several dynamic processes;* a flow of molten wax up the wick, heat from the flame melting wax at the top of the candle, convection of the air induced by the heat from the flame to cool the rim of the candle and form a cup for the molten wax, etc.
>
> (2006: 2–3, added emphasis)

As Baverstock argues, in spite of the complex dynamism involved in a lighted candle, it still delivers a constancy of light. Such stability can be observed in several other natural processes. Take my previous example:

Make water hot and it will tend to expand, evaporate and boil.

This process appears characterised by a constancy and longevity of outcome and yet, if we follow the argument of quantum mechanics, it also involves both flux and indeterminacy. To put this another way, we all know that water will eventually boil if you heat it, and yet it remains difficult to precisely predict the exact form of the quantum process through which boiling occurs. Constancy in such natural processes does not imply linearity, absolute fixity, or a lack of dynamism and flux. We can extend this argument further by considering what happens to water in the earth's atmosphere. On the one hand, we appear to have a constant process of evaporation, albeit one that is built from some 'chaotic elements'. On the other hand, this constant process forms part of patterns of weather which are highly dynamic and difficult to predict with any certainty. Once again, images of constancy and flux represent conjoint characteristics of such natural processes. In terms of temporal pace, natural processes seem to exhibit extreme variation, from phenomenal speed to extraordinary longevity.

To sum up, it has been argued that it is difficult to collapse the times of nature and society, or apply the same sense of temporal performance to the natural and social sciences. This is because the social arena appears to be associated with far greater historical specificity than that which we see in the rest of nature. Although the physical and biological domain are characterised by 'speed' and flux, they often seem to evince a longevity of process that is not matched within the social realm.

Social flux and constancy?

There is one further, and related, objection that might be applied to the preceding argument. Some sociologists argue that both flux and constancy apply to the social realm, and that in consequence, we find temporal parallels between nature and society. For instance, Urry asserts that our social lives combine the instantaneous flux of a 'wired' world with the slow moving 'glacial time' (2000: 158) that is found where people have the sense that social experience 'can and will be there in essence in many generations time' (2000: 159). Such parallels suggest that both natural and social time are characterised by flux and longevity. However this argument becomes complicated by those who have questioned whether the social arena is characterised by flux and an accelerating speed of change. In particular, Nigel Thrift (2001) has presented a detailed counter-argument to the 'social acceleration' thesis. In consequence, the ensuing discussion will first outline argument in favour of social acceleration, then consider Thrift's counter, and finally present a critique of both sets of argument. This critique will be used to suggest that, although humans have a capacity for 'speed' *and* 'slowness', we do not exhibit the 'glacial' sense of longevity that Urry (2000) seeks to associate with the social arena (see Chapter 3). Collectively, the ensuing arguments will therefore further question attempts to draw parallels, or equanimity, between social and natural time.

It is not difficult to argue that a modicum of flux inhabits our social world. For example, it is increasingly suggested that human social life is characterised by a remarkable rapidity of change. The social pace appears to be 'accelerating' as 'people race on a treadmill at increasingly frenetic speeds' (Macy, 1993: 206, quoted in Urry, 2000: 156). Speed seemingly becomes the constant desire (Virilio, 1986), 'going faster equals getting better, accelerating becomes improving, quickening cashes out value adding' (Luke, 1998: 172). This acceleration has supposedly now achieved such pace that 'anything is possible' (Thrift, 1999: 60), with the consequence that 'more persons, in more parts of the world consider a wider set of possible lives than they ever did before' (Appadurai, 1996: 53, quoted in Thrift, 1999: 63). For some, 'time is compressed and ultimately *denied* in culture, as a primitive replica of the *fast turnover* in production, consumption, ideology and politics' (Castells, 1996: 462–463, added emphasis).[7] Urry argues that such 'instantaneous time' is part of why we need a 'new agenda for sociology' (2000: 1). Earlier debates over structure and agency, methodological individualism or holism 'are unhelpful' (2000: 15). A new sociology needs to focus on networks rather than social structures and stress 'mobilities for the twenty-first century' (Urry, 2000) rather than the staticity of sociological concepts employed in the nineteenth and twentieth centuries. Other writers appear supportive of this desire to transfer our loyalties from static notions such as social structure toward a stress on fluidity, networks and 'flowmations' rather than 'formations' (e.g. Mol and Law, 1994; Castells, 1996; Luke, 1998).

Yet it is also important to note that there are those who doubt whether all is flux and speed in the social arena. Nigel Thrift has questioned 'the notion of speed' (2001: 53). Even though the latter may be 'part of the rhetoric of how Euro-American societies go on' (Thrift, 2001: 53), Thrift insists that it is not part of everyday practice. Instead he outlines a counter-thesis which challenges the range of voices clamouring for the significance of accelerating speed.[8] Specifically, Thrift refers to a number of social developments which he sees as encouraging a slowing down of social life. These include 'the growth of New Age religions' (2001: 44) and a range of body techniques such as 'dance therapy . . . , music therapy, massage therapy' (2001: 45), as well as an entire 'psychology of body language and gesture' that has 'gradually seeped into everyday life' (2001: 43). According to Thrift, such body practices 'stretch out the moment, most especially by paying detailed attention to it . . . Taken together, they may be seen as a slow-down of perception, as much as a speed up' (2001: 43). Yet these illustrations of bodily stillness are too open to question. First, they represent the aesthetic of a minority since they are largely confined to middle class groups who can afford, financially and temporally, to invest in them, or they are associated with the 'body cogniscenti' that are found in small New Age enclaves. Second, one could just as easily cite body techniques which celebrate an aesthetic of speed. This applies to sports activities (soccer, squash, running, etc.) which are far more commonly practiced than the contemplative pursuits that Thrift highlights. If there is a bodily slowing down, it is due to the exponential growth of 'Macbodies' and excessive weight rather than minority practices of contemplation. Third, body language techniques do not represent a new development since people have been learning them for centuries (Elias, 1994). Finally, Thrift's general thesis remains open to doubt because it does not appear to consider the possibility that many fashionable bodily techniques represent a *response* to a dominant culture of speed. In other words, people seek out massage or New Age practices precisely because of a feeling that their lives are going too fast, or are 'stressed' and overloaded by speed (Newton, 1995). In effect Thrift's argument could just as easily be used to support the prevalence of discourses of speed and the way in which they have placed a new value on the experience of stillness.

However the above critique of Thrift's thesis is not meant to suggest that human beings remain incapable of 'going slow'. Instead, it illustrates how human beings, as a consequence of our social plasticity, have the capacity for slowness *and* speed. Although this plasticity reduces the likelihood that any social config-uration will exhibit longevity, it does afford the possibility of enacting a slower or faster pace of social change. The main question is whether a greater social emphasis has been placed on 'speed' over recent centuries. As humans we have a remarkable ability to recreate our sociotechnical world and we have increasingly finessed this skill, especially since early modernity. To put this another way, we need to remember that speed, fluidity and inconstancy are not just 'twenty-first' century phenomena. Plasticity, mobility and 'flow' can be seen as sharply devel-oping human social characteristics since the Enlightenment and the Industrial Revolution (Nowotny, 1994). It was during the Enlightenment that the word 'progress' came to refer to progression through time rather than space (Arendt, 1970), a development that is subject to ironic treatment in Hogarth's paintings (such as *A Harlot's Progress*, and *A Rake's Progress*; Macey, 1994). Such sens-itivity to the ironies of change suggest an already jaded acclimatisation to the dubious benefits of accelerating human plasticity (cf. Nowotny, 1994: 85–86). It may be that twenty-first century people feel even greater 'acceleration' than that perceived in Hogarth's eighteenth century, but this does not imply that inconstancy, or concerns about it, constitute a recent phenomenon.

In sum, the human talent for plasticity is both historically situated and variable in its operations. Yet although human social change can slow down as well as speed up, this does not mean that it can evoke Urry's (2000) sense of 'glacial time', and its image of a social longevity that parallels that of nature (see Chapter 3). Even the more pressing cases for social constancy appear 'fleeting' when viewed from the millennial timescapes which we tend to associate with physical and biological process. For instance, we may think of our emotions as 'natural', or human beauty as 'timeless', or capitalism as the 'end of history', even though our emotions are culturally and historically conditioned (Lutz, 1988; Elias, 1994; Newton, 1998), human beauty was once perceived as Rubenesque rather than slim, and capitalism is a very recent development. From a millennial perspective, seeming 'natural' human constants appear transient.

Similarly, we like to think of other human concerns as 'timeless', such as the questions posed by religion or death. Yet we forget that in 1000 years time, the *form* of religious practice – as distinct from that of, say, carbon, water or DNA – is likely to have changed considerably, or in post-secular societies, it may even have disappeared altogether. In a similar fashion, the meaning of death is subject to change, as witnessed in the transition from the medieval experience of a 'public' death to its present privatisation 'behind the scenes of normal life' (Elias, 1985: 85), where it is sequestered or denied (Giddens, 1991; Bauman, 1992; Mellor and Shilling, 1993; Willmott, 2000). On the one hand, there are certain features which can appear part of the 'human condition' such as religion, social inequality, or ethnic conflict. On the other, these human 'characteristics' continually change. For example, the popularity of religions ebb and flow, the terms of ethnic conflict gradually evolve, and the definition and proportion of those in poverty does not remain stable. In general, the meaning of supposed human constants such as emotion, beauty, religion, conflict, poverty and death remain mutable and subject to social transformation.

To sum up, discourses of social speed and acceleration need to be seen in the context of the human ability to form and reform our sociotechnical world. Such observations raise the question of what it is about human beings which gives us this capacity for plasticity. If our social world is characterised by images of plasticity rather than constancy, why is this? The next chapter will address this issue by turning once more to the argument of Elias.

Conclusion

As noted in Chapter 3, there has been an understandable desire to treat the natural and social domain with equanimity and to dissolve the dualisms of the past. Yet the problem with pleas for 'generalized symmetry' is that their equanimity of perspective tends to deny the possibility of difference and thereby 'flatten out' nature and society. This chapter has argued that we need an alternative perspective that acknowledges the possibility of difference in our perception of natural and social temporality. In particular, the social terrain does not appear to be characterised by the relative longevity of process that we see in the domain of nature. In consequence, historically 'hard won' scientific temporal achievements, such as those of replicability and regularity, cannot be equally 'performed' across the natural and social sciences. As we move 'back and forth' between the natural and the social (Hampshire, 1971), we must therefore recognise that we may not be able to apply parallel epistemological strategies, and that our knowledge tactics may continue to differ between them. The implications of this argument for programmatic research will be further explored in Chapter 9.

The desire to flatten out differences between the natural and the social has been accentuated by images of post-Newtonian science which have encouraged a vision of natural processes as being governed by turbulence and impermanence. The appeal of such images to social scientists is understandable given the supposedly accelerating turbulence, instability and uncertainty of the social arena (Nowotny, 1994). In this context, drawing parallels between a post-Newtonian universe and social processes can look like an appealing means of getting beyond the 'Great

Divide' between the natural and the social realm. Yet there is a danger that such ambitions will deflect attention away from apparent differences within and between natural and social process. At the same time, it is easy to overplay the metaphors of instability, chaos and flux. All is not flux, and some natural processes seem to show remarkable longevity even though this 'stability is itself the product of a dynamic process' (Keller, 2000: 71). In other words, the 'dynamic stability' of many natural processes is not mirrored in the social domain, and the times of nature and society do not simply coincide.

These observations raise two additional questions:

1. Why does greater historical specificity characterise human sociality?
2. Do variations in social specificity, such as the seeming 'speed' or 'slowness' of social change, condition epistemological debate, such as that between social constructionism and critical realism?

In addressing these questions, the next two chapters will further explore the significance of the perception of temporality to sociological debate. Chapter 5 will address the importance of language and technology to our perception of social temporality. Chapter 6 will then consider the implications of this argument for epistemological debate, with particular attention to difficulties with critical realist contention.

5

LANGUAGE AND TECHNOLOGY

As humans, we can imagine and re-imagine our world. From historical novels to science fiction, we can communicate our imaginings of 'the world as it was, as it is, or as it may be' (Elias, 1991a: 129). Though some of our imagination feels cinematic (as with unconscious dreams), a good deal of it is reliant on our linguistic ability. Language has a transcendent quality in that it enables us to communicate intergenerationally. We can 'hear' the words of the dead and, occasionally, even make our own voice heard by those not yet born. At the same time, language is a principal agent in human plasticity. It enables people to 'free themselves from bondage to the moment' (Elias, 1991a: 129) and create and re-create their world. Elias likens language to the 'fifth dimension' of human experience since 'like time and space the tissues of symbols is all-embracing' (1991a: 96). This linguistic ability is of course constrained. As many have argued with respect to the human imagination, 'because it is finite it cannot reach the infinite' (attributed to Leonardo da Vinci, Cremante, 2006: 228). Yet it is still the case that language provides us with an extraordinary ability to survey and communicate.

In exploring these arguments, this chapter will attempt an answer to a question raised in the last, namely why is it that human social life can be so changeable and our sense of social time foreshortened. In other words, why is it that our social domain remains highly historically specific? I will suggest two human attributes as answers to this question, namely our linguistic skills and our talent for technology. In pursuing the former, I shall draw once more on Elias. In addressing the latter, I will examine Ian Burkitt's (1999) discussion of Evald Ilyenkov.

Symbol emancipation

Elias stresses that intergenerational communication through language is unique to humans, a skill 'unequalled in the world we know' (1991a: 91). He argues that although 'it is quite usual to speak of animal languages' (1991a: 86), it remains the case that 'no other animal species [than humans] has the biological means which are necessary for communication by means of learned languages'

(1991a: 86, added emphasis). Elias further suggests that our linguistic ability has freed the human species from a predominant reliance on genomic evolution, and the very slow time frame through which such evolution can sometimes occur. In other words, human discursivity is central to the relatively fast pace apparent within social change. Language represents 'humanity's *symbol emancipation*, its liberation from the bondage of largely unlearned or innate signals' (1991a: 53, original emphasis). In comparison to humans, 'animal societies are, as a rule, fairly rigidly set in a species–species mould' (Elias, 1991a: 31). Elias further suggests that 'one cannot observe among animals changes of the same scope as that from a feudal to a capitalist structure or from an absolute monarchy to a multi-party republic within the time-span of a few hundred years or less' (1991a: 31).[1]

One might question Elias's assumption about the rigidity of 'animal societies' and his 'questionable if not controversial distinctions between learning humans and instinctual animals' (Williams and Bendelow, 2003: 137). Yet it is important to note that Elias was keen to avoid a return to a dualism between human and animals wherein humans are seen as separate from, or 'above' animals.[2] Instead he argued that humans are different by virtue of their linguistic talents yet simultaneously interwoven with 'nature' and the animal world. In this sense, his argument is consonant with the view that 'humans are an exceptional species, but... they should nonetheless be viewed as one among many interdependent species' (Catton and Dunlap, 1980: 33). In addition, even though Elias may sometimes underplay the plasticity of animal societies, this does not detract from the significance of his argument that language and the manipulation of symbols are central to human plasticity and exceptionalism. Although animals such as 'crocodiles and monkeys might participate in *some* aspects of language' (Connolly, 2002: 61, original emphasis), this does not mean that the linguistic skills of humans, crocodiles and monkeys are in any way equivalent, especially as they inform change in their respective societies. Similarly, although our close primates, such as chimpanzees, have been taught to understand a limited vocabulary, and even speak some words, it remains the case that we are the only primate who routinely uses and develops complex linguistic codes. As Stephen Horigan notes, 'ape language experiments exhibit a marked degree of anthropocentrism' (1988: 100), and sometimes resemble a desperate attempt to impose a symbolic system on our closest primates. Yet quite apart from the resistance of other primates to such anthropocentric ambition, it remains the case that no other primate uses symbolic systems in the ways that humans do. As Elias notes, it is because of language that 'in the case of human societies a great social change can occur such as that from tribe to empire without any biological change' (Elias, 1991a: 31–32). In other words, it is this interrelation between linguistic flair and social change that appears particular to human beings.

At the same time, linguistic ability represents a remarkable biological endowment. It is 'the *organic structure* of human beings which makes knowledge possible... through language and... the transmission of knowledge from generation to generation' (Elias, 1991a: 90, added emphasis). Social change is therefore a consequence of the possibilities of human biology. On the one hand, the human brain facilitates a 'greatly extended human capacity for storing sound patterns and thought-images' (Elias, 1991a: 91). On the other, 'the human vocal apparatus, including its neural equipment, easily admits extensions and changes of any given fund of sound patterns' (1991a: 36). These biologically enabled cognitive and linguistic skills create the opportunity for human plasticity. As Elias puts it, 'human beings are *biologically capable* of changing the manner of their social life. By virtue of their evolutionary endowment they can develop socially' (1991a: 36, added emphasis). Language and culture represent a product of our particular evolution, and its biological affordances. Culture and biology do not therefore constitute opposites: they are entirely intertwined.

As Elias was aware, human emotions provide further illustration of the interweaving of biology and culture since emotion pervades our everyday experience (Lyon, 1996; Williams, 2003a). In other words, human thought is about more than just the cognitive sense of language since thought is nearly always imbued with affect and emotion. This emotional undercurrent may be experienced as background noise, but this noise rarely fades away entirely. William Connolly quotes Nietzsche's observation that 'between two thoughts all kinds of affects play their game; but their motions are too fast, therefore we fail to recognise them' (Nietzsche, 1968: 263–264, cited in Connolly, 2002: 66). Yet should we choose to 'listen', the emotional quality of our thought can be sensed by our body's resonances, such as the feeling in our guts or the sweatiness of our skin. To others, it may be 'felt' through our facial expression, the tone of our voice, or the intensity, or otherwise, of our eye contact. In this sense, thought and emotion are intertwined, and given that 'affect is part of our biology' (Connolly, 2002: 66), it reinforces the argument that culture and biology are inseparable.

Yet to return to Elias, it is still language that has a forceful claim on human social plasticity since it represents a biological endowment that frees human beings from the constraints of biology. Though operating from a rather different perspective, Gilles Deleuze and Félix Guattari make a similar point to Elias when they argue that 'in language, not only is expression independent of content, but form of expression is independent of substance' (1988: 62). Critically, 'the same form can pass from one substance to another, which is not the case for the genetic code, for example, between RNA and DNA chains' (Deleuze and Guattari, 1988: 62). We might question the latter argument by invoking neo-Lamarckian notions of epigenetic inheritance. Yet even a Lamarckian sense of epigenetics is not consonant with the 'independence' of language, its 'free-floating' form where referent is unhitched from object in a manner that creates an openness and potentiality for rapid social change. In contrast, though DNA, RNA and cellular reproduction are dependent on unstable processes (Keller, 2000), their net effect tends toward a constancy of process that can sometimes appear linear in its effects. Even when there is disturbance to a DNA sequence (through mutation) 'thanks to the blind fidelity of the mechanism, [it] will be automatically reproduced' (Monod, 1972: 109). Although certain life forms, such as viruses, may rapidly change, they still appear reliant for their replication on biological processes that may be of considerable duration, such as those involved in 'lytic' or 'lysogenic' cycles.[3] Furthermore, in many areas of biology there seems to be a *relatively* closed relation between biological 'information' and biological structure, such as occurs with the complex processes surrounding DNA and RNA in structuring proteins and cells. A similar relationship is not apparent in relation to language. Language as a 'code' does not determine social structure. As Deleuze and Guattari suggest, because the human 'form of expression becomes linguistic rather than genetic', it 'operates with *symbols* that are comprehensible, transmittable, and modifiable from outside' (1988: 60, added emphasis). It is the openness of this symbolic activity which allows for the possibility that social time will appear consonant with change because we can move beyond mere repetition and imagine 'new worlds'. As Slavoj Žižek puts it in a manner reminiscent of Elias, language allows humans to 'detach themselves from the immersion in their environs and thus acquire a proper symbolic distance toward it' (Žižek, 2004: 144).

To sum up, Elias's argument suggests that we cannot treat the natural and social temporality in equivalent terms because 'liquid language' (Bachelard, 1983: 189) creates a potential for rapid social change that limits the likelihood of *longue durée* social structures (see Chapter 6). As a consequence, the apparent longevity of natural processes is not similarly mirrored in the social arena. In furthering such argument, Elias illustrates how human biology is directly interwoven with human social plasticity because the latter relies on the biologically endowed human capacity for language.[4] This stress on a biologically enabled linguistic plasticity is also relevant to Hacking's distinction between natural and social kinds (see Chapter 3). As a further illustration of the significance of Elias's attention to language, it's worth briefly exploring the way in which it can inform Hacking's (1999) conjecture.

Elias and Hacking

The preceding discussion provides some purchase on the issues that are left unresolved in Hacking's distinction between 'social kinds' which are 'interactive' and 'natural kinds' which are 'indifferent'. As noted in Chapter 3, Hacking argues that knowledge of the social world is interactive: Knowledge about issues such as children's viewing of television informs and changes the behaviour of parents and children. In contrast, natural kinds such as quarks are indifferent in the sense that 'calling a quark a quark makes no difference to the quark' (1999: 105). In Hacking's conception, it is human awareness that is central to the interactivity of social kinds. Unlike quarks and microbes who do not 'know what they are doing' (Hacking, 1999: 106), our awareness enables us to interactively respond to social knowledge, and this distinction 'forms a fundamental difference between the natural and the social sciences' (Hacking, 1999: 32). In addition, this awareness means that social knowledge lacks constancy. It is a 'moving target' (Hacking, 1999: 114) because human awareness allows us to interact and change social kinds. They are slippery and, one might say, plastic.

Though Hacking's account is very interesting, it is foreshortened. It fails to explain what it is about human awareness that differentiates it from that of a quark or a microbe. It is to this omission that Elias speaks. Although Elias does not provide a full-blown theory of human awareness, he nevertheless focuses on a crucial ingredient of the instability of social kinds, namely human language. It is the biological capacity for language that enables human beings to reflect on, and react to, social categorisations. Elias not only stresses the centrality of language to the instability of social kinds, but also the way in which this key facet differs from the awareness of other animals. The more limited symbolic ability of most other animals means that open learning and plasticity do not predominate to quite the same extent. Language frees human beings from these constraints and enables us to create, communicate and respond to social know-ledge. In other words, language is central to the interactivity and instability of Hacking's (1999) social kinds. From an Eliasian perspective, it is surprising that Hacking did not draw on his earlier interest in language (Hacking, 1975, 1998) since attention to language provides a means to understand the instability and interactivity of social kinds. It is the biologically endowed capacity for language that explains why social kinds represent a 'moving target' (Hacking, 1999: 114) whereas natural kinds appear to us to exhibit a greater talent for stability.

Sands of time

Elias provides a number of other illustrations of the interrelation between language and human plasticity (Elias, 1991a, 1992). One of the most succinct is contained in his story of the 'Athenian hourglass'. It is particularly inter-esting for present purposes because it accentuates the association between relative constancy/inconstancy and nature/society, and the significance of language to this distinction.

As Elias notes, ancient Athenians used the hourglass as a means of ensuring parity between speakers engaged in debate. The advantage of the hourglass was that it enabled social exchange to be standardised because 'the sand running out indicated clearly when a speaker was running on beyond the appointed limit, longer than the other [speaker]' (1992: 102). In this way, they could make sure that, say, two opposing speakers spoke for the same amount of time. In effect, they used the 'repeatable' characteristics of 'time-meters', such as hourglasses, sundials or clocks, as a device to 'measure' the 'unrepeatable' quality of human exchange. Specifically, Elias argues that human speech is 'a continuous sequence of *unrepeatable changes*' (1992: 101, added emphasis) whereas the movement of sand through the hourglass refers to 'repeatable sequences of change which, in so far as *they are repeatable, are unchanging*' (1992: 101, added emphasis).[5] To put this another way, the social arena appears characterised by a series of unique events to the extent that they are rarely repeated in the same way. What we say or do about something is seldom the same on two different occasions. In contrast, physical processes, such as the boiling of water, or sand falling through an hourglass, do appear to us to be repeatable in that they seem to deliver the same 'outcome' again and again. We can invoke quantum mechanics to understand boiling water, or Newtonian mechanics to explore sand in an hourglass. In so doing, we might question whether these processes are 'unchanging' (Elias, 1992: 101, see above). The quantum process surrounding the boiling of water appears difficult to predict. Similarly, it is impossible to predict exactly which grains of sand fall through an hourglass first since we can only assess their predictive probabilities. Yet there remains a conditional regularity and specificity in their pattern of overall change and the 'outcomes' that we perceive.

This story provides further illustration of the way in which human language and speech appears more plastic and indeterminate to us than many physical processes. In addition, if we follow Elias, it suggests that human language is central to this plasticity because of its 'open', and therefore 'unrepeatable', form. To be sure, we could programme linguistic exchange by training speakers in a debate to say exactly the same thing in the same order in the same time interval. In this manner, we might produce a repeatable exchange similar to the programming language that enables computers to produce repeatable outcomes. If the speakers in a debate were so trained, they might produce speech patterns that were as predictable as sand falling through an hourglass. Yet such highly contrived predictability could only be achieved by severely restricting the potentiality of human language. As a consequence, the interaction would be rendered meaningless as a human debate. Furthermore if we follow hermeneutic tradition, the inherent attributes of human language are a semantic indeterminacy and ambiguity. For instance, the arguments of a speaker in a debate may well be subject to more interpretations than there are listeners in her audience. As Hans-Georg Gadamer argues, 'it is enough to say that one understands differently, if one understands at all' (Gadamer, 1986: 302, cited in Davis, 1996: 115) since language can always be subject to further interpretation. Language also produces change through the smallest of inflections. As Connolly observes, merely 'to place a new word or phrase into an established [intersubjective] network [of meaning] is also to alter the network itself in a small or large way' (Connolly, 2002: 71). In addition, as we listen to any speaker, we all tend to hear different things and often 'more' than the speaker intended, and in this sense language contains 'an inexhaustible surplus of meaning' (Levinas, 1994b: 109). Yet if we could eliminate this intrinsic plasticity from human language, its 'condition of flux' (Elias, 1991a: 61), we would remove much of its significance for human sociality.

Elias's story thus dramatises the differences between our perception of temporality in human sociality and other aspects of nature. The precision and replicability of the hourglass provide its utility as a measure of the unrepeatable character of human conversation. As Elias also reminds us, such regularities are interwoven with the broader relationship between natural science and the performance of regularity. For example, Galileo's famous experiments in mechanics relied on time-meters such as water-clocks in order to be able to show that, say, a physical object repeatedly dropped towards the earth with same acceleration (Elias, 1992: 107–115).[6] Following Elias, we have far greater difficulty in applying such temporal feats to the social arena. Unlike the hourglass or the water-clock, the replicability of human social exchange is continually corroded by the indeterminacy, 'excess' and plasticity of language.

Technolinguistics

The preceding discussion is not meant to suggest that Elias's argument is without limitation. In particular, his overall thesis is circumscribed to the extent that language is not the only source of human plasticity. As Eliasians such as Johan Goudsblom (1992) have observed, *technical* abilities such as the domestication of fire also defined human society and differentiated us from other animals. For example, the control of fire greatly increased human plasticity by enabling our forebears to clear land and to increase hunting skills. In addition, it extended the range of edible food through cooking and allowed earlier humans to create 'small enclaves of warmth and light' as 'a buffer against the extremes of cold and darkness' (Goudsblom, 1992: 39). More generally, human beings have transformed their worlds through a range of other technical artefacts such as utensils, weapons, printing, automobiles, and so on. Although Elias attends to the history surrounding such technology, he does not place a strong emphasis on it as a possible source of human plasticity.[7] In this context, Ian Burkitt (1999) provides a helpful corrective by showing how human plasticity derives from linguistic *and* technological competences that have afforded humans an unparalleled success in utilising the 'fruits of the earth'. Furthermore, this technological rapacity has enabled industrial and post-industrial societies to be far less dependent on the immediate demands of nature, such as the tillage of the soil or the continuous need to work to satisfy hunger.

Burkitt draws on Evald V. Ilyenkov's account of 'the thinking body'. As Ilyenkov stresses, 'there are not two different and originally contrary objects of investigation – body and thought – but only *one single* object, which is the *thinking body* of living, real man [*sic*]' (1977: 31, original emphasis). From this perspective, human plasticity derives from all the objects which humans have created, from dwellings and weapons to tools and utensils, *as well as* language and other signs and symbols. To put this another way, the constructionist elevation of language and symbols is inverted by Ilyenkov's extension of the Hegelian argument that the individual discovers himself 'as a *thinking* being in his actions' (Ilyenkov, 1977: 175). As Burkitt notes:

> Ilyenkov reverses the argument often run by Mead and other latter-day social constructionists that objects take on a meaning because of their inclusion in symbolic systems, thus giving primacy to signs. Instead, for Ilyenkov, symbols and words are sub-classes of all humanly created meaningful artifacts, rather than the primary base of all meaning.
>
> (1999: 36)

We can debate this 'action oriented' inversion. For instance, Ilyenkov notes that the individual 'does not act immediately according to any one prepared scheme, like an automaton or an animal, but considers the scheme of the forthcoming action *critically*' (1977: 49, added emphasis). Following Elias, such 'critical thinking' is reliant on our highly developed skills of symbolisation. In other words, the 'thinking body' can only invoke the world beyond it because language enables complex symbolic thought, and in consequence, language still appears as the primary proficiency underlying human exceptionalism. To use one of Ilyenkov's best-known examples, I can only 'describe a circle with my hand on a piece of paper' (1977: 69) because of my ability to *symbolise* circles, either through imagination, drawing, or mathematics. Similarly, as Burkitt acknowledges, the uniqueness of human artefactual creation derives from the way in which they are inscribed 'with a symbolic significance' (1999: 40). This occurs because 'language . . . has a profound influence on the human body' (1999: 40).

Yet even if language retains a primacy, Burkitt appears right to emphasise that it is insufficient. Our plasticity relies on an inseparable fusion of techno-linguistic skill, and in consequence, intergenerational knowledge is transmitted by the 'body' as much as the 'mind'. For example, human technolinguistic ability has enabled us to move at speeds well beyond those for which we are endowed by genetic inheritance and maturational development. Bicycles, cars, trains and planes have allowed us to traverse space at an accelerating pace whilst electronic skills have created the 'instantaneous' delivery of information around the globe (Urry, 2000). At the same time, we intergenerationally transmit this *embodied* knowledge. Many children grow up in worlds where artefacts such as cars surround them and they 'learn' this technology as much from bodily experience as the linguistic and symbolic representation of automobiles. In other words, human social flexibility is not only due to language. It also results from our ability to manipulate tools through dexterous hand–eye coordination. 'Technology and language, tool and symbol, free hand and supple larynx' (Deleuze and Guattari, 1988: 60) are central to human plasticity.

In terms of natural and social temporality, it is this technolinguistic aptitude that gave humans the ability to detect, *and use*, seemingly stable processes in the natural world. As noted, our forebears observed that the friction of two materials could 'spark' tinder and thereby create the remarkable sociotechnical achievement known as the control of fire (Goudsblom, 1992), and they may have gradually realised that this technique could be repeated with regularity given the conditional 'dynamic' stability of the natural processes surrounding fire. Through intergenerational communication, this human technolinguistic plasticity has increased via technologies such as the Athenian hourglass or the 'great inventions' of ancient China, such as the magnetic compass, paper, printing and gunpowder (Needham, 1956). Humans learnt that these technologies would produce the same result again and again due to the natural stabilities which they appeared to incorporate, such as the Earth's magnetic field or the explosive gases produced by gunpowder. In this sense, the history of science and technology addresses the relation between differing temporalities – human plasticity and flux becomes interwoven with the apparent flux *and* dynamic stability of many natural processes (see Chapter 4). In other words, it is the exceptional technolinguistic plasticity of humans that has enabled us to interpret and apply the relative stabilities of nature. Though other animals may not be as pre-programmed as Elias was wont to suggest, their lack of technolinguistic expertise has meant that they have been unable to mould natural regularities in the manner that humans have achieved.

It is the higher level of human technolinguistic talent that defines our plasticity. As Karl Marx noted with respect to (what we now know) as the great Chinese inventions:

> *Gunpowder, the compass, and the printing press* were the 3 great inventions which ushered in bourgeois society. Gunpowder blew up the knightly class, the compass discovered the world market and founded the colonies, and the printing press was the instrument of Protestantism and the regeneration of science in general; the most powerful lever for creating the intellectual prerequisites.
>
> (1861–1863: 22, added emphasis)

Though this quotation may overplay technological determinism, it is nevertheless illustrative of the potency of technical flair in relation to social change. Once again, humanity appears as a meeting of temporalities, wherein the accelerating plasticity of human society results from our technolinguistic ability to 'play' with the seeming stabilities of nature.

Conclusion

Within Eliasian thought, the divide between culture and biology collapses. Culture, like language and knowledge, represents a biological endowment, a consequence of an inter-millennial intertwining of biological and cultural evolution. Yet human culture, with its reliance on extremely complex symbolisation, remains an exception amongst animals. Although Elias stresses human interconnectedness with other animals, he also emphasises that humans have developed a complexity of symbolic thought unmatched in other animals, even amongst our primate cousins.

At the same time, language and symbolisation appear central to our perception of 'nature' and 'society'. Language is fundamental to human plasticity and our transcendence beyond biological determinism. Equally, it is the reason why Hacking's (1999) social kinds appear as 'moving targets' whereas natural kinds can seem relatively 'stable' and 'indifferent'. Language affords a remarkable plasticity and changeability in human social configurations. If we add technology to this argument, it is the openness of human technolinguistic society that makes it unlikely that the social domain will mirror that of nature, especially with regard to the longevity apparent in many natural processes. Longevity and constancy remain tenuous attributes of the social terrain because they can be continually corroded by the plasticity, indeterminacy and excess contained in human technological and linguistic skill.

In consequence, equanimous desires to flatten out differences between the natural and the social realm appear compromised. We tend to see the natural and the social differently and we have difficulty in 'playing' with temporality in a similar fashion in both domains. For example, although the demonstration of regularity and replicability remains precarious in the natural sciences, it is often impossible in many fields of social science. Following Elias, this is because of the open-ended indeterminacy of human language and its impetus toward a plastic sociality wherein any one social 'event' is unlikely to be repeated in quite the same way. In other words, the human social arena remains highly historically specific. As noted this specificity also derives from the human talent for technology. In this context, human plasticity partly represents the interweaving of human technolinguistic skill with the relative stabilities of many natural processes. For example, the human ability to control fire (Goudsblom, 1992) represents a conjoining of human plasticity with the apparently dynamic stability of natural processes, such as that which we *repeatedly* observe when we strike a match. In other words, human technological *plasticity* frequently assumes some *stability* in natural process.

As will be discussed in Chapter 6, the above arguments have interesting implications for the debate between social constructionists and realists (see Chapter 2). For instance, realists exhibit a penchant for notions of social stability such as those contained in references to social structure or social 'endurance'. Yet if language and technology corrode social stability, the question arises as to whether allusions to social constancy remain perilous. In addition, can they survive if one assumes that social change is 'accelerating'? In the next chapter, I will pursue these questions and attempt to show how perceptions of social temporality remain central to the perennial dispute between constructionism and realism.

6

TEMPORALITY AND REALISM

How does perception of temporality affect epistemological debate? To what extent do disputes, such as that between realists and constructionists, pivot around issues of temporality? This chapter will consider such questions by addressing three related concerns. First, critical realism will be analysed as a response to changing perceptions of temporality. Second, attention shall be paid to the way in which our sense of natural and social temporality informs sociologies of nature and interacts with realist and constructionist conjecture. Third, related epistemological excursions will be examined by questioning the validity of natural science concepts such as 'emergence' and 'complexity' when they are applied to the social domain.

Temporality and critical realism

Preceding chapters have suggested that we should remain open to the possibility of difference between the social and natural arena. At the same time, they have explored arguments which suggest that the twentieth and twenty-first century have been characterised by increasing 'speed' and instability. In what follows, I wish to apply these debates to critical realist thought. The latter is interesting because its defence of social stability appears problematic in a world of seemingly 'accelerating' change. If all is flux, preserving thoughts of stability can resemble an unwarranted nostalgia that is at odds with the 'new world' of flow, mobility and networks (Castells, 1996; Urry, 2000). Can we defend concepts such as social structure that assume some measure of stability? In spite of perceptions of accelerating social change, critical realists tend to assume that we can (Archer *et al.*, 1998). In so doing, they offer an avenue through which to pursue the relation of discourses of temporality to epistemological debate within sociology. In particular, critical realism provides a means to examine the effects of historical specificity within social science. In addition, the contention of critical realists is interesting because comparison between the social and natural domain forms a key part of their argument.

Critical realists are aware of the significance of perceived temporality, including the way in which it may differentiate between natural and social worlds. As Tony Lawson, notes:

82

Certainly, some allowance must be made for the fact that the natural sciences, by and large (but not exclusively), concern themselves with improving their theories of a relatively unchanging (or only slowly changing) reality while the social sciences concern themselves with understanding . . . a relatively fast changing reality, i.e. a highly space–time specific, world.

(1997: 224)

Or as Andrew Collier acknowledges, 'there is a vast difference in timescale between the "relative endurance" of social structures and natural ones' (1994: 244). To this extent, these writers corroborate the arguments of Elias that were explored in Chapter 4. Yet they differ from Elias in defending concepts which incorporate a stronger sense of *social* endurance, repetition, or regularity. Where Elias refers to social regularities, it is chiefly to the chains of interdependence which exist between people. He stresses that these interdependency chains are 'elastic, . . . variable, . . . changeable' (Elias, 1991b: 16). Social life is a result of the interweaving between these interdependency chains, and the complexity of this interweaving means that social outcomes are generally unplanned and unpredictable. Social relations are like a game where, though the players 'always have control over each other' (Elias, 1970: 81, original emphasis), they are nevertheless often unable to effect their preferred outcome.[1] In this context, it is theoretically possible that repetition and regularity would be observed such that similar social conditions effect similar outcomes. Yet this possibility remains unlikely because any moment in time represents a complex interweaving between numerous agents. *Social* complexity implies particularity, and given such particularity, the question remains as to why we should witness repetition, regularity or endurance of social relations across time. In other words, though Elias does exhibit a fondness for certain social regularities (Newton, 2003b),[2] his overall thesis is corrosive of the tendency to assume social stability and endurance since he tended to stress that 'we live in a world of continuous change' (Elias, 1975/2005: 03: 00). In contrast to Elias, many critical realists retain a preference for notions that contain a sense of social endurance. In particular, they support conditional social 'laws', 'recipes' and 'tendencies' and infer stability to social structure. In the ensuing discussion, I shall explore how these concepts are made problematic by discourses of temporality, particularly those relating to speed and acceleration. At the same time, I will compare the relative ease with which critical realist argument can be applied to the social and natural arena.

Drawing the line: laws, tendencies and recipes

As noted in Chapter 4, there has been increasing attention to the 'speed' of 'accelerating' social change (Virilio, 1986, 1991) and the popular, if debatable, image of a frenetic, 'go-faster' world (Thrift, 2001). Urry's sense of 'instantaneous time' provides a sociological imagination that stresses how 'products, places and people go rapidly in and out of fashion . . . time-horizons for decision-making dramatically shrink . . . and new technologies of information and communication instantaneously transcend space at the speed of nanoseconds' (2000: 125).

This 'fast pace' thesis raises the question of whether all social analyses must remain highly time-specific. If everything is continuously being socially transformed, can we entertain ideas of social relations that have constancy or will transcend time? In spite of Urry's (2000) image of human 'hyperplasticity', critical realists argue that we can. In addition, they have a first line of defence against the use of discourses of temporality as a means to question critical realist contention. In consequence, we need to address it before we can consider how temporality creates tensions for critical realism. This defence derives from Roy Bhaskar's distinction between the nature of being and of knowledge. Bhaskar adopts a position which is not extraordinary in itself, namely that human knowledge cannot encompass the ontological world as 'it is'. Yet what differentiates Bhaskar is his desire to preserve a distinction between 'contingent, historically transient' (Bhaskar, 1989a: 5) human knowledge and an intransitive ontological realm that is 'irreducible to patterns of events and active independently of their identification by human beings' (Bhaskar, 1989a: 11). Human knowledge remains an unstable account of an intransitive ontological realm, or the '*changing* knowledge of *unchanging* objects' (Bhaskar, 1989a: 11, added emphasis). In consequence, it could be argued that discourses of temporality, such as that of accelerating social change, are irrelevant to critical realism because it is ultimately concerned with the human attempt to *approximate* an intransitive realm of being. Critical realists can therefore argue that social 'acceleration' merely reflects the historically transient nature of human knowledge and its inconsistent speed of change, sometimes accelerating and sometimes slowing. Beyond this lies an unchanging realm which is unaffected by such variable human knowledge.

There remain two difficulties with this argument. The first arises because Bhaskar can be accused of creating a philosophical dualism wherein an ultimately unknowable intransitive 'other' is divorced from human knowledge. The question arises as to how one can posit an intransitive realm that is somehow unaffected by human knowledge and experience. In particular, how can there be an intransitive element to the social realm when it can only remain a human social construction (King, 1999)? As it is us who create our social world, how can there be an intransitive arena that remains 'beyond us'? It is one thing to suggest that natural objects are 'indifferent', as Hacking (1999) concludes. Yet it is another to assume a kind of 'ontological divorce' between an intransitive and transitive realm, especially when the intransitive includes the social domain. As Burkitt notes, Bhaskar's 'reality appears to be governed by its own laws in some independent realm that is distinct from humans' (Burkitt, 1999: 73). In sum, can one defend this seemingly *asocial* analysis?

The second problem is that a number of critical realists espouse a desire for human knowledge that is *time transcendent*. In other words, in spite of Bhaskar's separation of transitive human knowledge from an intransitive ontological realm, there remain critical realists who wish to specify knowledge of human *social* affairs which can stand the test of time. But can one create such time transcendent human knowledge? Furthermore, how can it be accommodated to Bhaskar's position which suggests that human knowledge is transitive and time-specific rather than intransitive and transcendent? Critical realists answer this question by arguing that time transcendent human knowledge can be produced by predicting the form of social relations which will arise *whenever particular social conditions are found*. Collier illustrates this conditional regularity thesis through the example of capitalism. Collier argues that:

> [social] laws can be formulated in terms which are universal, by virtue of being *conditional*: 'if the ownership of productive wealth is separated from the direct producers and divided between competing sellers of the products, then tendencies x, y, z will operate'.
>
> (Collier, 1994: 244, original emphasis)

In effect, Collier argues that there is a 'deep generative structure' to capitalism such that one can formulate conditional social laws as to its operations. If we find particular capitalist conditions, then we can propose a social law which states that 'x, y and z' will tend to happen under these circumstances. In consequence, even though social structures are 'only relatively enduring' (Collier, 1994: 244), they are time transcendent by virtue of operating *whenever* 'tendencies x, y, z...operate' (Collier, 1994: 244). Ted Benton makes a very similar point in arguing that social structures have 'tendencies and powers' which are *universal wherever the appropriate structures are instantiated* (1981: 18, added emphasis). Similarly Margaret Archer suggests that social and cultural 'recipes' 'will still work if tried a hundred years later when someone re-discovers it and has the motive to try it' (1995: 144). In effect, these writers argue that even if the social arena is characterised by flux and change, it is nevertheless possible to formulate time transcendent social laws, patterns and recipes. They suggest that whenever the 'right' conditions exist, these social 'tendencies' will be observed.

The difficulties of applying this kind of conditional argument to the social domain have however been noted for some time. For instance, writing in 1935, Collingwood observed the problem of trying to defend social statements that presume law-like or conditional regularity. Using the example of the Greek ideal of the city-state, Collingwood suggested that historical specificity precluded the possibility of their application:

> The political philosophy of Plato and Aristotle teaches in effect that city-states come and go, but the idea of the city-state remains for ever as the one social and political form towards whose realization human intellect, so far as it is really intelligent, strives. According to modern ideas, the city-state is as transitory a thing as Miletus or Sybaris. It is not an eternal ideal, it was merely the political ideal of the ancient Greeks.

Other civilizations have had before them other political ideals, and human history shows a change not only in the individual cases in which these ideals are realized or partially realized, but in the ideals themselves. Specific types of human organization, the city-state, the feudal system, representative government, capitalist industry, are characteristic of certain historical ages.

(Collingwood, 1946: 210–211)

While we might debate whether the Aristotelian notion of the city-state is quite as mutable as Collingwood suggests (Gadamer, 1986), the general point remains: social relations remain highly historically specific. As Collingwood further observes (in a manner slightly reminiscent of Elias):

The behaviour-patterns characteristic of a feudal baron were no doubt fairly constant so long as there were feudal barons living in a feudal society. But they will be sought in vain . . . in a world whose social structure is of another kind . . . social orders are historical facts, and subject to inevitable changes, fast or slow. A positive science of mind will, no doubt, be able to establish uniformities and recurrences, but it can have no guarantee that the laws it establishes will hold good beyond the historical period from which its facts are drawn. Such a science . . . can do no more than describe in a general way certain characteristics of the historical age in which it is constructed.

(Collingwood, 1946: 223–224)

In sum, as Collingwood argued, any social relation tends to reflect 'a certain stage in history' (Collingwood, 1946: 229), and cannot be read as indicative of a conditional universality whenever 'tendencies x, y, z . . . operate' (Collier, 1994: 244) because such tendencies are unlikely to reappear in a similar form. Yet the same does not apply to the natural domain. Consider again the statement, 'make water hot and it will tend to expand, evaporate and boil'. Collier uses almost exactly this statement in order to illustrate the 'tendencies' associated with a causal law (1994: 65). Yet as a *natural* tendency, it differs from a social tendency because, as critical realists sometimes acknowledge, 'social structures and mechanisms are *more highly space–time specific* than natural (e.g. biological and geological) ones typically are' (Bhaskar, 1989a: 175, original emphasis). For instance, it is probable that the statement, 'make water hot and it will tend to expand', will hold in another millennium, the only proviso being that water and heat still exist. Chaotic or complex behaviour does not negate the endurance of such probabilities (Eve, 1997). The heating of water is a 'chaotic process' yet still seems to inexorably lead to expansion and evaporation. Even within quantum mechanics, it is likely that the probability of a researcher seeing a wave or a particle will be the same in another thousand years given the same conditionalities. For though the object of study within quantum mechanics is inherently probabilistic, the properties of the distribution appear to be stable across time. In other words, although the outcome of a particular experiment may change from experiment to experiment, the probability of the outcome may well be similar in a thousand years time, even though scientific understanding of the processes involved remains historically contingent, and therefore subject to revision (Hacking, 1999; Wray, 2005). Yet such apparent durability is unlikely in the social arena. On the one hand, writers such as Fernand Braudel may be right to argue that certain social patterns, such as inequality, will persist since their elimination would require that 'all the social hierarchies will have to overthrown' (1985: 628). On the other hand, it is difficult to state what 'tendencies' will be associated with, say, wealth inequality in another thousand years, because they are likely to vary considerably, as reflected in the 'recent' uneven transition from tribal to feudal, to mercantile, industrial, financial and global capitalist societies. Beyond the general difficulties of explaining open systems (Bhaskar, 1978, 1989b), the specificity of the social means that there is very little probability of observing any particular social tendency a thousand years hence. In sum, what is the relevance of supposedly time transcendent social laws, patterns and recipes when they apply to highly specific moments in time and space?[3]

Some critical realists acknowledge that the social arena is 'a relatively fast changing reality' (Lawson, 1997: 224) and therefore more time–space specific. However they still stress social continuities and stabilities in spite of the fact that a 'fast changing' social arena implies specificity and a consequent inability to articulate social patterns or recipes that have constancy across time. Other critical realists address this tension by playing down the differences between the social and natural arena. For instance, Ted Benton acknowledges that 'long term historical prediction' is difficult in the social sciences because of the temporal variance of its subject matter (1981: 18). Benton then goes on to argue that substantially the same situation applies in the natural sciences: 'epistemologically speaking, the situation is quite comparable with the natural sciences. On the very much greater time-scale of biological, geological and cosmological change the comparable long-term historical prediction is equally suspect' (1981: 18). Yet this seems a strange comparison. To say that physical and biological science breaks down and is 'suspect' over millions of years can hardly be used as a justification for the failure of the social sciences to predict well even in the extremely short term. Many physical and biological processes appear to us to exhibit durability over the very long term, a situation which does not seem to apply within the social arena.

In a similar fashion to Benton, Tony Lawson maintains that the situation in the natural and social sciences is essentially the same:

> Certainly any social tendency in play will be dependent upon certain social structures being in place. But the operations of any natural tendencies will be conditional upon natural structures in *exactly the same way*. Thus, just as any inherent tendency for (capitalist) profit rates to

fall will depend upon capitalist structures (or other appropriate conditions) being sustained, so the disposition for, say, water to dissolve sugar will only be exercised where water exists. Both structures are *currently* present on planet Earth but (apparently) absent on planet Venus.

(1997: 223–224, original and added emphasis)

The problem once again with this argument is the seeming inconstancy of the social arena as compared with the natural domain (see Chapter 4). In other words, the two appear dissimilar because the relation between a social structure such as capitalism and its 'tendencies' looks likely to vary considerably across a *relatively* short space in time, as reflected in shifts from mercantile to industrial and to global capitalism, and so on. Both Lawson's examples may 'currently' exist on planet Earth, but only water seems likely to us to exhibit its tendency to dissolve sugar across future millennia.

In sum, it remains difficult for critical realists to transfer the time transcendent performances of natural science to social science. Conditional replicability and regularity are not easy feats to perform in natural science. In the social arena, they are extremely difficult even where one tightly constrains social process through, say, the activities of experimental social psychologists (Orne, 1962; Wetherell and Potter, 1992). Critical realist desires remain difficult to effect because social 'outcomes' reflect complex interweavings between numerous players (Elias, 1994). Of course, the natural world is also characterised by considerable complexity of process. Yet as the biology of cellular replication suggests, this does not mean that replicability and repetition are disabled in the natural world. In other words, the 'communication' involved is not entirely open-ended, and the complex cellular processes surrounding DNA, RNA, mRNA, etc., are based on a 'nucleotide language' that maintains an element of prescription (see Chapter 4). In contrast, human societies are remarkably open because of the 'free-floating' form of human and technolinguistic skill where expression is independent of substance (see Chapter 5). It is this open plasticity, combined with complex social interweaving, that mitigates against the likelihood of time transcendent laws, tendencies or recipes.

Social structure and endurance

It might however be argued that all is not yet slippery and changeable in the social arena. In particular, do there not remain *longue durée* structures such as capitalism? In consequence, is it not possible to speak of social stability and the endurance of social structures? At first sight, this appears an appealing argument. Yet there are a number of problems with it, not least of which is the tendency of *longue durée* structures such as capitalism to themselves be agents of social impermanency (Ruane, 2003). In addition, assumptions of social stability become more difficult to defend if one assumes an accelerating pace of social change. As Urry (2000) observes, sociological concepts which denote social stability appear increasingly compromised. If we live in a 'changeling' world, it becomes harder to argue that social structures are characterised by endurance. As some critical realists recognise, social concepts must be continuously revised because, as Hacking (1999: 113) suggests, they are 'moving targets':

> the faster nature, or greater space–time specificity, of social structures and mechanisms is itself sufficient for the hermeneutic moment to arise more frequently in social science ... As *structures and actions are continuously transformed* the social scientist will frequently need to re-investigate what is going on to *keep abreast* of the inherently non-predictable developments regularly taking place, including the transformation of human concepts.
>
> (Lawson, 1997: 225, added emphasis)

Yet the problem is not just that of 'keeping abreast' of social change. It is also that 'continual transformation' undermines the very relevance of concepts such as social structure. Their significance is called into question in a plastic world since social structures are traditionally seen as 'mechanisms that withstand the march of time' (Braudel, 1972: 353), or at least are resistant to it. The sociological centrality of structure, and structure/agency debates, is lessened if human hyperplasticity means that fewer and fewer 'social structures [are] sufficiently enduring for their examination to be feasible and worthwhile' (Outhwaite, 1987: 53). When social structures are fleeting, they lose much of their traditional meaning. Some writers may regret the increasing dominance of 'the terrain of the socio-cultural rather than the social structural' (Howson and Inglis, 2001: 314), but such dominance needs to be seen within the context of the perception of accelerating social change. If social scientists think we are moving toward a changeling world, the socio-cultural may advance, and the social structural wane. Human plasticity retains the potential to erode constancy and epistemological argument that assumes such constancy.

It is therefore not surprising that the issue of endurance has preoccupied critical realists (e.g. see Benton, 1981; Outhwaite, 1987; Collier, 1994). Indeed, for some it has become *the* concept to defend. For instance, Archer asserts that the social world only becomes empirically accessible to investigation because of the relative endurance of social relations and structures. Furthermore, she suggests that 'some version of "social science" could not even be voiced' if 'everything were subject to pure contingency' or where 'everything is flux' (1995: 166). Not surprisingly, in contrast to images of flux and turbulence, Archer highlights the existence of enduring roles such as that of employer and employee, or landlord and tenant. Such roles supposedly have a '*durability over time*, a capacity to endure despite ... changes in the personal features of their successive holders' (Archer, 1995: 276, added emphasis; cf. Lawson, 1997). Critical realists also suggest that we can speak of relatively stable social structures such as those which surround social class. On the one hand, class is socially constructed and its 'attributions, psychic identifications and claims may vary greatly' (Anthias, 2001: 386). On the other, the pace of change of such attributions and identifications can be relatively slow. As Gerard Hanlon observes, service classes are currently 'in the process of fragmenting' (1998: 58). Yet as he also suggests, such 'intra class fragmentation will . . . be a slow process – long-term party voters will not change their long-term political allegiances overnight' (Hanlon, 1998: 58). In other words, we cannot recreate our world in an instant and it is premature to suggest that the social landscape is already one of total turbulence and change.[4]

However further qualification needs to be made to these arguments. First, social structures may be defined by their endurance (Sibeon, 1999; cf. Giddens, 1984), but it is only when viewed from the perspective of an individual human lifetime that they appear stable. From the perspective of the 'very longue durée', social stabilities remain extremely short-term, a 'drop in the historical ocean'. Second, even situations of stability may themselves engender major social change, as illustrated by the argument that the social 'revolution' of the 1960s was conditioned by the economic stability of the 1950s and 1960s. Third, social relations that formerly appeared stable, such as that of the nuclear family, may become increasingly unstable if the pace of social change is accelerating. Fourth, the seeming simplicity of supposedly enduring roles, such as employer and employee, can hide increasing ambiguity and complexity. As Castells comments on our post-industrial landscape, 'who are the owners, who the producers, who the managers, and who the servants, becomes increasingly blurred in a production system of variable geometry, of teamwork, of networking, of outsourcing, and subcontracting' (1996: 475). Fifth, the particular form of 'enduring roles' can swiftly change depending on their social construction. For instance, the interdependency between employer and employee, or between landlord and tenant, can change rapidly through industrial relations or housing legislation, or through variation in the extent to which such legislation is locally enacted. To take a British example, employer–employee relations quickly changed during the Thatcher administration of the 1980s. Sixth, questions arise as to whether any social structure, even *longue durée* structures, hold relevance in 'faster-paced modern societies where change is quick and sometimes of paramount historical importance' (Green and Troup, 1999: 93).[5] In addition, even if there remain *longue durée* structures, they may contain the seeds of their own inconstancy. For instance, Braudel (1985) argued that capitalism was corrosive of older social structures even though he saw it as representing a *longue durée* structure. As Joseph Ruane observes, 'given that capitalism is a highly dynamic force and a potent solvent of traditional structures, this means that we now have a *longue durée* structure acting as a solvent of other *longue durée* structures' (2003: 13). Ruane suggests that this acknowledgement of the 'corrosive' effect of capitalism questions the relevance of *longue durée* structures as a source of constancy and social stability. As he notes, 'at this point the original notion of *longue durée* structures underpinning the constant, repetitive and quasi-immobile in social life is abandoned' (2003: 13–14).

90

Critical realists respond to such argument by pointing to further examples of relative social endurance (e.g. Lawson, 1997: 206–207). Yet demonstrating such endurance is not always straightforward. For instance, Archer (1995) argues that demography represents a *social* structure with 'a relatively *enduring emergent* property' (1995: 143–144, added emphasis). As Archer points out, a given population will be slow to change its age structure: a demography that is 'top-heavy' with a high proportion of older people will not normally change quickly to its opposite, a high percentage of young people. Unless the older people are decimated through disease, a sudden shift to a youthful population will not occur. Yet contrary to Archer, this is chiefly because of the endurance of biological structures, *not social structures*. If the eggs of human beings were 'hatched' within a week, and then reached sexual maturity within months, demographic structures relating to age could change much faster. In this case, a fast gestation and maturation would enable rapid changes in the proportion of young people. However the human pace of demographic change is limited by the slowness of human embryonic growth as well as the many years between birth and sexual maturity (Heer, 1975). This means that we cannot 'breed like rabbits'. The endurance of demographic structures derives therefore from their biological stability and the inability to 'speed up' gestation and maturation. We cannot yet re-write our biology, and this constitutes the principal reason why demographic age structures represent an enduring configuration. Demography is of course as much social as biological. There is no ontological divide and the social and biological remain completely intertwined. Yet it is the *biological* aspect of demographic age structures that largely guarantee their endurance, not as Archer suggests, its social structure. To put this another way, the problem with critical realist contention is its tendency to conflate understanding of natural and social temporality.

To sum up, critical realist desires for time transcendence provide an interesting illustration of the significance of temporality for current epistemological debate. At the heart of the debate between those who seek a 'new' sociology that abolishes the 'old' concepts of stability, and those who seek to preserve these traditional references, is contestation about perceived temporality. Critical realists wish to continue to entertain notions of stability and endurance whilst others, many of whom are sympathetic to social constructionism, seek to consign them to history. It is not surprising that realists argue that 'only on the metaphysical assumption that some relations are necessary and *at least relatively enduring* can we reasonably set out to practice science or to study society' (Archer, 1995: 166, added emphasis). This assumption is vital to their enterprise. Yet in a de-traditionalised and changeling world where everything becomes 'plastic', constructionism might become dominant because every social structure could be endlessly changed. If human social plasticity were total, the social arena would be open to continuous social reconstruction, and thereby also to constructionist argument.

Nevertheless, it is important to note that there are some counter-arguments to the foregoing, and that even if acceleration proceeds apace, it is perhaps

91

unlikely that *all* social stabilities will disappear. It is not yet possible to entirely dismiss 'the weight of the past' (Braudel, 1985: 628). First, the social is likely to continue to be conditioned by biological stabilities, such as those associated with gender, ethnicity, parenthood or, as noted above, human maturation. Second, the seeming 'dynamic' stability of many natural processes constrains our ability to socially reconstruct our world. In consequence, realists and constructionists are likely to continue their contestation through recourse to varying assumptions about temporality. On the one hand, there remain some limited social stabilities and it seems likely that critical realist argument will seek to capitalise upon them. On the other, these stabilities appear compromised by current discourses such as that of accelerating 'speed' and human plasticity. If acceleration is perceived to proceed 'apace', the debate is likely to sharpen between those who defend 'old' sociologies, such as that of social structure or even social laws, and those who proclaim a new sociology that either draws on social constructionism or stresses 'diverse mobilities' (Urry, 2000: 15). A central issue for these debates remains that of perceived temporality and the success of its use in bolstering competing positions.

Finally, it is of course worth noting that there is a broader interrelation between social theory and discourses of temporality. For example, could it be that the popularity of social theories more generally correlates with changing notions of temporality? The attention to ANT or Elias can be seen in this light. Considerable interest has been aroused by ANT, and as Dennis Smith notes, there has been a sharp 'upward trajectory' of interest in Elias since 1997 (Smith, 2000: 13). Both these approaches stress 'social ordering' rather than the stability of 'order' (Law, 1994: 2). The social world is recognised to be neither a shapeless pattern of 'shifting sands' nor a static landscape of stable social structures. Elias's (1994) concept of 'figuration' and the actor-network attention to reversibility (Callon, 1991) and 'ordering' may have gained popularity partly because they are sensitive to the mutability of social affairs. In a social world where it seems increasingly doubtful that 'fixed points can remain' (Urry, 2000: 17), social theories may prove more attractive if they can detect social patterns *within* a context of seemingly accelerating social instability. In sum, although it is unwarranted to see any social theory purely as a response to changing perception of temporality, it nevertheless may condition a range of theoretical debate.

Temporality and the sociology of nature

How does the foregoing argument affect current issues within the sociology of nature? In addressing this question, I shall briefly consider two examples, namely work on the sociology of the body and the sociology of the natural environment. In both these cases, sociologists are faced with the need to work *across* natural and social timescapes (Adam, 1990, 1998).

As Chris Shilling notes, 'the human body represents an excellent example of a phenomena that cannot be located exclusively in the social or the natural world'

(1993: 104). Yet sociologists who try to reconcile the 'culture' and 'nature' of the body have to address different senses of temporality. For example, to the extent that the sociology of the body is concerned with a *biological body*, one is dealing with bodily *processes* that appear characterised by a very slow pace of change, such as those surrounding the structuring of cells, protein and DNA. This slowness of change means that certain realist assumptions of structure, relative endurance, and conditional regularity are easier to defend. It can be conditionally assumed that synapses will continue to 'fire', cells will continue to replicate, or that more broadly, a breakdown in the relationship between biological flux and constancy will result in ill-health (see Chapter 4). At the same time, sociological inquiry that is based on strong constructionism appears constrained in relation to our biological bodies because they seem to contain longevities that put them beyond language alone. Human beings look likely to be largely composed of carbon, hydrogen and oxygen, no matter what we say or do. As will be argued in Chapter 7, even new genetics and genomics is not about to re-write these basic natural elements, or invent an entirely new biological language. In consequence, our bodies still contain substances which appear characterised by a notable longevity of process. Longevity implies extradiscursivity, and thereby, resistance to capture by social constructionism.

Yet the body is not just a biological entity but also a cultural object. The social interpretation of the body can rapidly change, as exampled by the increasing neuroticisation of the male body and the expectation that men as well as women must 'work' on their bodies (for an example, see any copy of *Men's Health* magazine and the frequent advice on how to, say, 'Upgrade your Abs'). The rapidity of such changes to cultural performance mean that realist assumptions of relative endurance or stable structures are far more difficult to maintain when the body is treated as cultural object. Because these performances are discursive, they are characterised by the plasticity associated with language. Establishing stability, laws or enduring 'recipes' within the *social body* remains difficult.

Culture, psyche and soma remain of course completely intertwined. Yet biological and social aspects of the body also represent the interweaving of different senses of temporality. In addressing the body, one is confronted with the difficulty of deriving a common epistemology across differing timescapes where part of what one is looking at may be stable for millennia, whilst other aspects may last no more than a few weeks (as with the fashions of body clothing). Those who attempt to explore *across* the biological and social must confront such difficulties, and therefore need to 'tread warily'.

Similar difficulties apply to other sociologies of nature, such as that relating to environmental degradation since we cannot easily 'reverse' environmental change within human lifetimes. On a relatively short time scale, it is difficult for us to reverse the effects of global warming through supposed carbon 'traps' such as forestry plantation. As Philip Fearnside, Daniel Lashof and Pedro Moura-Costa note, the impact of such carbon sinks will take effect 'decades into the future', whereas fossil fuel emission 'has immediate effects' (2000: 239).[6]

Similarly, the problems posed by nuclear waste involve a conflict between natural and social temporality. Nuclear installations contain a hybridity of physical and social processes (Callon, 1991) and thereby a hybridity of different temporal paces. 'Risk' derives directly from these different temporal paces since the *social context* of nuclear power could change *rapidly* to one characterised by political instability or military conflict, yet the temporality of nuclear radiation appears decidedly *long-term* (Adam, 1996, 1998). In consequence, as with the work on the body, sociologists addressing environmental degradation are involved, implicitly or explicitly, in developing epistemologies capable of working across these contrasting timescapes. For example, both realists and constructionists struggle to arrive at a position that can satisfactorily address the conjoint stability and instability inherent in the threat of nuclear radiation. Constructionist contention remains limited in dealing with nuclear radiation since its longevity places it beyond language. Although we socially construct nuclear technology, once nuclear waste exists, we cannot talk its radioactive effect out of existence, and therein lies the difficulty for 'the daughters and sons of our own and other species for thousands of years hence' (Adam, 1996: 326). Though the disposal of nuclear waste is a matter of social debate, our technological culture has not yet found a way to turn 'off' nuclear radiation. Little has substantively changed since Catton and Dunlap observed that the 'accumulations of toxic [nuclear] wastes... cannot presently be stored in [a] permanently safe fashion' (1980: 30). This raises the question of how constructionists epistemologically grapple with the extra-discursive. If they acknowledge the longevity and extradiscursivity of natural processes, they implicitly subscribe to a form of ontological oscillation that underscores 'the *reality* of environmental problems' (Burningham and Cooper, 1999: 305, added emphasis). If they 'bracket it out', realists may accuse them of failing to engage with the 'otherness' of nature, or being incapable of arriving at a political position which can present a critique of nuclear energy (see Chapter 2).

Yet at the same time, critical realists struggle in their desire to apply parallel argument to nature and society. Ironically if such parallels existed, the threat of nuclear waste would be lessened. For instance, if social structures were extremely stable over centuries, there would be less fear that nuclear installations would be endangered by military conflict, 'terrorism', or political instability. The problem of nuclear safety arises partly because natural stability appears to exist (i.e. radiation over several generations) but social stability does not. Nuclear waste thus points to the difficulties of critical realist epistemology in downplaying the different timescapes in natural and social processes. As argued above, this tactic is significant to their desire to construct notions such as conditional social laws, patterns, recipes, etc. Yet nuclear radiation points to the limitations of this tactic by reminding us that natural and social temporality are not 'quite comparable' (Benton, 1981: 18, see p. 87).

In sum, *the different temporalities which we perceive with the natural and social domain may favour different epistemologies, such as those associated with realism and constructionism.* It is not that epistemological position is determined by our perception of temporality, as Elias appears to suggest (see Chapter 4). Yet it may condition epistemological argument, favouring certain accounts over others. To put this another way, it is a considerable challenge to construct a single epistemological position capable of adequately addressing differences in natural and social temporality, and in this context, it is not surprising that natural and social scientists should turn to different epistemological frameworks. At the same time, it remains difficult to construct parallel worlds between the social and natural terrain (see Chapter 9). As a final illustration of these difficulties, I shall examine attempts to apply the concepts of emergence and complexity to social science.

Parallel worlds

Given the strength of anti-dualist argument, it is perhaps not surprising that sociologists should explore the natural sciences for argument which has correspondence with social science. 'Emergence' and 'complexity' represent two further concepts that have been borrowed from natural science and they are illustrative of the difficulties that can result from the desire for a common language. The first of these, emergence, is most frequently applied by critical realists. In arguing for social processes of emergence, critical realists draw on Bhaskar's (1978) argument that *both* the natural and the social world are stratified in such a way that relations between surface events and deeper ('generative') mechanisms is one of emergence, where the former presuppose the latter but are not reducible to them.

Perhaps the best-known critical realist use of emergence is contained in Archer's (1988, 1995, 1996, 1998) exposition on structure, agency and culture. Her account held appeal because it appeared to provide an answer to the old sociological conundrum of how we relate human agency to social structure (Giddens, 1984; Elias, 1994). Archer proposed that temporality could be used to differentiate social structure from human agency on the grounds that such structures frequently pre-exist current human actions. In other words, 'the majority of actors are the dead' (Archer, 1995: 148), and to follow Comte and Marx, we live in situations not of our own choosing. In consequence, *present* human agency occurs within social structures that were largely developed in the *past*.[7] Archer uses this observation to argue that 'people here present' and 'social structures' represent different social strata since the latter are 'divorced' from the former by virtue of being developed in the past. Social structures are therefore *emergent* because they are irreducible to the doings of contemporary actors yet have the 'generative' power to affect the activities of 'those here present'. For example, it is sometimes claimed that the European Union represents an institutional response to the experience of the Second World War. From a critical realist perspective, the actions of *present*-day European politicians and citizens are influenced by a *different level* of social strata, namely the *past* history of military conflict and the social structures to which it gave shape.

Stratification and emergence are concepts which can be easily applied to nature. For example, water cannot be *reduced* to its elements, hydrogen and oxygen, since it appears to operate at a different *stratum*. As Andrew Sayer notes, we cannot explain 'the power of water to extinguish fire by deriving it from the powers of its constituents, for oxygen and hydrogen are highly flammable' (Sayer, 1984: 109). Similarly though living matter can ultimately be reduced to 'simpler' inorganic molecules, it is nevertheless emergent from such inorganic matter if only by virtue of being 'alive'. Yet problems arise when this kind of conceptual language is applied to the social domain. As Tony King (1999) argues, there is a central flaw in Archer's use of a temporal argument to support realism because present social structures *can* be reduced to the actions of people in the past. On the one hand, the past does have independence in the sense that we cannot go back and change the ideas and actions of the long dead. On the other, this does not mean that *present* structures are not reducible to such people. As King notes, 'the "structure" which living individuals face, and which is supposed to be irreducible to other people is in fact, only these very other people interacting in the past' (1999: 210). In other words, present social structures are reducible to 'past people' for the simple reason that they were developed by them at various times in the past. In sum, people *are connected across time* rather than, as Archer implies, that time constitutes a 'divorce' which sets structures, or 'parts' of the system, apart from the 'people'. There is no such separation since life is lived continuously from one 'frame' to the next. For instance, if some people collectively create a new form of social structure, this does not mean that such a structure is not reducible to them if they suddenly were all to die tomorrow. Whether one wishes to stress historical continuity or discontinuity, the past does not constitute a divorce of people from social structure (Newton, 2004).

Yet the co-option of the language of emergence by critical realists reflects their tendency to believe that distinctions between social and natural structures are 'not a difference of principle, only of degree' (Collier, 1994: 245). If this is the case, then it is safer to assume that we can translate between natural and social science ideas. However such translation is at best questionable, and at worst symptomatic of the old social science tendency to ape the natural sciences. It might be thought that this vice would only pertain to committed realists, particularly those that exhibit a desire to perform natural science feats of endurance and replicability. But it can also be seen amongst those who wish to erect a 'new sociology' that moves beyond the limitations of the past. As we have seen, this desire characterises Urry's project (e.g. Macnaghten and Urry, 1998; Urry, 2000), spurred on by a sense that concepts such as social structure are increasingly irrelevant to sociology, whether they are perceived as 'emergent' or otherwise. In common with other writers (see Chapter 3), Urry uses the natural science concepts of complexity and chaos as aids to his new sociology. These concepts are seen as illustrative of 'becoming and rhythmicity', 'non-linear changes', 'counter-intuitive outcomes' and 'structural complexity' (Urry, 2000: 120–121). In the social arena, chaos and complexity are supposedly reflected in the processes surrounding global capitalism which appear 'non-linear, large-scale, unpredictable and partially ungovernable' (Urry, 2000: 208). Just as in the 'famous butterfly effect, where miniscule changes at one location produce . . . massive weather effects elsewhere' (Urry, 2000: 121), so 'small causes at certain places [under capitalism] produce large consequences elsewhere' (Urry, 2000: 208), such as that which followed the military develop-ment of Internet technology and 'the almost overnight collapse of all of Eastern Europe' (Urry, 2000: 209).

With its stress on chaotic behaviour and diachronic (and hence historical) analysis, chaos and complexity theory does appear to portray a natural universe that parallels that attributed to the social domain. The plasticity of the social seems to be mirrored by the seemingly chaotic and 'aperiodic' behaviour found in, say, physical turbulence or weather patterns. Just as writers on social theory such as Elias (1970) underline the 'unintended' order that derives from social interweaving, so writers on chaos theory can be seen to emphasise the 'search for *order*' which 'will show how patterns arise alongside unpredictable beha-viour' (Kellert, 1993: 112–113, added emphasis). But though these parallels are appealing, their relationship to chaos and complexity remains questionable. In the first place, complexity theory does not imply that things are necessarily 'unpredictable and partially ungovernable' (Urry, 2000: 208). As was noted in Chapter 4, although an automobile engine relies on chaotic dynamics, we can nevertheless generally predict that it will get us from A to B. As Eve notes, it is *not* the case that 'chaos means that nothing is predictable' (1997: 274). In particular, there is a distinction between 'nanosecond' unpredictability and everyday events which are entirely predictable. As Lovejoy (1999) concludes, the use of complexity theory to support social unpredictability and indeterminism is often inappropriate. In addition, as Matheson and Kirchhoff (1997) suggest, many of the 'metaphors' of chaos theory are neither particularly illuminating nor appropriate to the social arena, and their importation into social analysis may only serve to further confuse our understanding of natural and social tempor-ality. To put this another way, certain patterns in nature may appear chaotic, but their unpredictability derives from processes which remain extraordinarily slow to change. For instance, though weather patterns seem relatively unpredictable, they nevertheless rely on seemingly stable and predictable processes such as those entailed in the observation that 'the heating of water leads to evaporation'. In sum, as was argued in Chapters 4 and 5, the natural arena frequently seems to be characterised by a combination of flux and dynamic stability of process. Yet this combination does not apply to the temporality of social processes because there is an inherent indeterminacy and plasticity deriving from human techno-linguistic flair. The problem is that these significant distinctions between our perception of natural and social temporality are often ignored by those who stress the supposed parallels between complexity and predictability in nature and society.

Conclusion

Discourses of temporality remain central to social theory and the sociology of nature. If nothing else, it is difficult to collapse our perception of the times of nature and society, and this may condition the way in which we theorise the social landscape and its interrelation with nature. As noted in Chapter 5, these differences in perceived temporality are correlated with the exceptional attributes of human sociality, most notably our technolinguistic skill. Such talents advance the possibility of plasticity and inconstancy in our social affairs.

Yet a plastic social universe is not inevitable. The openness of human society creates the *possibility* of plasticity since it is up to us whether we favour tradition and conservatism or accelerating social change (see Chapter 4). Current debates, such as that between social constructionism and critical realism, exist in the landscape created by these possibilities, as do other contemporary social theories. Nevertheless, if perceptions of accelerating social change advance, traditional notions of social structure and stability may become correspondingly difficult to defend. The complications experienced by critical realists in advancing notions of endurance need to be seen in this context, and it perhaps not surprising that they have sometimes taken recourse to biologically informed concepts, such as that of demography, in order to uphold a sense of social stability. Similarly, social constructionism may be advanced by a sense of accelerating social change, as may social theories that stress the open-ended or unplanned character of social transformation.

To sum up, the differing temporalities that characterise our perception of the natural and social domain appear to condition the attractiveness of alternate epistemologies. Realism may prove more appealing to natural scientists than social scientists because the perception of temporality in the natural terrain can seem more conducive to entertaining notions of a dynamic stability *of process*, and thereby of conditional regularity. In contrast, an increasing sense of social plasticity may favour social theories that emphasise 'flowmations' and social (re)construction rather than stability and regularity. In this manner, we may continue to witness differing epistemological preferences between natural and social scientists (see Chapter 9).

Perceptions of temporality may also condition sociologies of nature (Adam, 1995). Sociological concern with the body, or with the environment, represent projects that have to grapple with different timescapes, and epistemological endeavour can be advanced or constrained by these variable temporalities. Constructionism is most obviously favoured when we consider the social construction of the body, or the environment, but less so when we examine a world beyond language, such as the longevity of biological process or the millennial timescapes of nuclear radiation. Similarly, although the longevity of natural process can favour critical realist desires for endurance, the differing perceived temporalities of the natural and social domain inhibit their attempts to draw parallels between social and natural process. Relatedly, a fair amount of the political debate surrounding nature exists within these competing images of temporality. For example, fears that we cannot reverse environmental degrad-ation arise because of the constancy and longevity of many natural processes. It is currently impossible to recreate vanishing species or reverse nuclear radi-ation, and many of our present attempts such as carbon 'sinks' and 'offsets' have their biochemical limitations. In this sense, nature can still appear stubborn, and this obstinacy is conditioned by our sense of its different temporality, and its unwillingness to change at the variable speeds of human social desire.

Yet it is also possible to imagine futurescapes where perceived differences between social and natural temporality could one day diminish. If we follow a 'genomic imagination' (Franklin, 2000), we can entertain visions of a 'biopost-modernism' where the biological might become as plastic as the social. However as will be argued in Chapter 7, although these bio-landscapes have novelistic appeal (Van Dijck, 1998), they seem unlikely to constitute a future cultural fashion.

7

GENOMICS

> Biological engineering is making possible unlimited remodelling of life forms; this may lead to a radical change in the conditions of life on the planet and, consequently, to an equally radical reformulation of all its *ethological and imaginary references.*
>
> (Guattari, 1992: 29, added emphasis)

The genome is difficult to define. Conventionally it refers to 'the sum of an individual's genes' (Rose, 1997: 102) but as some commentators have noted, the 'gene' remains a rather ambiguous, fuzzy and debatable term (Keller, 2000). Nevertheless, in this chapter I will draw on some of the contentious language of 'genes' and 'genetics' since alternatives such as 'exons' do not appear to be less problematic (Keller, 2006). Notwithstanding these problems of definition, it seems fair to say that attention to the human genome has occasioned some extraordinary sociological imagination, alternately evoking images of human freedom and entrapment (Mills, 1959). According to some commentators, its study will provide 'a *power almost godlike*' (Gee, 2000: 14, added emphasis, cited in Hendry, 2002: 188) through its ability to rewrite human biology. By promising to rewrite 'genetic' and cellular relationships which appear to have taken millennia to evolve, genomics has the potential to erode, if not collapse, some of the temporal distinctions between the biological and social domain. Most dramatically, it asks 'Why make the natural order as it now stands sacred?' (Daniel Cohen,[1] 1993: 227 cited in Rabinow, 1999: 53). Following a Darwinian perspective, there is no God-given human nature, and from the millennial perspective which Darwinism encourages, neither should there be long-term stability in the human genome. In other words, we have evolved and changed over millennia, and in consequence, why should we see our present genetic make up as sacrosanct. After all, 'what or who sanctifies?' (James Watson, 2000: 85, co-discoverer of DNA). In this sense, it seems to entail 'a fundamental rethinking of the identity of the human self and its place in larger natural, social and political orders' (Jasanoff, 2005a: 7).

Genomics also evokes spectacular futurist landscapes. It conjures up worlds where disease will be precisely targeted, human ageing retarded, and biology re-written. As Mike Fortun notes, 'the rhetoric of the promise is everywhere

100

in genomics' (2005: 158), encoded in visions of 'scientific breakthrough' and 'miracle cures' (Conrad and Gabe, 1999; Nerlich and Hellsten, 2004) and a general 'hodgepodge of metaphoric excess' (Rabinow, 2005: 99). It heralds questions such as:

> Will our children live to be 160? Will the replacement of damaged human body parts become routine maintenance?... Will some be left behind or choose to reject the technology of life extension? Will the human race divide into two distinct species?
>
> (Forum, 2006: *Tomorrow's People*, University of Oxford)

The above questions form the introduction to a conference organised in March 2006 by the *James Martin Institute for Science and Civilization* at the University of Oxford. The conference included presentation by speakers who envisage radical change in the near future, where people will communicate by 'wireless nano inter-faces' implanted in their brains, or a little more conventionally, where drugs will 'routinely alter our emotions and cognitive capacities' (Forum, 2006). Within these bio-futurist 'visions', genomics forms part of a genre of 'scientist fiction' involving elaborate 'boys own' fantasies of 'technoheaven' and 'technohell' (for instance, see Garreau, 2006). Although it is tempting to dismiss this genre as 'technohype', it remains the case that these imagined worlds conjure extraordinary social change wherein 'life becomes an object of innovation itself' (Brown and Webster, 2004: 166). In addition, as Fortun observes, the 'promise' of genomics cannot be reduced to 'either empty hype, or to formal contract, but occupies the uncertain, difficult space in between' (2005: 158; cf. Hedgecoe, 2004). If nothing else, there is a need to survey its 'technoscapes' (Appadurai, 1996) as performative instantiations of present-day desires (Michael, 2000; Brown and Webster, 2004).

Genomic futurism is also interesting because of the challenge it presents to some of my preceding argument, especially in its portrayal of a kind of 'biopost-modernism' where the biological becomes as plastic as the social. In other words, if we could really change the 'book of life', would biological process have any constancy? And if not, are we about to enter a world where everything, including the natural domain, becomes slippery and open to cultural desire? Given that 'the biological is not only mutable but can be imagined in new ways' (Brown and Webster, 2004: 75), is it the case that nature will one day merely constitute another cultural product (Rabinow, 1992)?

Spectacle

Scientist fiction becomes most graphic where it imagines 'posthuman' worlds where our biological 'failings' are corrected (Hayles, 1999). Through this process:

> progressive self-transformation could change our descendants into something sufficiently different from our present selves to not be

101

human in the sense we use the term now. Such an occurrence would more aptly be termed a pseudoextinction, since it would not end our lineage . . . *Homo sapiens* would spawn its own successors by fast-forwarding its evolution.

(Stock, 2002: 4)

In such stories, genomics provides the means to refashion our identity, both *social and biological*. Since 'the geneticised body is a plastic body' (Petersen and Bunton, 2002: 79), it can appear as an object of cultural whim and consumer desire. According to Stock, 'genetics is at our core, and as we learn to manipulate it, we are learning to manipulate ourselves' (2002: 4).

Stock's vision is of a 'technotopia' where genomics provides the means to perfect the human race through progressively redesigning the 'genetic' inheritance that we pass on to our children. In this respect, his argument accords with that of the *World Transhumanist Association* (WTA), an organisation dedicated to the progressive evolution of the human race. The WTA states that it has 3000 members based in more than 100 countries who support 'the moral right for those who so wish to use technology to extend their mental and physical (including reproductive) capacities and to improve their control over their own lives' (World Transhumanist Association, 2006). Nick Bostrom, Director of the *Future of Humanity Institute* (FHI) at the Faculty of Philosophy, University of Oxford, is the author of the WTA statement of values. According to Bostrom, 'transhumanists view human nature as a work-in-progress, a half-baked beginning that we can learn to remold in desirable ways. Current humanity need not be the endpoint of evolution' (World Transhumanist Association, 2006).[2] Bostrom elucidates a kind of Enlightenment thinking turned in on itself: the focus for progress is now ourselves, and since we are the champions of the universe, the progress of the world depends on our ability to *redesign* the human race. As noted in a WTA online exhibition, 'we will someday see that posthuman individuals will choose to evolve differently' (World Transhumanist Association, 2006).

Yet futurism can also be written in dystopian terms. A well-known example is provided by Lee Silver's (1997) portrayal of the *GenRich*. This futurist 'biocaste' will supposedly result from progressively redesigning the human genome so as to engineer a new sociobiological class. 'Germline therapy' will create a 'class of genetic aristocrats' whose 'genetic enhancements' enable greater athletic, intellectual, musical, artistic, or business ability than the remaining 90 per cent of the population, the so-called 'Naturals' (Silver, 1997: 5). Silver further portrays his *GenRich* as evolving into an entirely separate, and dominant, species who run 'the economy, the media, the entertainment industry, and the knowledge industry' (1997: 6). 'Naturals' are relegated to 'low-paid service providers or . . . laborers' (1997: 7). In this fashion, Silver's futurism presents a Huxleyan topography where social inequality becomes a hard-wired, and almost inescapable, biological reality.

Genomics evokes other fictive references such as John Wyndham's (1960) *Trouble with Lichen*. Just as Wyndham portrayed a world where people can double or treble their lifespans, so some life scientists have proclaimed that a new 'anti-senescent' age is at hand (Franklin, 2001; Brown and Webster, 2004; Cooper, 2006). They point to work on nematode worms that has found that their life span to be doubled where they possess a mutation on the 'daf-2 gene' (e.g. Kenyon *et al.*, 1993; Travis, 2003). Similarly, studies of mutations in animals that are biologically closer to humans have also been associated with increased longevity (such as with rodents; Holzenberger *et al.*, 2003), whilst research is ongoing into human longevity through exploring the genome of 100-year olds (*Les Centenaires*: Rabinow, 1999; cf. Perls and Terry, 2003), and into human stem cells, the '"immortal" nature' of which supposedly 'makes their study an imperative in the field of ageing research' (Rao and Mattson, 2001: 722, cited in Cooper, 2006: 3). This research heralds a new era of biopower where human beings might live 150 years whilst living 'active, healthy' life styles (Foucault, 1979; Rabinow and Rose, 2006). As Cynthia Kenyon explains, research on nematode worms has told us how our future might be:

These long-lived worms stay young longer. That's the thing that's so hard for people to grasp: its not just being healthy longer. *It's being young longer.* The worms have told us it's possible.
(Kenyon, Herbert Boyer professor of biochemistry and biophysics at University of California, San Francisco, quoted in Kingsland, 2003: 49, added emphasis)

Kenyon believes that the humble worm promises the 'elixir of youth' and she thinks that 'it would be fabulous to live to 150' (Kenyon, quoted in Kingsland, 2003: 49). Together with other genomics researchers such as Thomas Perls, she has founded a company, *Elixir Pharmaceuticals*, whose aim is to develop drugs which will delay the onset of aging and age-related diseases in humans (Kingsland, 2003: 46; Elixir Pharmaceuticals, 2005). The market appeal of such a pharmacological 'breakthrough' is dramatically illustrated by Stock:

Human cloning may one day tempt the occasional eccentric or those with unusual family histories or reproductive problems, but most people don't find the idea seductive. Not so with recapturing or preserving youth . . . as scientists repeated and expanded the research, the realization would start to sink in that the genomics revolution would soon be doing much more than telling us our cancer risks, curing genetic diseases, or personalizing drugs. Gradually, our agonizing about playing God and our worries about longer lifespans would give way to a new chorus; 'Where can I get a pill'.
(2002: 88)

Anti-aging pills would represent the perfect pharmacological goldmine because their target would be the entire human population. As Stock proclaims, 'Virtually every adult might take anti-aging medications for life – and a dollar a day from everyone older than forty-five is $30 billion in the United States alone' (2002: 89). In addition, extending joy and vitality would 'undoubtedly be good for the individual, family, and society' (Stock, 2002: 96).

The problem of course with these bio-emancipatory spectres is that there is always a dystopian alternative. For instance, Francis Fukuyama sees nothing but trouble with anti-aging potions. He argues that a world composed of a fit and healthy gerontocracy would be conservative in orientation and lacking in innovation (2002: 62, 96–97). In delaying our deaths, Fukuyama suggests that we could also end up giving people an extended old age in 'a state of childlike dependence' because we had 'found ways to preserve bodily health but could not put off age-related mental deterioration' (2002: 68–69). It's not difficult to add to these dystopian concerns. Anti-senescent desires could produce a gerontocracy in which younger people experienced diminishing political influence (Gems, 2003). In addition, they might radically increase environmental degradation because a strongly delayed mortality could double the human population that is alive at any one time. In this dystopian context, it might not be so 'fabulous to live to 150' (Cynthia Kenyon, quoted in Kingsland, 2003: 49).

In sum, the genomic spectacular spans the traditional range of science fiction, from utopias freed from human suffering to dystopias where our failings become biologically encoded. It can create images of a fabulous plasticity where we endlessly redesign ourselves or it can engender fears of a Promethean hell where anti-social desires are made flesh. Not surprisingly, these fantastical fantasies recycle popular literary references (Van Dijck, 1998). In other words, while genomic futurism is stimulated by *present* biotechnological technique, it is also strongly situated within *past* futurist debate (Paul, 2005). It asks, yet again, whether we are on the verge of finally controlling nature, or creating a new *Frankenstein* (Shelley, 1831), a *Brave New World* (Huxley, 1932) or the biochemically induced longevity of the *Trouble with Lichen* (Wyndham, 1960). In this sense, genomics appears as the biological underwriter of a narrative already well-established in risk mythology. At the same time, it reflects the way in which the present is increasingly conceived in futurist terms (Webster, 2005). Perceptions of rapid acceleration, together with concern about the 'risks' that accompany 'progress' (Beck, 1992), help to further a temporal consciousness in which present and future are increasingly collapsed. We seem to 'live' in future space and its potentialities define who we are and what we do 'now'. Commenting on genomics, Joan Fujimura suggests that:

> if we wait for the future to become the past, we leave the design of the future to others. *Especially* if one does not support the possibilities being imagined today, it is critical to study them. I am arguing for a sociology of the future.
>
> (Fujimura, 2003: 192, original emphasis)

104

Futurist anxiety is fuelled by those who suggest that there is 'a general belief [among geneticists] that voluntary abstention from germline modification in humans is unlikely' (Gordon, 1999: 2023). Others maintain that 'the "natural" desire for a perfect child has become a common refrain, as has the suffering caused by genetic diseases' (Kerr and Cunningham-Burley, 2000: 291). Such argument, combined with evidence of support for 'consumer choice' amongst geneticists (Wertz and Fletcher, 1998), leads Wolfram Henn (2000) to fear that DNA chip technology could eventually be used for the genetic enhancement of characteristics such as intelligence, height and body shape.

Such futurist scenarios move us yet nearer to fictive landscapes where genomics makes biology plastic and open to human whim. Yet there is an odd contradiction in this genre of futurism. On the one hand, it imagines expansive worlds where people can biologically reinvent themselves, either to the benefit or detriment of society. On the other, these *expansive* dreams frequently rely on *reductionist* accounts where the diversity of human life is diminished to genetic determination alone. Challenging such reductionism is important if only because it informs utopian and dystopian apparition through the portrayal of a world where 'nature will be remodelled on culture' (Rabinow, 1992: 241–242). At the same time, such visions raise the question of whether we shall see a 'bio-postmodernism' where cultural construction reigns supreme. If so, some of the distinctions maintained in Chapter 4 between natural and social temporality might be more difficult to entertain. In order to investigate this prospect, I shall first consider the mediatisation of genetics and its reliance on reductionist analysis. The ensuing discussion will then consider the possibility that we shall see a biopostmodern universe.

King gene

The mediatisation of genetics has generated a popular perception of 'genes' as a kind of 'master molecule' which linearly programmes life (Fogle, 1995). The gene appears as 'the ultimate identifier, establishing the essence and identity of a human body' (Van Dijck, 1998: 163). For example, the common use of the map metaphor by human genome scientists creates the image of a human body which can be fully charted, identified and known. In addition, as José Van Dijck suggests, 'the map metaphor suggests that it is only a small step from charting the human genome and locating generic aberrations to correcting these diseases' (1998: 122). This image of the gene is commonly portrayed across the range of popular outlets from print to broadcast to Internet media. As Petersen and Bunton note, media accounts rarely question the accounts of life scientists so 'that there is little reason for the reader to doubt the veracity of the scientist's claims' (2002: 115). In consequence, media portrayals tend to present an oversimplified account of genomic process that frequently downplays the 'multifactorial' and environmental influences on human behaviour and health (Van Dijck, 1998; Petersen and Bunton, 2002), and reinforce a sense of human identity as strongly predicated on genomic determination (Petersen, 1998;

Nelkin and Andrews, 1999). Yet this mediatised sense of the gene does not correspond to the argument of a number of molecular biologists and life scientists who stress the cellular complexity behind genomic replication (Keller, 1995). On the one hand, the idea of the gene as a 'master molecule' is understandable to the extent that we have inherited a Mendelian view of genetics combined with a powerful iconographic image of the double helix of DNA. In addition, as noted in Chapter 4, cellular replication can exhibit extraordinary fidelity. As Evelyn Fox Keller notes, 'viewed from the perspective of historical time [different species] display an unmistakable constancy in form and function' (2000: 12). Given this fidelity, one might well posit a master molecule like DNA that orchestrates a faithful replication. Yet this view is seen as too simplistic by some life scientists because it ignores the significance of all the cellular interactions that surround DNA. In the first place, there is a range of debate as to how we should conceptualise the human genome. In addition, as Steven Rose argues, 'what brings [DNA] to life *is the cell in which it is embedded*. DNA cannot simply and unaided make copies of itself: it cannot therefore "replicate" in the sense that this term is usually understood' (2001: 478, added emphasis). Instead, we have a 'fluid rather than a stable genome' in which 'genes . . . are in constant dynamic exchange with their cellular environment' (Rose, 1997: 125). As Catherine Waldby concludes, the idea of DNA 'as a sequestered and centralized set of top-down instructions has become obsolete' (Waldby, 2001: 788; cf. Dupré, 2006a). Or as Richard Strohman comments, the *reductionist* tendency to equate the 'book of life' with the 'concrete of DNA' is being replaced by a stress on the *flexible genome* which is a *necessary but not sufficient* explanation of human health and behaviour (2000: 101, original emphasis).

Nevertheless reductionism is still apparent in the treatment of genomics. As Taussig, Rapp and Heath note, the genomic imagination can entail subscription to 'a worldview in which human diversity is increasingly ascribed to genetic causality' (Taussig *et al.*, 2003: 61). Or as Richard Strohman remarks, his fellow molecular biologists and geneticists tend to 'believe that even the most complex human behavior can be reduced to genetic circuits' (2000: 109). Yet such assumptions remain problematic because it is difficult to attribute causal responsibility exclusively to 'genes'. As Jonathan Kaplan comments, 'while a gene may be associated with a particular variation on a trait in one environment, it may not be associated with it in another' (2000: 47–48). On the one hand, genetic influence is likely to appear stronger in highly homogenous environments because their very uniformity means that they are likely to have limited differential environmental effect. On the other, environmental influence may appear more significant if there is little genetic variance in a population (Sullivan, 2004). In other words, arguments can be made about the relative influence of 'genes vs. environment' but only with respect to a particular context. As Richard Lewontin argues, 'we can separate genetic and environmental effects statistically only in a particular population of organisms at a particular moment within a particular set of specified environments' (1991: 30). One traditional answer to this dilemma is to study monozygotic, or singe cell, human twins who are separated at birth and reared apart (thereby focusing on genetic uniformity that is subject to differing environmental 'effects'). Yet because such studies only approximate experimental conditions, natural science assumptions about causality still remain tenuous. As Rose *et al.* (1984: 269) observe, an adequate experimental design would be unethical since it would necessitate placing human clones in randomly selected environments. Furthermore, even in the unlikely assumption that we could apportion genetic vs. environmental influence, this does not mean that we would understand what would happen if we changed the human genome. As Kaplan argues, 'the heritability of a trait within a population will not permit you to make predictions about what will happen if changes occur in either the environment, the genetic distribution, or the way that the population is distributed with respect to the environment' (2000: 38; cf. Lewontin, 1991).

However some life scientists argue that we are relatively close to intervening in complex biological and behavioural arenas. For instance, Henn suggests that the advent of large-scale DNA sequencing and DNA chips means that 'genetic research is about to find the genetic needles in the haystack of complex human properties such as longevity, body shape or intelligence' (2000: 445).[3] Yet even if it were possible to determine such genetic influence, the effect of any change to the human genome is likely to remain context dependent, and consequently difficult to predict. In other words, human disease and behaviour appears multi-factorial involving complex ('epistatic') interactions within 'genes', as well as between 'genes' and proteins, and between intricate cellular processes and the wider natural and social environment (Kaplan, 2000). On the one hand, there are some diseases which appear to be related to single 'genes', or are *monogenetic* in form (i.e. one gene → one trait). On the other, writers such as Strohman argue that they account for 'less than 2%' of human disease (Strohman, 2000: 111). Such observations question arguments which propose that the human genome represents a 'lexicological enterprise' which, 'like any other dictionary or digest', can be manipulated 'at will' (Stafford, 1991: 212). Operating within natural science assumptions, there remain major questions regarding the feasibility of altering the human genome. It would appear that life cannot be *reduced* to a 'gene machine' (Strohman, 2000: 100).

Biopostmodernism?

In spite of the above argument, genomics can nevertheless figure as a possible engineer of, what might be very loosely termed, a 'biopostmodern' universe. On the one hand, the genomic imagination 'instantiates the definition of modern rationality' (Rabinow, 1992: 236), playing as it does on well-worn themes within Christian Enlightenment. It asks, yet again, whether we are on the verge of finally controlling nature (Kerr and Cunningham-Burley, 2000). In this sense, the genomic imagination appears as the biological underwriter of modernity: it reminds us that changing ourselves was always implicit in the Enlightenment project. Yet at the same time, in promising to collapse one of our last remaining stabilities, that of nature, and to re-write it through potentially endless reconstruction, our sense of the modern world is profoundly challenged. Rather than the once all powerful 'other', nature can appear 'antiquated, displaced, and superceded, . . . a mere shadow of the referent it used to signify' (Franklin, 2000: 190–191).

An unrestrained genomic imagination can consequently constitute the ultimate modernist herald of the postmodern. Just as modernism eventually heralded its own inquisitor, namely the postmodern injunction to 'doubt' reason and knowledge, so genomics can imagine the removal of all remaining foundations for our ethic and lifestyle. In addition, if we can think of reinventing our biological selves, can there be any stable ontological bulwark against a thorough-going 'strong' social constructionism (see Chapter 6)? Similarly can we even retain the notion of a universally shared humanity if *some of us* choose to re-write our biology (Turner and Rojek, 2001)? In this sense, though genomics appears as the realisation of a modernist dream, its *imagination* furthers a sense of the postmodern in both its epochal and epistemological terms. Everything, even nature, becomes slippery and open to cultural reconstruction.

Yet before we get carried away by biopostmodern fantasies, we need to recall that the genomic imagination still tends to rely on modernist tendencies, namely those of reductionism and determinism. To put this another way, the power of an unrestrained genomic imagination is achieved partly through a post-Enlightenment desire to reduce, and thereby 'engineer', life. Since modernist reductionism is less than ideally compatible with a postmodern sensibility, the genomic imagination is not yet the perfect suitor for postmodernism desires. In addition, as Anne Kerr and Sarah Cunningham-Burley (2000) note, genomics can just as easily reconfigure elements of the pre-modern and the counter-modern as the postmodern. They suggest that 'a sense of fatalism about genetic disease . . . *internalises older [pre-modern] notions of destiny*' (2000: 284, added emphasis). Such pre-modern notions as 'destiny' are also accompanied by counter-modern tendencies, especially if the new genetics is equated with 'new eugenics'. In this scenario, genomics could herald 'de-civilizing' tendencies (Elias, 1996) as 'barbarism . . . gains access' by re-clothing 'eugenics . . . [in] the robes of health, productivity, the promise of profit' (Beck, 1995: 33).

The genomic universe can however still evoke a characteristic that is loosely associated with the postmodern, namely a tendency toward slipperiness and instability. In consequence, it could be suggested that it questions the perceived temporal distinctions proposed in Chapter 4, particularly the suggestion that biological process appears characterised by a constancy and longevity that is not similarly mirrored within the social arena. As noted above, if one assumes that new genetics herald an ability to re-write 'the book of life', will this not gradually erode images of biological constancy? Similarly, if we can collapse evolutionary processes that took millennia to evolve, can we still speak of biological longevity? In sum, will both the biological and the social be characterised by an increasing sense of plasticity?

Genomics and constancy

The genomic imagination evokes futures where the body is consumed according to cultural fashion. Yet as noted above, the problem with this image is its tendency to rely on a reductionist text where the 'reprogramming' of our 'genes' becomes codeterminous with the recreation of ourselves. Furthermore, it remains unlikely that nature and culture will be 'equally subjected to re-imagination (Van Dijck, 1998: 177) because people will probably want to retain constancy in human biology. In other words, would we ever want 'unfaithful' bodies? Even if we were to create a completely new body, would we not still desire constancy? When our bodies lack constancy of process, the results for the individual can be serious ill-health, and much medicine is concerned with trying to 'fix' such bodily inconstancy. Medical technique desires constancy by 'stabilising' complaints such as coronary arrhythmia or a hyperactive thyroid.

It is of course possible to envisage alternate sci-fi worlds where our bodies might change according to the task at hand. For instance, perhaps our eyesight would be able to 'switch levels' and suddenly see things at a microscopic level, or our fingers might become smaller and longer so as to deal with some intricate feat of dexterity. This would represent bodily plasticity nearly on a par with that of language. Yet this does not mean that constancy and replicability would go out of (cultural) fashion. We would not want to suddenly go blind when we 'switched' to 'microscopic perception mode' or find that, in 'elongated finger mode', our fingers had turned into 'elongated pincers that had become incapable of grasping anything' (Deleuze and Guattari, 1988: 72). In other words, constancy is likely to remain a *socially desirable* feature of our biology even if it could be subject to redesign, or endlessly adaptable to the task in hand. As was argued in Chapter 4, the same feature is not a *necessary* characteristic of our social lives. Instead, the open-ended flexibility afforded by human technolinguistic skill means that social stability and constancy is something that must be continually performed. Most significantly, plasticity in the social arena does not equate with 'dysfunctionality'. In contrast, an unfettered biological plasticity implies impairment since our bodies would cease to maintain their 'health'. Human health is likely to continue to be associated with constancy in biological functioning, however 'precariously' this is achieved.

To sum up, the genomic imagination does not threaten to collapse all apparent differences between social and biological temporality. On the one hand, it may offer some ability to short-circuit some genomically informed processes that seem to have taken millennia to evolve. On the other, it is less likely that genomics will remove the temporal differences that were highlighted in Chapter 4, especially the greater constancy and longevity of process that we seem to see in the biological and physical domain. In part this is because it appears unlikely that we would desire inconstancy in our relationship with the natural world. We may still want a 'stable' biology, and solid ground, and gravity to hold our bodies down. As the horrors of tsunamis and earthquakes remind us, an unpredictable natural world may not be something that we wish to entertain. In sci-fi landscapes, we might imagine extraordinary 'future-plastic' worlds composed of, say, 'artificial' replacements for 'building blocks' such as carbon, oxygen, or even for the cellular processes surrounding DNA. Yet it seems improbable that we would wish our natural world to be as plastic as the possibilities of our culture. Dynamic stability in bodily functioning remains associated with physical health, and the appearance of a truly plastic physical universe would be one where we could never be certain of such simple 'bearings' as how we cross the street.

It therefore remains doubtful whether genomics will herald some revolutionary change in bodily or physical plasticity. However this does not mean that it is without social implication. In particular, considerable concern has been expressed as to the moral consequences of genomics. According to some writers, changes to 'our nature' represent a threat to human dignity and our sense of who we are. Others suggest that the legacy of eugenics remains strong, and that in consequence, the 'new genetics' will come to constitute a 'new eugenics'. In what follows, I shall consider these concerns since they are germane to our perception of the natural and social domain. At the same time, I shall address an old dispute around which they pivot, namely the question of whether nature can be foundational to our lives.

Genomic foundations?

The genomic imagination reinvigorates the question of whether nature can provide a foundation for our ethic and our knowledge. For in spite of long-standing accusations that such aspiration represents a 'naturalistic fallacy' (Moore, 1903: 13), there remain authors who wish to ground human behaviour in nature. An illustration can be found in Bryan Turner and Chris Rojek's (2001) attempt to construct a foundationalist ontology. In brief, Turner and Rojek (2001) attempt to solve the following dilemma: how can we arrive at a foundation for human rights given the postmodern/social constructionist challenge to the notion of ontological foundation? Or as Turner and Rojek put it, how can we reconcile a 'foundationalist ontology and a social constructionist epistemology' (Turner and Rojek, 2001: 120)? In part, their answer is to suggest that there are universal aspects of humanity such as our sense of insecurity and frailty, and our suscept-ibility to pain. In consequence, 'the body and the environment are the *concrete foundations* of life with others' (2001: 111, added emphasis)'. They go on to suggest that it is our shared universal experience of frailty and pain that justifies a universal theory of rights. They use the example of the pain of tooth decay to illustrate this argument:

> From an orthodox Foucauldian perspective, mouths as such do not exist: as a site of professional practice, the mouth is a late invention of dental science... [However] the pain of dental decay... is not simply the effect of discursive professional practices. It has a phenomenolo-gical reality and presence that demands urgent action... No amount

of philosophical talk about its constructed character will convince us otherwise: *a pain is a pain is a pain.*

(2001: 119, added emphasis)

Nature thus provides us with a foundation for human rights in spite of constructionism and cultural relativism: we cannot 'escape the meat' (Birke, 1999: 145) and the frailty of our bodies. Yet as critics such as Jack Barbalet (1998) maintain, there are difficulties in sustaining this thesis. On the one hand, the experience of pain does remain universal. On the other, its experience has changed considerably in the last 200 years. For example, dental pain is no longer intense or long-lasting for most people in the developed world. We have changed our dental habits through preventative medicine, and dentistry is now sufficiently advanced to reduce dental pain considerably. The same does not apply in the less developed world. In consequence, the experience of pain and frailty depends considerably on its social context rather than being 'a universal condition of the human species' (Turner and Rojek, 2001: 125). It is not simply the case that, beyond all 'philosophical talk . . . a pain is a pain is a pain. (Turner and Rojek, 2001: 119) or that 'pain is less culturally variable' (Turner, 2003: 280). Instead, we all suffer pain but some of us suffer it a lot less. In consequence, against Turner and Rojek, our shared ontological frailty does not necessarily create 'interdependencies and interconnectedness' (2001: 125). In addition, it is important to remember that we live in a world already characterised by gross inequalities in health (Rose, 2005). As Eric Grace argues, 'the United States deploys about 14 per cent of its total economy to maintain the world's most technologically advanced medical system. Yet . . . the infant mortality rate in the United States is higher than in 21 other countries, and black babies are more than twice as likely to die in infancy as white babies' (1997: 96). In addition to such internal divides within a single country, there are also major 'North/South' divides in access to medical technology (Petersen and Bunton, 2002).

In this context, the deployment of genomics may only serve to further erode notions of universal humanity. In so doing, it places additional doubt around Turner and Rojek's (2001) quest to recover a foundational ontology based on human frailty. Yet Turner and Rojek are not alone in wishing to preserve our sense of universal humanity. For example, Frances Fukuyama argues that genomics presents a direct threat to 'the unity . . . of human nature' (2002: 172), including universal experiences such as pain and suffering. Evoking Turner and Rojek's (2001) argument, Fukuyama suggests that 'a person who has not confronted suffering or death has no depth. Our ability to experience these emotions is what connects us potentially to all other human beings, both living and dead' (2002: 173).

Yet as noted above, medicine has already compromised this 'unity' of human experience because the experienced of pain and death is not universally shared in the same way. In the developed world, pain is lessened and the meaning of death can be sequestered or denied (Elias, 1985; Giddens, 1991; Willmott, 2000). In

111

addition, if we follow fictions such as Silver's (1997) *GenRich*, germline engineering has the potential to permanently remove any vestige of universal humanity through the progressive creation of new biological castes. Not surprisingly, 'bio-conservatives' such as Fukuyama wish to halt the prospect of such alarming changes on the grounds that it would constitute an affront to the 'idea of the universality of human dignity' (2002: 156). Seemingly, we would 'lose our humanity' because genomics threatens 'some *essential* quality that has *always* underpinned our sense of who we are' (2002: 101, added emphasis). Similarly, David Le Breton argues that genomic 'post-humanism is a morality that is contemptuous of humanity, a morality that is no longer founded on the finality of the human being, along with the intrinsic dignity of each particular individual' (2004: 3).

However if we take evolutionary thought seriously, it challenges such contention. In particular, it suggests that there is no 'finality' to humanity because our evolution remains accidental rather than prescribed. As Steven Rose comments on Stephen Jay Gould:

> Gould argues that much evolutionary change is contingent, accidental, and that, as he puts it, if one were to wind the tape of history backward and replay it, it is in the highest degree unlikely that mammals, let alone humans, would evolve.
>
> (Rose, 2001: 482)

In other words, even though there appears to be a millennial constancy to many biological processes, it remains the case that biological evolution is historically specific (see Chapter 4). The processes surrounding genomics may have remarkable longevity, but the evolutionary 'outcomes' of these and other processes are still the product of particular times and places (which may advantage some organisms rather than others). Evolutionary argument therefore suggests that 'the human germline is not sacrosanct' (McGee, 2000: 99) and that our current biology is accidental rather than celestially ordained. In so doing, it questions whether changes to human biology represent an attack on human dignity. As Slavoj Žižek puts it,

> if the claims of biogenetics hold, then the choice we are confronting today is not between human dignity and the "posthuman" technological generation of individuals but between clinging to the *illusion of dignity* and the accepting the *reality* of what we are.
>
> (Žižek, 2004: 130, original emphasis)

In sum, it remains difficult to maintain naturalist foundations for our lives, whether in relation to human rights or human dignity. In this context, genomics reinvigorates the Humean argument that recourse to natural foundations for our ethic represents a naturalist fallacy. In so doing, it questions the deployment of naturalist reference by writers as various as Turner and Rojek (2001), Fukuyama

(2002) and Le Breton (2004). Yet although it is doubtful that human biology can provide a foundation for human morality, it remains the case that the potential redesign of our biology still occasions a good deal of social concern. As noted, a number of writers fear that the new genetics heralds a new eugenics. Given that these anxieties have come to constitute one axis of debate about the relationship between the social and the biological, it is worth surveying their argument.

In addition, controversy over eugenics relates to that concerning the naturalist fallacy. Sagoff suggests that eugenics debates draw on a very lengthy tradition of debate that asks whether 'the natural is considered normative' (2005: 77). For instance, should we follow Hippocratic and Platonic tradition and see science as 'nature's helpmeet' (Sagoff, 2005: 77)? Or should we follow Lucretius and Bacon and regard 'the physician as standing apart from, and often in opposition to nature' (Sagoff, 2005: 78)? Sagoff argues that the former view counsels restraint and care in our 'interference' with nature. The latter perspective suggests that 'improving on nature is perfectly intelligible' and sees any interference as a question of 'the balance of risks and benefits' (Sagoff, 2005: 78).[4] Dystopians, and many of those concerned about eugenics, tend toward the former view, while utopians accentuate the latter. However as we shall see, other writers suggest that both the utopian 'hope' and the dystopian 'fear' are seriously overplayed.

Our dystopian future?

As Dorothy Nelkin and Susan Lindee (1995) observed, a consequence of the Nazi association with eugenics is that we have largely forgotten the popularity of eugenic discourse in the late nineteenth and early twentieth century. Nelkin and Lindee noted that 'a 1928 survey of 499 [US] colleges and universities found that 343 offered courses in genetics and eugenics' (Nelkin and Lindee, 1995: 21; cf. Kevles, 1995; Buchanan *et al.*, 2000). In addition, some commentators fear that eugenic attitudes still remain culturally persistent and that, as a result, the 'new genetics' may easily come to represent a 'new eugenics'. (Neuhaus, 1988; Duster, 1990; Degler, 1991; Allen, 1999; Le Bretton, 2004). They argue that this eugenics will be based less on the state-sponsored terror of the Nazi era than a new 'market eugenics' (Henn, 2000: 446) where consumers are increasingly 'free' to choose the 'design' of their children, thereby delivering an individualised realisation of eugenic ambition.

It is certainly not difficult to find evidence of eugenic thinking among contemporary life scientists. For instance, Stock discounts the possibility of a new eugenics yet simultaneously illustrates his own eugenic proclivities. He argues that the key difference between the new genetics and the old eugenics is that the development of the former will be governed by individual consumers rather than the imposition of the state. Following Stock, the free market, commerce and consumer choice represent our guarantor against future terrors rather than the means of their deliverance (cf. Hughes, 2004). He reasons 'that most parents would make the safe choices' (2002: 112), and as a consequence, the new genetics will not produce either 'Frankensteins', or Huxleyan or Nazi control. Yet there are numerous problems with Stock's thesis. First, an alternate genomic imagination suggests that the net result of the commercialisation of new genetics may be eugenicist 'bads' rather than the new genetic 'goods' envisaged by Stock. As Silver repeatedly stresses, his hard-wired *GenRich* are the consequence of consumer choice: 'it is individuals . . . *not governments* . . . who will seize control of these new technologies' (1997: 10, original emphasis). Commerce and consumer choice could therefore represent the perfect means to deliver an irreversible, biologically determined, social inequality that is based on 'market eugenics'. Second, Stock's genomic vision contains echoes of the Nazi desire to control through the manipulation of biology. For instance, according to Stock it will be 'natural' for parents to use germline engineering to screen out deviance in their children. He suggests that 'parents will want to moderate temperament and personality . . . they may worry about raising a difficult, inflexible child or wonder if extreme traits will handicap their kids' (Stock, 2002: 119). In his Brave New World of normalcy, future humans will no longer be 'handicapped' because they stand out from the herd. Deviants need not worry: they have no biological future. The Huxleyan analogy is complete when Stock further asserts that 'efforts to moderate personality extremes will not rest on genetic manipulations alone. Psychopharmacology too will carry us in this direction, with its antidepressants, mood stabilizers, sedatives and antianxiety drugs' (2002: 120).

In spite of the distance which Stock seeks to create between his project and the Nazi 'slur' on eugenics, his dreams remain reminiscent of Nazi ambition. Following Stock, it seems that the desire to control, to purify and to remove deviance is still perfectly acceptable so long as its implementation is achieved by an alliance of science, commerce and 'free' consumers. His thesis provides support for Nelkin and Lindee's contention that US culture is imbued with a 'genetic essentialism and biological determinism' that make it receptive to 'the rise of a new eugenics' (1995: 171; cf. Badagliacco and Ruiz, 2006).[5] As Petersen and Bunton note, the concern of various commentators is that a new eugenics would lead to the reproductive *exclusion* of 'categories of "the undesirable" ' (2002: 195) through the biological reinforcement of normality. Consumer choice might enable parents to 'screen out' the 'deviant' and the disabled, and if a 'queer gene' were ever found, it would allow liberalised 'free consumers' to police (hetero)sexuality (Steinberg, 1997; Shakespeare, 1998).

Yet the question arises as to whether both utopian and dystopian visions remain overplayed. As Nik Brown observes, 'the whole area is literally spilling over with heated aspirations, promises, expectations, hopes, desires and imaginings' (2003: 4) and it is therefore not surprising that it has 'created exaggerated expectations that it could not possibly fulfil . . . in the near term' (Sagoff, 2005: 70). Nikolas Rose suggests that those who fear a new eugenics are 'fighting the battles of a previous war' (2005: 6) by using a discourse that is informed by hyperbole rather than feasibility:

The troubled discourse of bioethicists, popular science writers and social theorists in the developed world tends to be futuristic. It often rests on overstated claims about the marvels that bioscience and biomedicine is about to achieve. Contemporary biotechnology – no doubt following a pattern familiar from other technologies – thrives on such exaggerated expectations of epochal changes just around the corner. These claims generate publicity, inflate share prices, mobilise funding agencies, enhance careers and, no doubt, generate a sense of excitement and mission for those working in the field (Brown, 2003). While it may be true that many of the phenomena of life – from reproduction to emotion – now seem to be understandable as mechanisms, in most cases we are a long way from being able to re-engineer them at will.

(Rose, 2005: 7)

It is not difficult to find examples that illustrate how genomic futurism can overplay the benefits, or the threats, posed by new genetics. An illustration of the latter is provided by Jürgen Habermas's (2003) argument that it is immoral to use germline engineering to redesign our future progeny because it 'intervenes in the somatic bases of another person's spontaneous relation-to-self and ethical freedom' (2003: 13). Habermas suggests that human morality is based on the assumption that human beings are 'independent subjects who are capable of saying no' (2003: 57). This morality is negated by germline engineering because genetically redesigned children would be unable to 'say no' to the ways in which they had been re-programmed before their birth.[6] As a result, the reprogrammed child would 'no longer [be] capable of understanding herself as the undivided author of her own life' (2003: 91–92). But whatever the merits of this argument, it appears to rely on a 'Genes R' Us' reductionism that assumes that human 'redesign' is not far away. For instance, Habermas warns that:

if we consider that medical mavericks are already busy working on the reproductive cloning of human organisms, we cannot help but feel that the human species might soon be able to take its biological evolution into its own hands.

(2003: 21)

Ironically, this argument is reminiscent of Stock's thesis except that it proceeds from dystopian rather than utopian concerns. The problem with both accounts is that they fail to note how their *expansive* expectations about the redesign of the human race rely on *reductionist* assumptions about the genetic determination of human life. In consequence, they place insufficient emphasis on the range of argument which suggests that genomics represents but *one element of* the complex, interactive and iterative influences on human health and behaviour.

Further doubts about the possibility of utopia or dystopia arise because of the uncertain development of genetic technique and commerce. Since a direct association between genetics and health appears to apply to relatively few diseases, genomics may represent one more addition to our medical arsenal rather than a revolutionary 'breakthrough'. Some life scientists suggest that 'where more complex traits such as intelligence are concerned . . . we may never be able to use gene transfer for enhancement' (Gordon, 1999: 2023) whilst others note that where complex conditions such as schizophrenia are concerned, 'the data suggest that multiple genetic factors and environmental triggers are involved, and the use of genetic engineering to reduce the occurrence of the disease presents a formidable technical challenge indeed' (Ehrlich, 2000: 323). In addition, the technologies which might underlie germline engineering, such as in vitro fertilisation (IVF), are very difficult to effect. As Rose comments, '75%–80% of treatments fail in each [IVF] cycle in the UK' (2005: 7) and it remains unlikely that women would wish to undergo what presently remains an invasive, 'artificial' and distressing treatment merely for the sake of the 'cosmetic' enhancement of their children. As Steven Pinker observes, 'anyone who knows someone who has undergone IVF knows that this is a traumatic, painful, and rather unpleasant procedure' (2003: 8). There are also significant risks: Brown and Webster note that 'egg extraction . . . might lead to haemorrhage or pelvis inflammatory disease' (2004: 62).

In addition, there are also questions about the commercial potential of new genetics. In particular, there are suggestions that genomic commerce has been over-hyped and over-sold in a similar fashion to the 'heady' days of the e-commerce 'bubble' (Rasnick, 2003; Gottweis, 2005). Though US venture capital funding of biotech companies amounted to $2872 million in 2000 and $2160 million in 2001 (Glasner and Rothman, 2004: 109), Simon Williams suggests that 'many early claims . . . have been somewhat exaggerated' (2003a: 166). Similarly, Herbert Gottweis suggests that 'stock prices of genomics companies have been rising across the board until 2000, only to take a deep dive afterwards' (2005: 180), and Glasner and Rothman note that 'few . . . [biotech] pharmaceuticals, so far, have turned out to be big money makers' (2004: 96; cf. Ernst and Young, 2003). As Rose observes, 'promissory capitalism demands results in the short term' (2005: 18) and many biotech firms have struggled to deliver. In seeming recognition of this problem, some biotech companies have openly declared that they do not anticipate making a profit 'for a period of years, if at all' (Geron, 2003: 1, cited in Cooper, 2006: 15). In addition, other critics have questioned whether there is sufficient pressure on the major pharmaceutical companies to innovate when much of their profit derives from the 'recycling' of existing drugs (Angell, 2004). In sum, although genomics has raised a range of moral concerns, these anxieties are lessened when new genetic technologies fail to deliver or be adopted. As Gottweis notes with regard to gene therapy, while 'its potential ethical–social implications . . . are enormous, . . . these debates are largely theoretical due to gene therapy's sobering lack of success to actually cure diseases' (2005: 11; cf. Sagoff, 2005).

Furthermore, there remain several institutional obstacles to the redesign of the human race, whether eugenically motivated or otherwise. For instance, in the UK, a host of government committees survey the future biopower of genomics and pronounce upon the governance of health and agriculture.[7] In the USA, Martin (1999) notes that work on human germline intervention has been stalled ever since the publication in 1982 of *Splicing Life*, the report of the US President's Commission for the Study of Ethical Problems in Medicine, and Biomedical and Behavioral Research (Capron, 1990; Cook-Deegan, 1990, 1994). He suggests that the combination of opposition from religious groups, environmental activists and prominent scientists has meant that 'all serious work on germ line therapy ceased' in the 1980s (1999: 21).

Yet it is still possible for dystopians to argue that a new eugenics is feasible without reliance on germline engineering. They may suggest that new eugenic scenarios could result from *existing* techniques of preimplantation genetic diagnosis (PGD) since these could be used to select human embryos with 'desirable' characteristics. Such 'reprogenetics' is far less risky than trying to alter the human genome since one is selecting embryos rather than 'reengineering' the germline through, say, the creation of an additional 'chromosome 47'. Fertilised embryos are created outside the womb, nucleotide sequences are examined (using polymerase chain reaction to 'amplify' this information), and 'healthy' or 'desirable' embryos are then implanted. In consequence, it might offer 'a much simpler way of offering the family reproductive choice' (Thomas, 2000: 102). In its current use, PGD is deployed in order to prevent very serious genetic diseases. However Henn fears that rapid developments in DNA sequencing and chips will enable researchers to determine the markers, or genetic interactions, that surround complex properties such as body shape or intelligence, and that consumers will then select embryos which contain these markers (cf. Winter, 2000). He notes support for 'consumer choice' amongst geneticists (Wertz and Fletcher 1998), and cites research which suggests that a significant proportion of the public in developed and developing countries favour using PGD for conditions 'such as two missing fingers, short stature, obesity, or even limited musical talent' (Henn, 2000: 445).

Dystopians can also further challenge the argument of those who discount their fears. For instance, although Rose is dismissive of the dystopian threat, his argument illustrates how PGD could be used to progressively design out 'human defects'. As Rose observes, there are genetic markers for breast cancer, BRCA1 and BRCA2, and women with these markers are thought to have 'a 70% as opposed to 10%' risk of breast cancer (Rose, 2005: 12). Rose poses the question of whether PGD 'should . . . be used in such cases to implant only male embryos' (2005: 12) where there are indications of BRCA1 or 2 risk. Yet from a dystopian perspective, such 'opportunities' are reminiscent of eugenicist desires to remove the 'defective'. Debates in popular science media continue to further such dystopian concerns. For example, Michael Le Page, a features editor at *New Scientist* magazine, suggests that parents already feel that 'they have a duty to ensure [their] child is healthy . . . and want to ensure that they don't get . . . faulty genes' (Le Page, 2006). From a dystopian perspective, such reports reinforce the fear that we are 'shifting . . . from seeing a child as an unconditionally welcome gift to seeing him as a conditionally acceptable *product*' (Kass, 2003: 42, added emphasis). In so doing, PGD could repress women through it's use in prenatal sex selection (Corea, 1985), or be used to commodify children through demands for 'an *a la carte* child who conforms to "parental" desires, and whose appearance conforms to societal norms' (Le Breton, 2004: 6). In addition, 'strong' bio-conservatives such as Leon Kass and his colleagues suggest that PGD 'might be a privilege enjoyed exclusively by the rich' (2003: 59), leading to 'a society divided between the economically and genetically rich . . . and the economically and genetically poor' (2003: 59). In other words, such bio-conservatives portray a world divided between *GenRich* and *GenPoor* based on *existing* IVF/PGD technology.

To sum up, the genomic imagination engenders considerable contestation. Nevertheless, it does seem reasonable to argue that the proclamations of many gene utopians and dystopians rely on a technicist futurism which overplays the commercial promise of genomics and downplays the complex 'multifactorial' nature of human health and behaviour. In part, the development of genomics may depend on the interplay of commercial desire, state intervention and regulatory pressure (Brown and Webster, 2004; Jasanoff, 2005a, 2005b; Waldby and Mitchell, 2006; Kent *et al.*, 2006).[8] In this context, developments in South Korea, Singapore and China are of as much, if not greater interest, than those in the west (Salter *et al.*, 2006). It remains to be seen how many countries will apply clear regulatory logics and whether there will be some states where policing of reproductive technologies is either limited or ineffective (Leather, 2004). To the extent that the latter applies, it could become difficult to entirely discount dystopian fears, especially if IVF/PGD, or related technologies such as in vitro maturation, were to become more effective, inexpensive or less invasive.

Conclusion

The futurist terrain of the genomic imagination contains an extraordinary admixture of scientific and commercial imperative, and its target is 'nature itself'. This marriage of finance and scientific knowledge evokes images of financial 'bonanzas' that draw on a research climate already conducive to commercialisation (Rose, 2001). For gene dreamers, current pharmacology will be as nothing compared to the biopower of genomics to transform 'health and happiness'. Yet if we assume that the human genome is not sacrosanct, why stop there? Why should we accept the current limits of our biological evolution particularly when the pressures of natural selection are redundant in the developed world (because the vast majority reach sexual maturity before they die)? In consequence, why do not we envisage the 'transhuman' redesign of the human race so that we can erase our imperfections once and for all? From both a Darwinian and modernist perspective, it can make sense to enhance *Homo sapiens* so that we achieve control not just over nature, but over ourselves.

In this fashion, the genomic imagination creates extraordinary spectacle, from redesigning our children to the perpetuation of youth and the conquering of disease. In so doing, it suggests that life is something which can be re-written according to commercial design and 'the anarchic whims of consumers and clients' (Habermas, 2003: 48). Within this futurism, it can appear as though the unravelling of the double helix of DNA by James Watson, Frances Crick, Rosalind Franklin and Maurice Wilkins has led to a 'biological *ars combinatoria*' (Stafford, 1991: 212, original emphasis) with the potential to re-write the text of 'life itself'. In this sense, genomics seems to offer the final realisation of Marx and Engels' dictum that under capitalism 'all fixed . . . relations . . . are swept away . . . [and] all that is solid melts into air' (Tucker, 1978: 476; Burman, 1982)? To put this another way, genomics can be seen as combining two variants of the thesis that the postmodern was always contained in the modern? First, it draws on the sense that 'liquid capitalism', and its (somewhat overplayed) image of unconstrained global flows (Castells, 1996; McGuigan, 1999; Urry, 2000), was always inherent in capitalism. Second, it draws on the notion that the re-imagination of human nature was always implicit in the modernist control of nature. In this sense, it is not surprising that variants of the genomic imagination have inspired awe at the vision of new, and potentially revolutionary, 'liquid landscapes'.

Yet these images of 'bio-liquidity' remain contested. Critics suggest that they often end up presenting over-hyped accounts which fly in the face of scientific feasibility. They argue that, whether we are concerned with returns on commerce or on human health, genomic outcomes look prosaic rather than revolutionary. In addition they suggest that there are few signs of the consumer demand needed for market eugenics, or that genomics will herald a new paradigm for the pharmaceutical sector. Furthermore, the development of genomics is not based on the unrestrained flow of capital but instead appears influenced by regulation, variability in marketisation, and the extent to which different national states adopt strongly interventionist policies, either ethically or economically (Waldby and Mitchell, 2006; Salter *et al.*, 2006). Such observations do not mean that utopian aspiration or dystopian fear is entirely without foundation but it does suggest a need for considerable caution in interpreting the fantastic scenarios that populate their discourse (Brown and Webster, 2004).

In part, the contestation over genomic futurism reflects differing perceptions of the way in which the logic of liberal capitalism will intertwine with genomic development. For some, the 'logic is [now] different' since (neo)liberal capitalism is *not* the means to deliver the 'wholesale management of population qualities' by the state (Rabinow and Rose, 2006: 211). In consequence the state terror of eugenics will not return (cf. Stock, 2002). For others, it is the very individualisation of the eugenic programme which they fear. They suggest that it is consumer choice that will slowly but surely deliver 'market eugenics', and that liberal capitalism will be central to this endeavour. From the latter perspective, the fear is that consumer choice will deliver a market eugenics that is under-taken precisely in the name of 'the logics of vitality' (Rabinow and Rose, 2006: 211). Why should not parents demand the right to 'the maximization of quality of life' (Rabinow and Rose, 2006: 211) for themselves and their children by 'buying' into the promises of genomics? In other words, if power is productive, it can be productive in different ways. In consequence, dystopians can still argue that a Foucauldian sense of biopower provides the very means for deliverance of the eugenicist fear, the only difference being that the 'new' eugenics proceeds through the management of life rather than former fascist cults of death. In response, critics are likely to suggest that these fears are still far too overplayed in the context of current genomic development.

Whatever the case, it seems fair to conclude that genomics does not currently suggest that we are moving toward a biopostmodern universe where biology becomes consonant with the liquidity of language and text. First, there is a contra-diction inherent in current biopostmodern images which tend to rely on the reductionist hype that surrounds genomic discourse. Second, a biopostmodern landscape remains unlikely because biological and physical constancy is unlikely to go out of fashion. We may not want to 'fall off the world' or watch our bodies 'disintegrate', except as observers of science fiction. Even if nature were to become 'after culture' (Rabinow, 1992), we may not wish to revise its temporal operations.

Finally, debate about genomics reinforces the need for caution in the social science interpretation of life science. As noted, the problem with utopian and dystopian concerns is that they tend to place too much reliance on reductionist argument. Such observations raise the question of how social scientists should approach life science, particularly given its traditional proclivity toward reduc-tionism. The next two chapters will explore this issue. Chapter 8 considers different tactics for life science engagement, one based on the tactical co-option of reductionism, the other on its rejection. Chapter 9 then considers an area of life science which challenges reductionism through its very complexity, namely the intricate neurological processes that comprise the human brain. In addition, Chapter 9 will examine 'parallelist' strategies as means to relate the 'mind' and the 'brain', based on a comparison of the variable 'Spinozist sympathies' of William Connolly, Antonio Damasio, Paul Ricoeur and Jean-Pierre Changeux.

8

TRANSGRESSION

In Chapter 4, I argued that, in spite of anti-dualist desire, we should not endeavour to collapse the natural and the social within a singular realm that admits no difference. I suggested that the latter project is likely to be circumscribed by the difficulty of applying the same sense of temporality to the social and natural domain. In particular, it was suggested that the historical specificity of the social domain did not appear to be mirrored in the same way in nature, and that the times of nature and society do not simply coincide.

Yet if we assume difference, what does this imply for attempts to relate nature to society? Can we overcome the traditional divide? Are such transgressive desires feasible or foolish? Posing such questions is easy. Answering them is, of course, rather difficult (see Chapter 2). What can be said is that transgressive desires appear to be growing in fashion. In addition to the prevalence of anti-dualism (see Chapter 3), there have been a variety of attempts by social scientists and philosophers to advance transgression, especially through attempts to engage with life science. At the time of writing, this is particularly apparent in the social science interest in brain sciences, as is reflected in the UK in seminar series such as the ESRC series on 'Neuroscience, Identity and Society'.[1] Social science attention to neuroscience has been stimulated in part by a perception that the brain sciences have moved beyond their formerly reductive stance to embrace more complex accounts that acknowledge the significance of social and environmental issues.

Yet it is still the case that reductive accounts populate significant areas of life science research. In consequence, in what follows I shall firstly consider the question of how sociologists and social scientists should engage with, or move beyond, reductionist life science. Chapter 9 will then examine recent developments in relation to supposedly more 'complex' neuroscience, with particular attention to the argument of William Connolly and Antonio Damasio, and the interdisciplinary 'conversation' between the phenomenologist, Paul Ricoeur and the neuro-biologist, Jean-Pierre Changeux.

Cautionary tales

In his oft-cited paper, Ted Benton called for a rapprochement between sociology and biology, but noted that the latter should be given a 'cautious welcome'

(1991: 1). To those unfamiliar with sociological debate, or perhaps to evangelical 'interdisciplinarians', this need for caution may appear odd. Yet as Phil Sutton explains, 'Benton's welcome is a necessarily cautious one if a simple return to an older biological reductionism is to be avoided' (2004: 95). In other words, a central question in transgressing the boundary between sociology and biology is how one approaches the reductionism that has, traditionally, informed the latter. In this chapter, I shall consider two opposing stances that are relevant to such transgression, namely tactically co-opting reductionist life science, and deliberately trying to engage with a non-reductionist biology. Although this analysis will point to the difficulties of these endeavours, and will display many of the traditional tactics of academic critique, it is not my intention to suggest that meaningful dialogue between life and social science is impossible. Instead, the ensuing discussion aims to highlight the continuing difficulties that need to be addressed if this project is to be realised.

It remains desirable that there should be engagement between social and life science if only because of the interconnectedness of the natural and social domain (Elias, 1992). As noted in Chapter 1, the human body can be both extra-discursive and deeply embedded in the social fabric, as witnessed in the human smile, our biological capacity for language, and the body scripts of birth, maturation and death. Such examples underscore the social salience of the extra-discursive body, and how any account of the social world remains deficient if it ignores the fact that human beings have biological bodies, and that our bodies are centrally implicated in human communication, development, maturation, reproduction and aging (Bury and Wadsworth, 2003). In addition, it remains difficult to engage with the politics of nature, such as that relating to environmental degradation, gender and health, unless we engage with natural science debates that surround such concerns (see Chapter 1). These are all 'big' issues, and in spite of sociological tradition (Turner, 1991), it remains remarkable that the body was for so long treated as a 'passive shell' (Shilling, 1993: 29), almost like a mechanical vehicle upon which human life depended but in which nothing of any sociological significance could be found.

In sum, we constrain our imagination and analysis if we refuse to examine the way in which human biology interacts with sociological concerns. At the same time however, we need to recall the limited success that sociologists have so far had in tackling biological issues. For example, environmental sociology represents the field with the lengthiest history of 'frontier crossing' forays. Commenting on this field, Frederick Buttel observed that:

> while the injunction to incorporate biophysical variables as causal factors makes intuitive sense at the metatheoretical level, it has *proven to be very difficult to bring this proposition to bear at a more straightforward theoretical and propositional level*... there is much work to be done in specifying the array of mechanisms through which social and biophysical

forces interact, and in being able to specify propositions about the conditions under which particular mechanisms come into play
(1996: 70, added emphasis, cited in Murdoch, 2001).

As Jonathan Murdoch later concluded, 'while various attempts have been made to link nature and society more closely together within environmental sociology, it now appears as though there is a general acceptance of rather traditional divisions between these two domains' (2001: 111). Such comments do not mean that it is impossible to break down barriers between the natural and social terrain, but they do suggest that there may be difficulty in the enterprise.

In this chapter, I wish to explore why addressing biology remains a 'daunting' task (Benton, 1994: 30) and why it has *so far* met with limited success within sociology. I shall first consider Elizabeth Wilson's (2004) attempt to tactically engage with reductive life science. As a contrast to Wilson's stance, I will then explore work that aims to marry a non-reductive biology with the study of the sociology of the body, especially as it informs the relation between psychosocial experience and human health.

Engaging life science: tactical co-option

Drawing on a range of feminist debate, Elizabeth Wilson (2004) has presented what might be termed a 'negotiation strategy' for successful engagement between the humanities, social science, and life science. An introduction to her negotiating position can be found by considering work that, in some ways, represents its opposite, namely Elizabeth Grosz's (1994) attempt to develop a culturally aware understanding of biology that is attentive to feminist concern. Grosz accepts the need for feminists to engage with biology yet also argues for different ways of conceptualising biology. In particular, she argues that feminist accounts of the body 'must be extricated from the biological and pseudo-naturalist appropriations from which it has historically suffered' (Grosz, 1994: 20). For Grosz, this requires the *abandonment* of 'the restricting or containing studies of the body within the biological and life sciences' (1994: 20). She seeks out alternate accounts of biology through reference to a wide social science and philosophical terrain, drawing on Freud, Lacan, Merleau-Ponty, Nietzsche, Foucault, Deleuze and Guattari, and Kristeva, amongst others. In other words, Grosz's strategy is to tackle the reductionist tendencies of life science by *replacing* them with the expansive terrain of psychoanalytical and poststructural work. Yet such alternates raise their own questions. First, the use of psychoanalytical references has a tendency toward a rather rigid Cartesian dualism, as is observed in Freud's account of 'neurones'. Second, it remains uncertain as to whether a *replacement strategy* that exchanges reductionist life science for poststructural 'expanse' can provide an easy basis for dialogue with life scientists (see Chapter 9).

The same criticism does not apply with equal force to Wilson's (2004) account of a 'neurologically oriented' feminism. Like Grosz, Wilson draws in part on

Freud and she is similarly concerned about the way in which feminist debate is dominated by literary and constructionist argument:

> My point is that the cultural, social, linguistic, literary, and historical analysis that now dominate the scene of feminist theory typically seek to seal themselves off from – or constitute themselves against – the domain of the biological.
>
> (2004: 8)

Yet Wilson's strategy opposes that of Grosz. Instead of rejecting biological reductionism, she tactically embraces it. Wilson believes that feminists can utilise the 'reductive formulations' (2004: 14) of much life science and her argument combines positivist life science with constructionist, historical and literary analysis. In so doing, her analysis raises the question as to the efficacy of this 'counter-strategy'. On the one hand, Wilson provides fascinating and original analyses that go significantly beyond many existing texts in teasing out the relationship between the social and biological. This is particularly the case where Wilson explores how human evolution combines biological and social process (and thereby furthers the project of writers such as Wasburn, Lorenz, Elias and Burkitt). On the other hand, Wilson's project becomes problematic where it relies on reductive life science. Although Wilson is attentive to critique of positivist life science, she still tends to evoke many of the limitations that are highlighted by such critique. For instance, she directly links human psychological depression to animal research by comparing studies of the gradual 'kindling' of animal behaviour with the onset of human depression. Drawing on Peter Kramer's (1993) *Listening to Prozac*, Wilson discusses the 'kindling' of seizures in laboratory animals:

> It has been demonstrated experimentally that epileptic seizures can be induced in normal animals through exposure to a series of small, initially nontraumatic electrical currents. The first shock does not induce a seizure, but over time, without increasing the level of the shock, the animal begins to respond with seizures that are initially small and contained but that eventually become more severe and widespread. Once the brain has been so 'kindled', smaller and smaller electric shocks will induce seizure.
>
> (Wilson, 2004: 24)

Wilson connects this animal experimentation to human depression by drawing on Kramer's argument that 'depression . . . can be induced in normals [humans] . . . through a series of small stimuli, none of which at first causes overt symptoms' but which become 'more complex over time' (Kramer, 1993: 114). Wilson further suggests that 'perhaps the brain may be kindled for depression through the stresses of everyday life' and later concludes that 'like [Freud's]

neurasthenic patient, the depressive patient is a casualty to nervous weakening'
(2004: 25).

In this example, Wilson repeats many of the errors that follow from the
application of research on animals to human beings. In particular, she effectively equates an electric shock received by a laboratory rat with 'the stresses
of everyday [human] life' (2004: 25). But can the reduced settings of animal
laboratory experimentation be equated with the social complexity that surrounds
the experience of human stress? Even Kramer at one point notes that 'the
stress to which animals are subjected, electrical current, is not the same as the
stress that depresses humans' (1993: 115).[2] Furthermore, can the biologically
reduced setting of a suffering laboratory rat be equated with the 'cultural, social,
linguistic, literary, and historical' (Wilson, 2004: 8) assumptions that inform
feminist and sociological study, whether in relation to human stress, depression
or any other concern. Even if human behaviour is no more complex than that
of rat, can we assume that there are no significant differences between these
two animals? And can we generalise from the deliberately reduced setting of an
animal experiment to the 'field' behaviour of either rats or humans? In other
words, Wilson's easy transition from animal research to human psychology masks
a host of debatable assumptions, and ignores the considerable tension between
biological reductionism and feminist argument. Wilson asserts that 'critical and
political responses to *Listening to Prozac* have been much less... interested
in, neurological detail' (2004: 27). Yet Wilson could also be accused of an
insufficient attention to 'neurological detail' by failing to interrogate Kramer's
utilisation of psychophysiological research. As Margot Lyon observes, Kramer
adopts a position which, if not biologically determinist, is nevertheless one
where the biological is seen as 'causally prior' to the social (Lyon, 1996: 64).
Even though the socio-cultural plays a part in Kramer's account, 'the underlying explanation for behaviour is... biochemical and genetic' (Lyon, 1996:
63; cf. Breggin and Breggin, 1994). Moreover, Kramer's thesis is conducive
to the medicalisation of social life wherein individuals are 'defined and treated
through illness constructions grounded in... neurochemical features' (Lyon,
1996: 64). To the extent that such medicalisation downplays, or denies, the
social context, it reproduces dualist and biologically reductionist analysis. In
particular, Prozac may be symptomatic of processes of commercialisation wherein
the consumer is offered supposed 'relief' whilst the social context of depression is largely ignored (Moncrieff, 2006). In addition, as Tim Kendall (2006)
notes, if unpublished trials are included in the assessment of the efficacy of
anti-depressant drugs, many appear to have a negligible demonstrable effect.
At worst, the net effect may be that women, who still report most depression
(Murakumi, 2002), become part of a commodification process which benefits
from their suffering whilst deflecting attention away from the social relations
that surround their distress. Once again, the question remains as to how a reliance on texts such as that of Kramer (1993) can be equated with a feminist
concern.

Elsewhere in her wide ranging analysis, Wilson provides further illustration of the difficulties inherent in combining reductive areas of life science with literary and social science argument. These examples show the tension that arises when the expansive analysis of literary and social science discourse is applied to the reductive conclusions that can still inform life science. For instance, in a chapter on sexuality, Wilson re-examines Simon LeVay's (1991) report in *Science* which suggested that neurological differences explain our sexual orientation. Based on research on rhesus monkeys (Slimp *et al.*, 1978) and indications that the 'interstitial nuclei in the anterior hypothalamus' (INAH 2 and INAH 3) of the human brain are larger in men than women (Allen *et al.*, 1989), LeVay hypothesised that INAH nuclei size relates to sexuality, being larger in straight men and lesbians (those attracted to women) and smaller in straight women and gay men (those attracted to men). LeVay tested this hypothesis in research on the post-mortem brain tissue of 41 individuals, including men whose medical records indicated they were gay (having died from HIV/AIDS), and men and women who were *presumed* to be straight (LeVay, 1991: 1035). He noted that INAH 3 was 'more than twice as large in heterosexual men as in the homosexual men' and that 'there was a similar difference between the heterosexual men and the women', implying that, *'at least in men, . . . sexual orientation has a biological substrate'* (LeVay, 1991: 1034, added emphasis).

Wilson notes that the LeVay's study suffered from a host of limitations which 'have been exploited in many critical commentaries' (Wilson, 2004: 53). Yet aside from these numerous internal shortcomings (such as the assumption of hetero-sexuality, the lack of lesbians, etc.), there remain serious constraints in LeVay's (1991) experiment. These include the belief that sexuality can be defined by two distinct bipolar categories, heterosexual and homosexual which effectively 'elim-inates the possibility of a person with a sexuality neither heterosexual nor homo-sexual' (Halley, 1994: 536–537, cited in Wilson, 2004: 55). As LeVay himself noted in commenting on the limitations of his study, 'the use of postmortem material, with the consequent impossibility of obtaining detailed information about the sexuality of the subjects, limits the ability to make correlations between brain structure and *the diversity of sexual behavior that undoubtedly exists within the homosexual and the heterosexual populations'* (1991: 1036, added emphasis). In addition, LeVay's work was informed by animal research on gender-typical sexu-ality. As Jennifer Terry notes, 'assuming that gender typicality is the same across species allows researchers to ignore or misunderstand variance among individual animals and across species. This is precisely what happens in much of the research on human sexuality and sexual orientation that relies on the use of rodents' (2000: 161, cited in Wilson, 2004: 56). Wilson documents many of these limita-tions in LeVay's (1991) research in detail. Yet given these serious shortcomings, the question arises as to why she uses his study as an exemplar in the first place. The answer appears to rely in her argument that category differences in biolo-gical form, such as those related to the INAH nuclei, may have effects that are not bipolar in kind. In so doing, she draws on Michael Fortun's notion of the 'chiasmus' as a site where 'two distinct concepts can't be distinguished from each other, but feed off each other, send silent coded messages between themselves, and set possibilities in motion' (2003: 23). Wilson argues that Fortun's chiasmus provides a model for LeVay's study with its 'complex structuration of rudimentary divisions and their vicissitudes' (2004: 59). Yet this argument still does not answer the question of the relevance of the LeVay's study with its numerous shortcomings, reductionism, and questionable reliance on animal experimentation. Given its constraints, its ability to inform a 'neurologically oriented' feminism appears limited. In addition, it remains doubtful as to whether one can project the *expansive* discussion of Fortun (2003) on to the *reductive* assumptions of animal experimentation. LeVay's findings derive from a very particular context and there is no given reason why they should apply in another context (Cartwright, 1999; Lewontin, 1991), never mind one that draws on the expansive imagination of historical and social science, as is the case with Fortun (2003). It is difficult to justify the application of an expansive social science imagination to a reductive natural science setting, especially where the former expands so far beyond the latter that it renders it meaningless except as a literary trope.

To sum up, Grosz (1994) and Wilson (2004) provide differing strategies for engaging with biological terrain. Grosz avoids biological reductionism whereas Wilson engages with it. Yet there are difficulties with both approaches. Grosz's argument can be questioned because it often adopts a 'replacement strategy' rather than one which provides a serious engagement with life science. Wilson can be criticised for drawing dubious parallels between experimental/animal research settings and human psychology as well as ignoring the tension between the expansive terrain of social science discursivity and the reductive settings of studies such as LeVay. On the one hand, those concerned to interweave the sociological and biological may not wish to return to a Durkheimian 'anti-reductionism taboo' (Catton and Dunlap, 1980: 19) where *only* the social is deemed to be of sociological significance. On the other, there remain forms of biological reductionism that are difficult to equate with sociological or feminist concern.[3]

Given the difficulties of Wilson's attempt to tactically engage reductive life science, it is not surprising that a number of writers have tried to marry sociological concern with a less reductive biology. Prominent amongst these forays is work on the sociology of the body, that has endeavoured to correlate the historical and social context of people's lives with their psychological and physical health. The remainder of this chapter will critically examine this work and consider the extent to which it represents a successful engagement with a less reductive life science.

Beyond the ethereal and the elusive: towards the transgressive corporeal

In what follows, I shall explore attempts to materially 'ground' the sociology of the body that proceed by addressing the relationship between the psychosocial,

social inequality and health. It will be argued that although adventurers in this area have a 'noble purpose', they have tended to underestimate the differences in perspective between sociological and psychobiological analysis. Related difficulties can also be observed amongst those more broadly concerned to embed human beings within their natural environment, such as Peter Dickens' (2000) re-evaluation of social Darwinism.

Various writers have criticised the tendency in work on the sociology of the body to see the body as infinitely plastic, whereby it largely appears as 'a "made up body" linked to a "made up self" ' (Bury, 1995: 44). Though such writers may acknowledge that the body is socially constructed and is *partly* made and re-made through discourse, they also argue that there are limits to this process (see Chapter 2). Thus Chris Shilling notes that 'the body may be surrounded and perceived through discourse, but is *irreducible* to discourse' (1993: 81). For these writers, the problem with work on the sociology of the body is that a strong social constructionist emphasis has rendered a biological and corporeal sense of the body 'theoretically elusive' (Kelly and Field, 1994: 34) with the consequence that it has 'a rather "ethereal" existence' (Williams, 1996: 41). Simon Williams further argues that medical sociologists have perpetuated the rift between the social and the life sciences through their 'tendency to relegate the body to biology' (1996: 41; cf. Bury, 1997: 199). Instead Williams argues that 'sociology should be fundamentally embodied' (Williams, 1996: 42). This desire to 'truly embody' sociology will be referred to as the project of a nascent *transgressive corporeal sociology.*

The study of emotion represents a common interest amongst those associated with this project because of its perceived relevance to crossing the 'divide' between the biological and the social. As Simon Williams argues (drawing on Margot Lyon):

> Emotion, it is clear, provides . . . a 'bridge' between the social and the biological domains, 'resituating' the body in the world *whilst avoiding reductionist pitfalls* en route . . . A sociological commitment to emotion, therefore, provides an 'alternative analytical framework that both challenges assumptions regarding the division between biology and being, and provides a new perspective on the interrelationship of these different orders of phenomena (Lyon, 1996: 69).
>
> (Williams, 2003a: 146, added emphasis)

It is this non-reductionist 'bridge' that explains the appeal of emotion to 'transgressive corporeal' sociologists. Yet although I have sympathy with these concerns (Newton, 1998), I also feel that there are difficulties in exploring the bio-corporeality of the body. It is one thing to note that the biological and life sciences are contested terrains, and that within this 'family' of knowledge there are 'branches' which allow for the possibility of 'an extension . . . to include psychological and social processes and mechanisms' (Benton, 1991: 20). But it is another thing to actually make this 'extension' and develop approaches that enable a successful 'cross-over' to be achieved. As Shilling notes, 'as yet, there are no *fully developed perspectives* on the body which seek to combine the biological and social sciences in the manner suggested by Benton' (Shilling, 2003: 93, added emphasis). In what follows, I shall try to show why, as with environmental sociology (Murdoch, 2001), it has been difficult to formulate such a 'fully developed perspective'. In so doing, I will utilise material from an earlier paper (Newton, 2003a), as well as a rejoinder to this paper by Williams (2003b). As noted in my earlier paper, the work of Peter Freund provides a useful introduction to the transgressive corporeal project.

For Shilling, Freund's work can be seen as providing one means of developing 'a bridge between naturalistic and social constructionist views of the body' (Shilling, 2003: 93). Equally, for Williams and Bendelow, Freund points the way toward a ' "socialised" . . . biology rather than a reductionist sociobiology' (Williams and Bendelow, 1998: 144). Freund himself argues that 'sociology . . . cannot afford to regard *human physiology* as irrelevant or duck its relevance by *artificially "bracketing"* such issues' (1988: 856, added emphasis). He develops his case by conjoining a traditional sociological concern with power relations to a concern with emotion, physiology and health. Freund (1990) argues that our experience of emotion is linked to class, gender, age and ethnicity, because the latter affect our social status and our ability to invoke tacit 'status shields' (Hochschild, 1983). Freund, like Hochschild, emphasises the psychological cost of emotional labour in terms of its 'stress' on the individual.[4] But unlike Hochschild, Freund explores the interrelations between power, emotional stress, *and our physiology*, in order to produce a 'sociopsychosomatic' politics of health (Freund, 1990: 471). He suggests that the experience of emotional labour has psychophysiological accompaniments which, if protracted, are likely to lead to 'adverse somatic changes' (1990: 466) and ill-health.

The assumption of a link between the psychosocial and health is shared by Benton, Shilling and Williams. For instance, Benton noted the significance of ' "stress" in the aetiology of many chronic and life-threatening physical illnesses' (1991: 5), while Shilling (1993) drew on a range of work in examining the supposed relationship between stress, emotion and ill-health. Williams argues that 'the emotionally expressive body translates broader psychosocial and material conditions of existence, including conflict situations, into the recalcitrant language of *disease and disorder*' (Williams, 1998: 131, added emphasis). All these authors also point to the links between *power relations*, emotion and health, thereby furthering Freund's call for a 'sociopsychosomatic' politics of health. For instance, Benton emphasises the interaction of 'stress, anxiety and isolation' and power relations such as 'pertinent aspects of the class system' (1991: 6). Similarly Williams, and Williams and Bendelow, argue that emotions have a 'central role in linking the health and illness of the . . . agent with wider structures of power and domination, civilisation and control in society' (Williams, 1998: 131;

Williams and Bendelow, 1998: 144). Finally, Shilling (1993) drew on Freund and Hochschild in support of such a relationship.

In pursuing such argument, these writers 'engage with', rather than 'bracket out', life science. In other words, they reject strong constructionist reticence or the defence of agnosticism, and deliberately use psychophysiological study in order to show how human health is affected by the interplay of power relations and psychosocial issues. In reviewing their work, it is therefore initially important to consider a key element of this relationship, namely that between the psychosocial and health. In my earlier critique (Newton, 2003a), I turned to the field of psychological stress in order to examine this issue since it represents the field of inquiry in which the vast majority of work linking the psychosocial and the biological body has been undertaken. As Jon Elstad notes, 'the sociologically oriented tendency within stress research can be regarded as the original source of the psycho-social perspective' (1998: 603), and reference to stress and disease is not uncommon amongst texts on the sociology of medicine and health (e.g. Locker, 2003).

The assumption that psychosocial stress leads to ill-health has been a continuing feature of stress discourse since the inception of stress studies. Early work on stress was strongly naturalistic in orientation, as illustrated in the work of Walter Cannon and Hans Selye (Pollock, 1988; Newton, 1995; Viner, 1999). Subsequent work promoting the health link was associated with psychophysiological research drawing on Selye, most notably the Swedish analyses of Lenart Levi and Marianne Frankenhaeuser. These researchers studied the relationship between psychological stress, catecholamine output (e.g. adrenalin, noradrenalin) and illness indicators (Newton, 1995). Levi and Frankenhaeuser, had difficulty in establishing this relationship with Levi, for example, acknowledging that 'the causation of disease by such [psychosocial] stimuli is not proven' (1974: 73). Researchers associated with the Swedish school, such as Robert Karasek and Bertil Gardell continued to pursue this hypothesis, though with a less than conclusive success (e.g. Karasek et al., 1987). Subsequent research has observed correlations between stress and psychophysiological measures opposite to that which might be expected (Baum and Grunberg, 1997; and see p. 138). For example Fletcher and Jones (1993) found that stress was associated with lower rather than higher blood pressure. As I previously argued (Newton, 2003a), other attempts to reliably establish a stress–health relationship have been problematic. Briner and Reynolds summarised the heavy layer of doubt which surrounds this central assumption of stress research:

> the evidence for the relationship between general stress and health is not particularly strong: Lazarus and Folkman (1984, p. 205) describe the link between stress and illness as ' . . . still only a premise, albeit widely assumed'; . . . Pollock (1988, p. 391) states that the link is "unclear and unproven": Schroeder and Costa (1984, p. 853) write that ' . . . the link . . . has been exaggerated'; and Cohen and Manuck (1995) observe

that '. . . convincing evidence that stress contributes to the patho-physiology of human disease is sparse, and, even where evidence exists, relatively small proportions of variance are explained'.

(Briner and Reynolds, 1999: 652)

Stress researchers acknowledge the lack of understanding of their putative stress–health relationship. For instance, one review admitted that '*at the moment*, there are only hints and guesses' as to the way in which stress may affect the immune system or lead to physical ill-health (Evans *et al.*, 1997: 306, added emphasis). The phrase, 'at the moment' is significant. It reflects stress researchers' continued optimism even though they have lacked 'evidence'. That is to say, in spite of the inability of five decades of research to establish clear pathways between stress and illness, most stress researchers still clearly want to believe in it. To do otherwise would be to question the rationale of their project.

In a rejoinder to this argument (Newton, 2003a), Williams (2003b) argued that I had paid insufficient attention to work that supported the influence of psychosocial factors, such as that of Richard Wilkinson (1996, 1997a, 1997b, 2000a, 2000b). Williams also drew on Elstad's argument that 'recent reviews leave few doubts that psychological stress . . . can influence disease-related patterns' (Elstad, 1998: 601, cited in Williams, 2003b: 553). Moreover, the supposition that stress and 'negative' emotion lead to physical ill-health is supported by popular experience, such as that of having a headache or a backache after 'moments of stress' or 'painful emotions'. In such moments, we may be particularly aware that our bodies are like 'a living memory pad' (Bourdieu, 1990: 68). In addition, these psychosocial experiences appear to have physiological correlates. As Elstad comments, 'examples are found as regards the cardiovas-cular system (e.g. systoloic/diastolic blood pressure), the endocrine system (e.g. secretions of catecholamine and cortisol) and the immune system' (1998: 601, cited in Williams, 2003b: 553). Based on this and related argument, Wilkinson argues that 'there is a large body of evidence demonstrating that various forms of psychosocial stress can have a powerful influence on death rates and rates of illness' (1996: 5). However the existence of adverse temporary psychosomatic experiences does not necessarily mean that stress or emotion has any permanent impact on the immune system or that they lead to longer-term physical ill-health. For instance, while many of us may find our lives 'very demanding', this does not mean that such demands will seriously affect our physical health. As Elstad himself notes, 'the problem is . . . to demonstrate that such [physiological] changes are large enough and longterm enough to affect health in a significant way' (1998: 601, cited in Williams, 2003b: 553), and as he further observes, 'Wilkinson's underlying social theory is not always convincing' (1998: 611). Furthermore, given that stress research has a very lengthy pedigree, and that it has been difficult to demonstrate long-term stress–health links, it is perhaps not entirely surprising that critics have questioned the relationship between the psychosocial and ill-health, especially when there have been a number of observed 'decouples' between 'stressor levels' and physiological correlates, such that a heightened level of the former is associated with a *lower* level with the latter (see p. 139). As Elstad remarks, there have been 'divergent findings' and 'strong conclusions are difficult to draw' (1998: 601).

Yet as Williams rightly notes with respect to his argument and that of my own, 'there is probably less difference between us on this count than may first appear' (2003b: 553). I would argue that it still remains an open question as to whether psychosocial issues moderate the relationship between social inequality and ill-health, and one should not discount this possibility. The problem is that stress researchers have tended to assume that a psychosocial–health relationship *does* exist. Similarly, transgressive corporeal sociologists have extended this assumption to encompass the broader relationship between the psychosocial, social inequality and health. Just as psychological stress researchers want to believe that stress causes ill-health even though 'at the moment, there are only hints and guesses' (Evans, Clow and Hucklebridge, 1997: 306), so do transgressive corporeal sociologists seem to assume that the psychosocial, power relations and health are interrelated even though '*it is not yet conclusive*' (Shilling, 1993: 116, added emphasis) and '*the precise links require further specification*' (Williams, 1998: 134, added emphasis). It is this background assumption that I sought to question in my earlier critique (Newton, 2003a). In particular, it seems premature to state that 'socio-economic factors affect health *primarily* through *psychosocial rather than material pathways*' (Williams, 1998: 133, added emphasis; cf. Williams, 2001: 71) when, (1) this argument is premised upon research arguments which have been criticised (Newton, 2003a), and (2) there remains evidence for the contrary argument. As Peter Carroll and his colleagues argue (Carroll *et al.*, 1996), 'material pathways' can appear more significant than psychosocial influences, as reflected in the health-related differences associated with variation in income, housing, educational opportunity, diet, etc., between social classes. In consequence, they suggest that 'the most compelling intervention strategies . . . are unlikely to be psychological' (Carroll *et al.*, 1996: 34).

Yet whatever the status of the relationship between, inequality, the psychosocial and health, it was *not* the primary concern of my earlier critique. Instead I was chiefly concerned with the problems that could result from its co-option by sociologists. In particular, there remains a tension between the espoused position of transgressive corporeal sociologists and the studies they co-opt in support of their argument. Transgressive corporeal sociologists have expressed desires toward 'fundamentally re-thinking the "biological" in non-reductionist terms' (Williams, 1998: 134; cf. Benton, 1991; Williams, 2001), or to being 'careful in appropriating analytic concepts and discourse' (Freund, 1990: 471), and developing a biologically informed sociology that is clearly differentiated from the reductionism of sociobiology (Shilling, 2003). In this respect, their work follows Benton's (1991) call to engage with non-reductive life science. At the same time however, it illustrates the difficulties of this project. In engaging with psychosocial studies, transgressive corporeal sociologists have drawn, directly *or* indirectly, on the language of psychological stress (Elstad, 1998; Newton, 2003a). As I have argued elsewhere (Newton, 1995), this language, as with much traditional psychosocial study, remains that of the 'closed individual', *homo clausus* in Elias's (1970) terms, as reflected in the reductionism, individualism, ahistoricism, apoliticism, etc. of its conceptualisation. In consequence, the danger in citing this kind of psychosocial argument is that one ends up drawing on assumptions that can only remain in conflict with the pursuance of a non-reductionist, contextualised, biology. In particular, it seems odd that some transgressive corporeal sociologists appear aware of the narrow terms in which stress discourse is written, and more generally attentive to the social construction of health and medicine, but do not appear to feel that such cognisance implies a need to question the whole stress–health relationship. For example, Freund and McGuire (1991) and Freund (1998) are attentive to the construction of stress, health and medicine and its apoliticism, scientism and decontextualisation. Yet they do not seriously question whether stress leads to ill-health even though this supposed relationship is the means through which stress and health discourse gains much of its rationale and legitimisation.

These difficulties can be further illustrated by considering Freund's reference to the so-called 'fight or flight' response (Freund, 1990; Freund and McGuire, 1991). Though this entails something of a detour, it is worth exploring the fight/flight concept since it is illustrative of the problems encountered within transgressive corporeal sociology. This concept refers to the argument that human beings have evolved a particular physiological response pattern to danger or threat. It suggests that a pattern of heightened physiological arousal evolved in such situations in order to enable us to 'fight' or 'flee' ancient threats (such as that stereotypically associated with the 'marauding mammoth'). It is further surmised that this response pattern is inappropriate to dealing with the stresses of contemporary society since we cannot necessarily fight or flee, say, work 'stressors'.

As with a number of stress researchers, Freund makes a large theoretical jump in assuming that our supposed contemporary inability to 'satisfy' the fight/flight instinct has potentially pathological consequences. Citing Leder (1984), he argues that the fight/flight response represents a source of stress which may lead to 'gastritis, high blood pressure, perhaps a heart attack' (Leder, 1984: 39, quoted in Freund, 1990: 462). There are two problems however with such argument: first it is reliant on the debatable assumption of stress–health links, and second the fight/flight concept incorporates much of the reductive naturalism found in the writer who is generally credited with its invention, namely Walter Cannon (Newton, 1995). *Contra* Benton, Cannon's work *cannot* be said to reflect a desire to 'think holistically about living organisms' (Benton, 1991: 17), since his arguments are based on a naturalistic, reductionistic and desocialised account which explains human behaviour chiefly in terms of instincts. For Cannon, the fight/flight response represented an instinctual reaction to threatening environmental stimuli. According to Cannon, the 'emotion of fear is associated with the *instinct* for flight, and the emotion of anger or rage with the *instinct* for fighting or attack' (1914: 264, added emphasis). Stress researchers have long used this argument in order to explain stress as the outcome of a mismatch between our present-day psychology and 'outmoded' 'Stone Age' biological instincts, such as the fight/flight instinct. Arroba and James provide a typical example of this argument:

> Modern offices and factories may be very different from the environments our ancestors inhabited, but *our bodies are still programmed to cope with primitive and dangerous places.*
>
> (1987: 6, added emphasis; cf. Benson, 1979: 143)

This idea of 'Stone Age' bodies suffering in the modern-day office is very popular, even though it totally overlooks the social and technological complexity of, say, Stone Age society (Sahlins, 1972; Pollock, 1988). Within such discourse, stress is portrayed as the result of our 'natural', but outmoded, animal instincts. In sum, such arguments present a *crude dualism* that reduces the 'problem' of present-day social complexity to the outmoded biological body, as supposedly witnessed in the anachronistic fight/flight instinct. The biological reductionism of such discourse makes it far closer to sociobiological argument and evolutionary psychology than to what one might expect in a putative non-reductionistic bio-corporeal sociology (Dupré, 2001).

In Chapter 3, I questioned an overweening commitment to anti-dualism on the grounds that it can obscure the possibility of difference in our perception of nature and society. However such argument does not imply that we can defend a crude dualism that presents a sharp divide between our biology and our sociality. Yet this is precisely the logic of the fight/flight concept through its insistence that ill-health derives from a 'schism' between our outmoded biology and our contemporary social sophistication. Freund and McGuire effectively reproduce this crude dualism through their argument that 'modern conditions do not always make the adaptive response of *fleeing or fighting* a practical one' because of 'the rules of "civilized" behavior' (1991: 83, added emphasis).[5] Such citation of the fight/flight instinct is not however an isolated enrolment of reductive and dualistic research amongst those arguing for a more bio-corporeal sociology. For instance, both Freund and Shilling draw on the work of Frankenhaeuser and her colleagues in order to support links between, work, stress and ill-health 'indicators' (Freund, 1988: 852; Shilling, 1993: 123). Yet Frankenhaeuser's work is situated within the same dualistic tradition as those who draw on Cannon. For example, echoing the naturalism of Canon's fight/flight instinct, Frankenhaeuser argues that ill-health arises because 'bodily responses may . . . be totally inappropriate for coping with the pressures of life today [due to] the mismatch between our *old* biology and the demands of the *new* sociotechnical world . . . ' (Frankenhaeuser, 1989: 748, added emphasis). Once again, a crude dualism is presented that contrasts our outmoded biological body with the contemporary 'stressors' that derive from our socially and technically complex world. It does indeed seem that there has been a strange schism between our social and our natural development whereby our tired old bodies have not 'kept up'. Stress and maladaptive emotions would be rendered harmless if we could just have some 'new model' body.

Reference to the fight/flight syndrome is still employed amongst those concerned to develop a biologically oriented sociology. For example, Mildred Blaxter argues that it is 'common to most mammals' and 'adverse consequences for health result if arousal is sustained or recurring' (2003: 74). It is also found even amongst more contextualised accounts of stress. For instance, Williams (1998) has drawn on the studies of Karasek and his colleagues. Their work has the advantage of appearing more contextualised through its elaboration of the Scandinavian studies of stress researchers such as Gardell and Gustavsen (Newton, 1995). However their theorising still inherits the reductive dualism associated with earlier Scandinavian writers such as Levi and Frankenhaeuser. For example, they argue that the problems of 'controlling' 'stressors' are 'of course aggravated by the fact that our work stresses now are *not* related to the need for rapid fight/flight physical reactions *for which we are physiologically adapted*' (Karasek and Theorell, 1990: 86, added emphasis). Once again, the problem appears to be that our 'physiological adaption' is outdated, appropriate for such pre-modern 'fight/flight' needs as avoiding marauding mammoths, but not to modern 'work stresses' where our biology only provides 'aggravation'. On the one hand, our neuroendocrinal processes can appear responsive to social demands (Newton, 1995). On the other, the fight/flight concept presents a very simplistic portrayal of this relationship. In particular, it too easily accepts that there are long-term health consequences to neuroendocrinal activity, and it ignores the remarkable social complexity of earlier human societies. In effect, it relies on a crude dualism that reduces social ills to our outmoded biology.

In sum, though clearly resistant to positivism and naturalism, the desire of Freund, Williams, and Shilling to cross the divide between the social and the biological has, understandably, led them to marshal existing psychophysiological research in support of their argument. The problem remains however that this research still has a tendency to rely on the kind of positivist, naturalist and dualist argument from which, elsewhere, they are keen to distance themselves. To take a further example, Freund (1988, 854–855, 1990: 464, 1998: 277) and Williams (1998: 129, 2001: 71) draw on animal studies such as that based on baboons (e.g. Sapolsky, 1982, 1992). Wilkinson argues that this kind of primate study 'fits well with the increasing success of psychosocial factors in explaining health inequalities' (2000b: 999) and notes that 'stressful social hierarchies predispose to poorer health among troops of baboons as well as in human societies' (1996: 5).[6] Yet as I suggested in my earlier critique (Newton, 2003a), an unqualified reference to animal studies presents a questionable account of human health and can appropriate rather inappropriate analytic concepts – features which appear to contradict Freund and Williams expressed concerns. In his rejoinder, Williams argued that I had taken insufficient account of the need to question 'the categorical (sociological) division or opposition between humans and animals' (2003b: 556). Williams further suggested that 'we are, after all, despite our vanities or self-conceits/deceits, animals belonging to the primate order' and he also notes that 'some non-human animals... are capable of quite sophisticated forms of learning' (2003b: 556). I would agree with these sentiments.[7] But this does not make the citation of animal studies any less problematic. Although animal studies may inform human health where we share similar biological processes, it needs to be remembered that different species have biologically and culturally evolved within differing ecological settings. In particular, humans have developed levels of linguistic and technological skill that are unmatched in other animals, and in this sense, there is a case for human exceptionalism (see Chapter 5). In consequence, a 'stressed' rat or baboon is likely to represent a very different phenomenon to that of a 'stressed' human, especially when the former are assessed in the laboratory and the latter 'in the field'. There remain notable variances across animal species, and such variances compromise attempts to extrapolate from animal experimentation to human behaviour. These difficulties in comparative analysis are compounded by the numerous difficulties of measuring diffuse psychosocial concepts such as stress or emotion, whether in humans or animals (Newton, 1989, 1995; see p. 125).

The problems of an inappropriate reliance on reductionist studies are not unique to those addressing the sociology of health. They can also be found among other writers exploring the broader relationship between human beings and their natural environment. For example, Peter Dickens presents an uncritical reproduction of the central tenets of stress discourse in his attempt to develop 'an alternative kind of "social Darwinism" ' (2000: 97). Dickens argues that 'recent work shows that continued exposure to stressful circumstances can severely affect the body's immune system' (2000: 108). Like Freund, Benton and Williams, he links the deleterious effects of stress to social inequality arguing that 'lack of social power is a key reason for the link between inequality and bad health in Western societies' (Dickens, 2000: 108). Yet in developing this thesis, Dickens (2000: 108) calls on exactly the same positivist stress discourse as Freund, Benton, Williams and Shilling, through reference to early 'key' writers such as Hans Selye (Viner, 1999) as well as later researchers schooled within the same psychophysiological tradition as Selye, such as William Lovallo (e.g. 1997). In addition, Dickens presents an unquestioning précis of the dualist fight/flight response, noting that 'humans, like most other animals, have evolved powerful responses' of 'preparing themselves to stay and resist or to flee and capitulate' when 'confronted by a physical, mental or emotional threat' (2000: 108). Such evocation of the fight/flight response is hardly surprising given that it forms a key part of the psychophysiological discourse upon which Dickens bases his argument (e.g. see Lovallo, 1997: 61–68). In sum, an acceptance of stress orthodoxy is not unique to sociologists of the body but instead would appear to permeate the argument of other writers concerned with the relation between the social and natural domain. The problem with such co-option is that its reductionism, individualism and ahistoricism remain ill-suited to the pursuance of a non-reductionist account that transgresses between biological and sociological accounts of nature.

In sum, it appears that desire does not easily translate into practice amongst those who advocate the co-option of a less reductionist, more holistic and complex biology. This observation begs the question of how we can traverse the traditional schisms between sociology and the life sciences without recourse to dualism and reductionism (Benton, 1991). However before we can consider this issue, we need to consider how we can 'socially know' the biological body. To put this another way, the question remains as to how we can 'interview' the body.

Moving from the social to the biological body

A central problem for the project of transgressive corporeal sociology is that there is no easy way to 'know' the biological body, or know how it relates to the social. To put this another way, any non-reductionistic and contextualised corporeal sociology must still contend with the fact that it is very difficult to interrogate the body, and this places constraints on transgressive corporeal sociology projects such as the study of emotion, power and health. For contrary to the continuing desires of some biologists, physiologists, and psychologists, the social cannot easily be reduced to the biological (Benton, 1991). As Andrew Sayer puts it, 'our thoughts and actions presuppose certain chemical transformations in our brains but are not reducible to them; in answering someone's question we are responding to the question not their brain chemistry' (1997: 479). In other words, individual brain cells do not think, even though collectively they provide the biology through which thought may emerge (see Chapter 9). Yet the traditional 'biological answer' to this conundrum is to 'interpret' the body through physiological indicators. However such indicators are not straightforward to analyse which means that there is no easy way to read the psychosocial from the biological. As Armstrong argues, it is difficult to reliably infer 'the relationship between "internal states" and experience' (Armstrong, 1987: 1217). Citing Pennebaker (1984), Armstrong notes that 'there is increasing evidence that the experience of [medical] "symptoms" is not anything like as highly correlated with internal biochemical state as once believed' (1987: 1217). This is hardly surprising since the same physical or physiological 'response' may accompany varied human experience. For instance an increased heart rate might reflect physical exercise, sexual activity, or strong anxiety. Similarly, measures of stress and strain may reflect physical rather than psychological demands upon the body (Karasek and Theorell, 1990: 63).

These and other difficulties make it is as specious to talk of linear relationships between the body and the social as it is to speak of the same within the social. As physiological psychologists such as David Krantz and Jennifer Falconer observe of the cardiovascular 'response' of the body:

> adjustments in the energy needs of bodily tissues (e.g. during exercise or psychological stress) result in a complex pattern of cardiovascular adjustments involving neural, endocrine, and mechanical patterns. *Changes in any one component of the system necessarily affect other components of the system.*
>
> (1997: 194, added emphasis)

In other words, any desire to relate the social and the biological must confront the complexity of their interwoven relationship (Schwartz, 1982).[8] Transgressive corporeal sociologists are of course likely to agree with this aim given their espoused desire to avoid reductionism. Yet embracing physiological complexity remains far from straightforward if only because it occasions a number of problems for assessment. For instance, amongst the more commonly employed physiological measures are cardiovascular response (such as blood pressure and heart rate), and hormonal response (such as catecholamines and corticosteroids). Andrew Baum and Neil Grunberg note that the latter constitute the 'most commonly studied neuroendocrines in stress research' (1997: 177), and in consequence represent the area where the vast majority of research linking the psychosocial and the body has been undertaken. Yet assessments of the relationship between hormonal measures and stress can be *biased* by a host of 'extraneous variables'. Such extraneous variables include 'factors such as gender, race, weight, age, health status, and consumption of salt, caffeine, nicotine, and so on, as well as exposure to exercise' (Krantz and Falconer, 1997: 200).[9]

Psychophysiological researchers have developed methods to address such 'sources of error'. In addition, there are 'improved' and less 'invasive' methods of data collection such as the use of saliva rather than urine samples. Yet there remain a variety of questions regarding such research. The classic one is that of the 'validity' of the laboratory setting in which much of this research is undertaken. Not surprisingly, just as in experimental social psychology, the physiological laboratory setting is revealed as a notably social encounter (Orne, 1962). For instance, a variety of research, from Ayman and Goldshine (1940) onwards, has observed that cardiovascular responses measured in the laboratory or clinic can be considerably higher than those taken 'at home', a phenomenon referred to as 'white coat hypertension'. For experimental physiologists these are sources of 'observer error'. Yet such 'errors' question the legitimacy of experimental physiological research just as much as they do in experimental psychological research. Just because we are interviewing the body rather than 'task reactions' or 'verbal response' makes little difference to the issue of the validity of the laboratory settings of experimental research. For example, some research suggests that physiological measures may be 'corrupted' by the anticipation of being involved in a stress experiment (Obrist, 1981). The usual questions about the artificiality of experimental laboratory settings therefore remain.

In addition to the above constraints, there are other questions over how reliably we can interview the body, and thereby relate the social to the biological. For instance, physiological stress researchers such as Baum and Grunberg (1997) are aware of certain difficulties in 'interpretation'. They note that behavioural, psychological and physiological data do not always 'converge', but rather 'decouple'. In particular, measures of the body may indicate that 'it' is 'stressed' even though the individual concerned shows *no* signs of behavioural or psychological stress. Baum and Grunberg's answer to such conflicting data is, in effect, to argue that the *body must be 'right'* where physiological indicators suggest stress. They note that:

> if a subject reports no distress but exhibits elevated catecholamines or cortisol, the situation can be explained in several different ways. It could reflect denial as in a participant who denies or represses experienced distress... Alternatively, arousal could be due to some other variable, such as experiences immediately prior to assessment, activity level and exercise, diet, drug use, or other extraneous factors. Or, in chronic stress situations, elevated hormone levels could reflect new baseline levels and long-term enhancement of endocrine activity...
>
> (1997: 188)

In other words, Baum and Grunberg consistently assume that it is the extraneous variables that disguise the 'truth' of physiological assessments of the body. However such 'decouplings' and 'divergences' can equally well be read as a reflection of the difficulties of interviewing the body. For example, there is rarely likely to be a simple correspondence between biological processes and social ones since both arenas are characterised by complexity, involving the neural, the cardiovascular and the neuroendocrinal, as well as the complexity of social interweaving (Elias, 1994). In sum, when we look at how the social relates to the biological, we are examining the interrelation of very complex processes (Benton, 1991). In this context, the question arises as to *why* one should be able to observe a linear correlation between such bodily and social processes. Given such complexity, it seems more reasonable to expect that a correlation will *not* be observed, or that the body may appear 'stressed' but the individual not.

The entire enterprise is also compromised by the difficulties inherent in the physiological project, particularly the taking of 'basal' or baseline measures. Such measures are intended to provide a reading of the individuals 'resting' state when they are not 'stressed' by social, biological or physical contaminants. An individual's physiological response to experimental 'stressors' can then be compared to her baseline or resting state. Achieving a reliable baseline measure requires that all the extraneous variables noted above are either controlled or within 'normal' levels. At the same time, accurate baseline measures are critical to physiological assessment since otherwise one cannot be sure that a particular reading does represent an 'elevated' level. Yet such accuracy is difficult to obtain. Normalcy is compromised since the nomothetic is elusive: for instance, extraneous variables such as caffeine or nicotine are particular to the individual and therefore difficult to reliably assess and control. Baseline readings of an individual at 6.00 AM after a night's 'rest' may be abnormal because their caffeine and nicotine levels are abnormally low. Aside from biological contaminants, there is also the difficulty of controlling for social 'stimuli'. Indeed, the search for a physiological space devoid of extraneous social contamination almost resembles a quest for an *asocial* and *abiological* 'holy grail'. A 'pure' baseline seeks a highly idealised state where social, physical and biological contaminants do not interfere. Given the difficulty of attaining this state, it is perhaps not surprising that research such as Baum and Grunberg (1997) should encounter the problem of 'decouples' between the physiological and the social/psychological. In this context, one might ask whether the search for uncontaminated baselines represents a dream of purity that is elusive, if not chimeric.

Highlighting this array of difficulties is not meant to detract from the desires of transgressive corporeal sociologists. Rather my concern is to reinforce arguments about the inherent complexity of the relationship between the biological and the sociological (Benton, 1991; Shilling, 1993; Williams, 2001), and the consequent need to 'tread warily'. At minimum, there is a need to avoid the simple appropriation of psychobiological research. This remains the case because psychophysiological research can *still* exhibit a propensity to read the social (e.g. psychological stress) from the biological (physiological 'indicators') through a quasi-linear (looking, say, at 'moderator' variables) or reductionistic 'lens' which detracts from the complexity of the interweaving between the social and the biological.

Conclusion

The significance of the body for the social underscores the need to formulate lines of inquiry capable of integrating the two. This chapter has examined two approaches to this project, one based on the tactical co-option by social analysts of reductive biology, the other based on its avoidance. With the first strategy, a central question is that of how we are to marry the expansive tendencies of social science with the reductionist proclivities that can still characterise life science. Elizabeth Wilson (2004) bravely tackles this project, yet illustrates its shortcomings. In addition, there are problems with reductionism which are, as John Dupré notes, 'merely practical' (1996: 107). As Dupré argues, 'to make sense of macroscopic phenomena we must categorize them in terms that are, from the microscopic view, radically heterogeneous' (1996: 107). From this perspective, one needs to ask why the microscopic should ever easily map on to the macroscopic, especially *between* natural and social science?

An alternative approach to Wilson's (2004) tactic is provided by 'transgressive corporeal' sociology. This approach not only attempts integration but also addresses Benton's (1991) call to break down the division between life and social sciences. Writers such as Shilling, Freund and Williams have clearly been sympathetic to this latter 'cause', and to the argument that there can be no epistemological reason to erect a barrier between the biological and the social. In areas such as the sociology of health, it may seem wilful ignorance to sidestep or 'bracket off' the interaction between the social, the emotional, and bodily physiology. Equally, a sociology of emotion, or sport, or aging that ignores the inner working of the body can appear one-sided.

In addition to wanting to truly cross the 'Great Divide', Benton, Shilling, Freund and Williams seem concerned to counter strong constructionist treatment of the body. They are either openly critical, or questioning of, approaches where 'the body is viewed simply as a "blank screen" or "sign receiving system" ever open to being constructed and reconstructed by external texts or discourses' (Shilling, 1993: 39; cf. Soper, 1995). At the same time, their arguments move beyond the agnosticism associated with social constructionism (see Chapter 2). Transgressive corporeal sociologists directly engage with, and utilise, life science research. Yet their work also illustrates some of the perils of this exercise. In particular, in spite of an avowed wariness concerning biological reductionism and decontextualised research, their work reproduces some of these assumptions as they inform psychophysiological research. The consequence is that we still appear 'close to the starting point' (Shilling, 1993: 106) in formulating a 'sociopsychosomatics' of the body and health. Not only can we not straightforwardly rely on existing psycho-physiological research in order to enter the biological terrain, but we also face considerable difficulty in knowing the body and the biological. The complexity of the relation between the body and the social is such that a particular physiological measure cannot necessarily be read as the 'response' to a certain kind of social 'stimuli', such as a 'stressor' or 'maladaptive' emotion. For neither the social nor the biological appear to operate in this *singular* fashion even if, as Stefan Beck and Jörg Niewöhner note, 'linear understandings of physiological change underpin most explanations of disease aetiology' (2006: 223).

In sum, the limitations of singular accounts need to be replaced by those which move toward the complexity of both the biological and the social arena (although, as argued in Chapter 6, this does *not* imply that we should uncritically import natural science notions of complexity into social science analysis). We are often likely to be looking at a constellation of issues and processes, as exampled by the way in which back pain may reflect a complex interweaving of 'evolutionary defect', physical, social and emotional 'demand', and non-linear physiological processes. The perils of the traditional physiological enterprise derive from the difficulties of isolating singular relationships (such as that between stress and hormonal secretion) within a biosocial arena characterised by pervasive complexity.

Yet there are also areas of biological research that stress complexity, such as that provided by neurological work on the human brain, and brain imaging studies. In addition, there has been increasing interest in the development of a more 'socially oriented' neuroscience (Decety and Keenan, 2006). Given that the human brain is characterised by extraordinary complexity, such neuroscience may seem an ideal partner for social scientists seeking to avoid the reductive. The next chapter will therefore present a foray into this arena by exploring neo-Spinozist discussion of a very old issue, namely the relationship between the 'mind' and the 'brain'.

9

NEUROLOGICAL
ADVENTURES

At the time of writing, there are continuing calls to 'facilitate interaction between social scientists and life scientists . . . and move beyond the defensiveness that has been called "the science wars" ' (Harrington *et al.*, 2006: 4). To this extent, Benton's desire for 'a re-alignment of the human social and the life-sciences' (1991: 26) appears alive and well. In addition, in spite of the cautions noted in Chapter 8, it can be argued that social scientists need to challenge the stereotype which suggests that epistemological and methodological flaws pervade life science. As Harrington, Rose and Singh suggest:

> Social scientists . . . need to consider how far new norms of transdisciplinary collaboration emerging in the life sciences (e.g. systems neuroscience, field biology) may demand a rethinking of conventional philosophical categories of analysis. Is genetics deterministic? Is the message of brain science 'reductionist'? Or, when we use such terms, are we working with a kind of cartoon of the life sciences that belies its actual and increasing complexity?
>
> (Harrington *et al.*, 2006: 1)

It was argued in Chapter 8 that certain areas of life science research do indeed remain reductionist and determinist, and apolitical, ahistorical, decontextualised, and so on. Yet this does not apply equally throughout the life sciences (Benton, 1991), and it is perhaps as ridiculous for social scientists to tar all of life science with such connotations as it is for life scientists to believe that all of 'the social sciences don't "believe in reality" or turn everything into a "social construction" ' (Harrington *et al.*, 2006: 4). Although there may be marked tendencies in both 'camps', there can also be divergences. Furthermore, according to writers such as Gibbons *et al.* (1994) and Sayer (1999), it is possible to construct a transdisciplinary, or even postdiscipinary, space where meaningful dialogue might be undertaken.

As noted in Chapter 8, there is a perception that certain areas of life science are becoming less reductive, thereby raising the possibility of meaningful dialogue between social and life scientists. Some social scientists and philosophers believe that a rapprochement between life and social science looks feasible, especially within neurology, the brain sciences, and 'social neuroscience' (Decety and Keenan, 2006). In this chapter, I shall explore the possibility of such rapprochement in four ways. First, I will examine William Connolly's attempt to 'pursue *conversations* between cultural theory and neuroscience' (2002: 9, original emphasis). Second, I shall contrast Connolly's (2002) account with that of the neuroscientist, Antonio Damasio. Although both these writers claim to be influenced by Spinoza, their orientation and conclusions markedly differ, seemingly conditioned by their disciplinary allegiances, Connolly to cultural studies and politics, Damasio to neurology and biology. Third, I will address arguments in favour of interdisciplinary engagement. And finally, I shall explore an interdisciplinary conversation between two avowed Spinozists, namely that between the phenomenologist, Paul Ricoeur and the neuroscientist, Jean-Pierre Changeux (2000).

In this manner, the chapter will circumnavigate around aspects of Spinozism and it is therefore necessary to first note a particular limitation in Spinozist thought, namely its failure 'to take time seriously' (Hampshire, 2005: 147). In particular, it is difficult to accept the Spinozist conjecture that 'it is a *timeless*, logical necessity that the order of nature should be what it is' (Hampshire, 2005: 132, added emphasis). It may be that Spinoza projected atemporal argument because of the influence of notions of celestial eternity (Spinoza, 1996). Equally, it may be because his life preceded the temporal emphasis of, say, Darwinian evolutionary thought, or the effects 'of modern technology in so rapidly changing human nature and the conditions of life in society' (Hampshire, 2005: 147). This may explain why 'he seems to us now to have greatly underestimated the time scale in human history' (Hampshire, 2005: 147). Nevertheless this does remain a rather significant oversight. Yet notwithstanding Spinoza's temporal 'blind spot', neo-Spinozist argument is still of interest to our present concerns. As we shall see, it may provide one programme by which to address the earlier conjecture of this book, especially the proposition that we see differences in natural and social temporality (see Chapters 4–6).

Neurosocial parallelism

In his text, *Neuropolitics*, Connolly notes that 'from time to time I have looked into brain research only to move away. It seemed to be sucked into a reductive model of science' (2002: xiii). Yet he senses that something has changed and 'that exciting things were happening' (2002: xiii), as exampled by the writings of neuroscientists such as Antonio Damasio, Francisco Varela, Evan Thompson, Eleanor Rosch, Joseph LeDoux, and V. S. Ramachandran. For example, in Damasio, Connolly notes resonance with the work of Henri Bergson and William James, especially in Damasio's (1995, 2000) attention to the significance of affect and temporality to cognitive processes. Connolly also documents what he sees as a more general shift in conceptualisation within the neurosciences. For instance, he quotes the observation of the neuroscientist, Rafael Nuñez, that in:

the last couple of decades...there has been a tendency to move from a rational, abstract, culture-free, de-centralized, non-biological, ahistorical, unemotional, asocial and disembodied view of the mind towards a view which sees the mind as situated, decentralized, real-time constrained, everyday experience oriented, culture-dependent, contextualized, and closely related to biological principles – in one word, embodied.

(Nuñez, 1999: 59)

At the same time, other neuroscientists remind us of the extraordinary complexity of brain processes:

A piece of your brain the size of a grain of sand would contain one hundred thousand neurons, two million axons, and one billion synapses, all 'talking to' each other. Given these figures, it's been calculated that the number of possible brain states – the number of permutations and combinations of activity that are theoretically possible – exceeds the number of elementary particles in the universe.

(Ramachandran and Blakeslee, 1998: 8)

In working toward a cultural 'conversation' with this complex neurology, Connolly draws on a range of philosophical thought, especially that of Spinoza, Hampshire, Nietzsche and Deleuze. For present purposes, Connolly's reflections in relation to Stuart Hampshire are of particular interest. In an essay attacking classical materialism, Hampshire explored the relation between our complex, changing, thought processes and the materiality of our brain states. In so doing, Hampshire drew extensively on his long-standing interest in Baruch Spinoza, whom Hampshire saw as:

particularly skilled in *shifting attention back and forth* from the consideration of persons as active observers of the physical world to the consideration of them also as observed objects, with their bodies in a dual role, as both purposefully used instruments of exploration and also as observed objects.

(Hampshire, 1971: 213–214, added emphasis)

For Connolly, the advantage of Hampshire's *modified* Spinozism lies with its conceptualisation of parallelism. In particular, Hampshire develops a:

Perspectival parallelism [that] drops [Spinoza's] reference to a singular substance with two parallel attributes. [Instead] it asserts that human beings are unable to translate first-person experiences of perception, thinking, and judgment neatly into third-person observations of the physiochemical processes operative while those activities proceed. This is because the thinking in question *draws upon and flows into a larger context or cultural world* than that encompassed by the physiochemical processes under observation. Nevertheless, a significant change in the physiochemical process is met by some change in thought process, and vice versa.

(Connolly, 2002: 88, added emphasis)

Connolly argues that 'recent research into body/brain processes' supports this parallelism since it points to 'the complexity and variable speeds of the body/brain/culture network' (2002: 89). Since body, brain and culture are of variable geometry and temporality (see Chapter 4), Connolly suggests that only a parallel account can hope to capture this diversity and complexity. Drawing on Nietzsche, Connolly also brings in the significance of affect to thinking, and the ways in which our emotions simultaneously re-frame a range of cognitive and bodily processes. Yet he suggests that this complexity is beyond scientific modelling:

> Affect is a wild card in the layered game of thinking. Since the effects of one system are bounced or bumped into other systems with different speeds and capacities of reception, you would have to form a god's-eye view of the entire complex as it unfolds in action to 'explain' its operations at any specific time. The geology of thought is thus susceptible to third-person understanding, but the interlayering of unconscious and conscious thinking in motion may transcend the reach of the most confident models of scientific explanation.

(2002: 90)

In making these observations, Connolly appears to argue that a full transgression between life and social science is invalidated by the multi-layered and complex nature of human thought, neurology and biology. In order to achieve such transgression, Connolly suggests that an omniscient perspective would be required which could survey the interrelation between culture, history, individual biography and social, cognitive and neurological process. For example, to the extent that we memorise aspects of culture, or our own biography, their recall may often be non-chronological. In thinking through any thought, we encounter a non-chronological mish-mash of jumbled thoughts that reflect our biography and culture, and this mish-mash may also interact with complex emotional resonances and bodily and neurological process. At the same time, our thinking rarely resembles a logical, rational, or linear practice. Instead, our cerebral 'chatterbox' frequently contains anomalies, contradictions, 'slippages' and ambiguities. Connolly argues that an omniscient survey of such complex processes is beyond any science, and that we must therefore have recourse to some form of parallel explanation. In other words, although social science and socially oriented neuroscience may increasingly concur in an emphasis on the non-reductive, the social, and the historical, it will remain difficult, if not impossible to fully transgress their traditional boundaries. Instead, we must follow 'Hampshire's recommendation to *move back and forth* between experimental/theoretical exploration of body/brain mechanisms and phenomenological attention to the experience of thinking and judging' (Connolly, 2002: 91–92, added emphasis).

Connolly's promotion of Hampshire's 'perspectival parallelism' is particularly interesting in view of the argument expressed elsewhere in the present book. In Chapters 4 and 5, it was argued that there remain differences in our perception of temporality between the social and natural realm (as a consequence of the remarkable plasticity afforded by human technolinguistic skill). It was also suggested in Chapter 6 that such differences in our perception may condition the attractiveness of alternate epistemologies, such as that of social constructionism and critical realism. If this is the case, some version of parallelism can seem a conducive strategy. Rather than simply reverting to dualism, a parallel approach suggests that we can constantly journey 'back and forth' between our two, utterly interwoven but distinguishable, constituencies. In addition, unlike ANT, parallel strategies are not constrained by the difficulties of projecting symmetry onto a natural–social terrain that may not be symmetrically governed, especially as regards its variable temporality (see Chapter 4). Furthermore, if we accept that we experience differing temporalities and epistemological ease between the social and the natural, it may be that some variant of parallelism represents the *only* possible tactic that we can employ. If we cannot assume similar temporal or epistemological orientation, how can we devise singular, omniscient, accounts of our natural and social universe?

At first sight therefore, Connolly's neo-Spinozist parallelism constitutes an appealing strategy. Yet in deploying this parallelism, Connolly draws attention to some of its possible limitations. He suggests that Hampshire's 'modified Spinozism . . . encourages cultural theorists to explore accumulating evidence of significant correlations between the observation of body/brain and the lived experience of thinking' (Connolly, 2002: 8). But in undertaking such explorations, Connolly largely focuses on the 'experience of thinking', especially as it is observed in relation to film studies. As a consequence, neurological studies increasingly make only a 'guest appearance' in Connolly's discussion. For instance, Connolly presents an interesting analysis of affect and thinking through reference to the film, *Five Easy Pieces*. In a relatively brief aside, he subsequently notes that 'recent experiments by neuroscientists such as Antonio Damasio and Joseph LeDoux confirm the indispensability of affect to thinking' (2002: 76). However, such 'cameo' roles for neuroscience do not really follow 'Hampshire's recommendation to move back and forth' (Connolly, 2002: 91) between neuroscience and the experience of thinking. This observation makes one wonder if this is a likely outcome of parallelism, given that those undertaking this endeavour may easily retreat to the comfort of their own discipline, whether cultural study, sociology or neuroscience.

Nevertheless Connolly does make a number of very interesting arguments concerning work on neuroscience, as in his use of Damasio to reflect on the differing timescapes of our conscious awareness and bodily process, where a thought may seem lighting fast to our awareness but 'it is actually quite extensive if you think of it from the perspective of the neurons which make it possible' (Damasio, 2000: 126, cited in Connolly, 2002: 34). He loosely links such observations to film study by, say, exploring the play on temporality in Orson Welles's *Citizen Kane*. Yet neuroscience increasingly takes a minor role in his discussion. It could of course be argued that default to one's own disciplinary training is always likely, if not inevitable, in any attempt to relate the biological and the social. But equally, there remains a suspicion that it is more likely to occur with a strategy of parallelism since the biological remains on the 'other side' of the (still present) 'border', a territory to which it is easier to make occasional forays rather than an active and continuing exploration.

In this context, it is interesting to note that in attempting to formulate a neurology of emotion, Antonio Damasio (2003) also deploys Spinoza, and in a fashion that resembles that of Connolly. Just as Connolly favours the cultural, so Damasio favours his own disciplinary background, namely the neurological. This is most obvious where Damasio applies biological metaphors to social analysis. For instance, in *Looking for Spinoza*, Damasio repeatedly emphasises the importance of biological homeostasis and he directly applies this biological concept to his examination of the social domain. It seems that social institutions such as 'religion, justice and socio-political organizations' are merely 'mechanisms for exerting homeostasis at the level of the social group' (2003: 166). Following Damasio, it appears that social complexity can easily be reduced to biological metaphor.

Damasio's parallelism also favours the biological when he considers the relation between thought, emotion and feeling. First, he differentiates between emotion and feeling by declaring that 'emotions play out in the theater of the body' and 'feelings play out in the theater of the mind' (2003: 28). It seems that 'emotion and feelings are closely related but *separable* phenomena' (Damasio, 2001: 781, added emphasis), the former the province of the neurochemical, the latter of our conscious representation *of* our neurochemistry. Although this argument can appear consonant with a neo-Spinozist parallelism, it is also apparent that Damasio evokes a more traditional schism between consciousness and the biological body. This is reflected in his reference to the 'fight-or-flight' mechanism (Damasio, 2001: 781) which, as we saw in Chapter 8, can induce a crude dualism, and also in Damasio's evocation of mechanistic images of human behaviour. We are told, for example, that 'emotions allow organisms to cope successfully with objects and situations that are *potentially dangerous or advantageous*' (2001: 781, added emphasis). Yet the stock reply of many social scientists to this bipolar world of 'danger' or 'advantage' might be to say, 'If only life were that simple!'

Underlying Damasio's account is an 'arboreal' account of human biological functioning that is a long way from Connolly's (2002) preference for a Deleuzian sense of the 'rhizomic' and 'dendritic'. Indeed, following taxonomic traditions in biology, it is clear that Damasio is not 'tired of trees' (Deleuze and Guattari, 1988: 15). At the 'lowest branches' (2003: 31), Damasio portrays basic metabolic processes, reflexes and the immune system; at the 'middle-level branches' he finds 'behaviors normally associated with the notion of pleasure . . . or pain' (Damasio, 2003: 32), such as the pain of bodily injury. Higher up come *drives and motivations* like those for 'hunger, thirst, curiosity . . . , play and sex' and beyond that are 'emotions-proper' such as 'joy and sorrow and fear' (Damasio, 2003: 34, original emphasis). At the top of the 'canopy' are 'feelings'. Yet although feelings represent the apex of Damasio's hierarchy, it is apparent that Damasio presents us with a 'bottom up' arborial account that privileges the biological and the neurological. Emotions are described as a neuro-chemical complex, the outcome of 'a complex collection of chemical and neural responses forming a distinctive pattern' (Damasio, 2003: 53). Similarly, feelings represent the cognitive response to the biological dynamism 'below', 'mappings of the myriad aspects of body states in the sensory regions designed to receive signals from the body' (Damasio, 2003: 87).

Damasio's argument can appear consonant with Spinoza's proposition that 'the human mind does not know the human body itself . . . except through the ideas of affections by which the body is affected' (Spinoza, 1996: 47, prop. 19). Yet Damasio's account contains very little of Connolly's (2002) attention to the complexity of thought, and its anomalies, contradictions, 'slippages', ambiguities and other rhizomic 'rumblings'. Instead, Damasio appears chiefly concerned with whether thought is 'efficient' or 'inefficient'. For instance, we are told that 'feeling sad . . . is often about an *inefficient* mode of thought stalling around a limited number of ideas of loss' (Damasio, 2003: 89). Sadness is *not* portrayed as the result of a complex and shifting array of glimpses of memories from our childhood and adulthood, jumbled up with the swirling eddies of our present experience. Instead, it is merely a consequence of inefficiency and lack of imagination (perhaps ameliorable to being 'rectified' by reductionist psychotherapies, such as 'neuro-linguistic programming', that replace 'negative' with 'positive' imagery). However to be fair to Damasio, his thesis is not a uniformly reductionist account of human thought. In particular, following Spinoza, he stresses that 'mind and body are *parallel and mutually correlated processes*, mimicking each other at every crossroad, as two faces of the same thing' (2003: 217, added emphasis). Nevertheless, Damasio's version of parallelism reveals a mark preference for the biological over the cerebral, cultural or sociological, and a tendency to reduce the latter to the former. He repeatedly suggests that it is the body and the biological that are the primary concern to both emotion and feeling.[1] In general, it seems that there is a relatively straightforward unidirectional causal equation such that 'emotion/bodily/biological response → feelings', rather than vice versa.[2]

In sum, although Connolly seeks to draw similarities between his own conjecture and that of more philosophically oriented neurologists such as Damasio, their emphases appear very different, seemingly conditioned by their primary disciplinary allegiance, Connolly to cultural studies, and Damasio to biology. Though he continually emphasises affect, Connolly gives a primacy to thought, culture and language, as reflected in his lengthy discussion of film studies. In contrast, Damasio sees feelings as a *response* to bodily activity rather than as an *expression* of thought. Feelings are the response to all the biological goings-on further down Damasio's arborial structure, and in Damasio's thesis, it sometimes seems that we are the mere playthings of our biology. Although both writers portray themselves as following a kind of neo-Spinozist parallelism, there is a marked difference in emphasis in their argument. For Connolly, there remains a tendency to portray the causal direction as one of thinking leading to a bodily response, even though he acknowledges that thinking reflects an interweaving of culture, memory and 'muscles, skin, [and] gut' (Connolly, 2002: 36). In contrast, for Damasio, this causal direction is reversed: it is our bodies' response that occasions feeling and thought – the latter are just a 'mental representation of. . . physiological changes' (Damasio, 2001: 781). To the extent that these different emphases are in line with each author's disciplinary bias, it suggests that a neo-Spinozist parallelism may be insufficient as a device to erode the borders between the biological and the social. Instead, it may help to promote the 'magpie' behaviour where writers import occasional 'nuggets' from other disciplines, but remain firmly embedded within their own disciplinary camp. Parallelism may therefore be limited as a means to encourage a thorough-going transgression. However set against this argument is Connolly's suggestion, following Hampshire, that 'full' transgression can only hold chimerical appeal, a desirable illusion rather than a feasible strategy. In effect, Connolly's thesis resurrects the question of whether transgression is possible and whether some kind of border zone must consequently remain in place.

The discussion in Chapters 3–6 poses further questions for a prospective 'perspectival parallelism'. In particular, how easy is it to move 'back and forth' across the natural and social domain if the territories on either side operate according to different epistemological rules? As was suggested in Chapters 4 and 5, it can be difficult to apply temporal scientific feats, such as replicability and regularity, with equanimity between the natural and social terrain since the latter remains far more highly historically specific (as a consequence of the plasticity occasioned by human language and technology). In journeying across the 'border zone', we cannot necessarily apply the same epistemological frameworks or research technique, and parallelist adventures are likely to require considerable refinement. Furthermore, it seems probable that relatively few natural and social scientists have a thorough understanding of the research philosophy and technique that applies across both their respective constituencies. Yet to the extent that knowledge of differing epistemologies and techniques is required, exploratory expeditions may be constrained.

Such observations raise the question of whether the chief limitation in 'neurological adventures' is that of disciplinary allegiance. As commentary on social neuroscience has stressed, 'social scientists and neuroscientists... must understand each other even more fully than at present in order to determine the questions and approaches that might work best' (Raichle, 2003: 759). In other words, if writers were more willing to embrace the position of other disciplines, might it be possible to arrive at a more fruitful interchange? In so doing, might we also 'soothe the suspicions that handicap informed dialogue between the social sciences and the life sciences' (Harrington *et al.*, 2006: 4)? Or alternatively, is it the case that interdisciplinary exchange represents another chimera that only presents the semblance of a conversation? In order to address these critical questions, the remainder of this chapter will explore the tensions that surround interdisciplinarity, first by engaging with the argument of its advocates, and second, by examining an example of an intimate interdisciplinary exchange between two writers, each of whom 'announces himself at the outset as a Spinozist with respect to the mind/body problem' (Connolly, 2002: 204), namely the earnest conversation between Paul Ricoeur and Jean-Pierre Changeux (2000).

Interdisciplinary manoeuvres

biologists and sociologists sometimes act as if they were guardians of national territories separated by clear-cut boundaries'.

(Elias, 1991b: 25)

in reality, biological and social processes depend on each other; they dovetail into each other when human beings first learn to speak a language'.

(Elias, 1991b: 19)

As a prelude to the ensuing argument, it is necessary to note two things about interdisciplinarity. The first is that disciplinarity represents a development that has grown in ascendancy since the later nineteenth century, and perhaps especially after 1945 (Fuller, 2003; Sayer, 1999; Changeux and Ricoeur, 2000: 8). Disciplinary coherence has therefore not always existed and some express a desire to turn the clock back toward an 'older historical sensibility toward disciplinarity, one that diminishes the phenomenon's significance in the ontology of knowledge production' (Fuller, 2003: 3). Yet the question remains as to whether it is possible to reverse history in the manner that interdisciplinarians desire.

The second observation is that there is a significant limitation with the *normative* aspect of interdisciplinary debate. In particular, there remains an inevitable tension between the normative advocacy of inter/trans/post disciplinarity and its descriptive analysis. The work of Michael Gibbons, Helga Nowotny, Peter Scott, and their colleagues provides an example of this tension, and in consequence, it is worth first examining their thesis in a little detail (Gibbons *et al.*, 1994; Nowotny *et al.*, 2001).

In order to successfully realise their 'Mode 2' transdisciplinarity, Nowotny *et al.* assert that natural scientists '*must* recognize that... social knowledge is also involved' and they '*must* overcome their fear of contamination by the social' (2001: 235, added emphasis). Aside from looking surprisingly like a social science manifesto, there remains a significant tension between such prescriptive exhortation and the argument that these authors sign up to elsewhere, namely that knowledge needs to be understood within the *local* context of its production.[3] In particular, in spite of emphasising contextual differences between scientific fields, Nowotny *et al.*, go on to promote their 'Mode 2' transdisciplinarity as the favourite template for all 'socially robust' science. In keeping with this mission, fields that appear less socially and politically efficacious are disparaged.[4] The implication seems clear: in the brave new world of science, all fields must move toward Mode 2 if they are to prosper and survive.

The tensions that result from this normative position recur throughout Nowotny *et al.*'s argument. For example, it is never convincingly explained why the currently wide diversity of scientific practice will come to coalesce around Mode 2 transdisciplinarity. In other words, if scientific fields are deeply embedded in local contexts, as Nowotny *et al.* (2001) attest, this localisation will continually inhibit normative ambition.[5] In consequence, it remains unlikely that Mode 2 can be applied across the spectrum of natural and social science – or that 'Mode 1' ever represented a common set of criteria. The problem is that normative ambition, whether toward inter, trans or postdisciplinarity, has a tendency to play down the possibility that its prescriptions will only ever be relevant to relatively small scientific niches. Yet this represents the most likely outcome of normative interdisciplinary prescription given the large diversity of knowledge regimes that apply across the natural and social sciences (Whitley, 2000).

Beyond science wars?

Although the normative dimension of interdisciplinary ambition remains problematic, this does not mean that interdisciplinary conversation is without benefit. And an interesting illustration of such a conversation is contained in an ambitious text, entitled, *What Makes Us Think?* This book records the lengthy 'conversation' between the philosopher of anthropology, Paul Ricoeur and the neurobiologist, Jean-Pierre Changeux (Professor of Neurobiology at the Collège de France). The remainder of this chapter will focus on this discussion. What is curious about their conversation is the intransigence of the epistemological conflict between its authors, in spite of their stated desire to achieve interdisciplinary accord. It would of course be possible to select other exemplars where such conflict is less pronounced. For instance, Pierre Jacob and Marc Jeannerod's (2003) *Ways of Seeing* reports the highly productive deliberations between a philosopher and a neuroscientist concerned with the philosophy and neurology of visual cognition. There appears to be considerable consonance between its authors, perhaps because, as a philosopher, Jacob believes that 'cognitive neuroscience is the biological roots of the current cognitive sciences' (Jacob, 2003: 3). In this context, it is perhaps not surprising that interdisciplinary adventures can be successfully realised. Yet the question remains as to whether this constitutes the exception rather than the rule. In many situations, and perhaps especially in projects between sociologists and life scientists, there may remain significant differences in orientation (Whitley, 1982). The discussion between Ricoeur and Changeux speaks to this context. It illustrates the struggle to attain a 'meeting ground' in the face of differing ontological and epistemological attachments. Their text is also interesting in the light of my earlier discussion: although both declare strong Spinozist sympathies,[6] 'differences soon emerge in their interpretations of that doctrine' (Connolly, 2002: 204). In sum, Changeux and Ricoeur (2000) provide an apposite commentary on the constraints of interdisciplinary exchange.

In *What Makes Us Think?* Ricoeur and Changeux state that they are committed to furthering an interdisciplinary dialogue guided by their belief that such discussion can reveal 'much material... for fruitful interdisciplinary research' (Changeux and Ricoeur, 2000: 133). In addition, their text projects an image of productive interchange. Apparent harmony is maintained because both writers create the impression of wanting to move beyond conflict and the maintenance of disciplinary turf, and this image is furthered by their polite discourse and the maintenance of a generally mannered exchange. It is also the case that there are some areas of agreement, most notably in relation to ethics. This occurs because Changeux does not seek to reduce ethics entirely to the neurosciences (e.g. see Changeux and Ricoeur, 2000: 241). Instead, he couches his overall argument within an evolutionary framework. Détente is also encouraged because Ricoeur appears ambiguous with respect to naturalist argument while Changeux frequently bases his ethic on a naturalist imperative.[7]

Yet in spite of this ostensible accord, there remain sharp differences between their perspectives. For Ricoeur, the neurobiological concerns of Changeux can only be treated as a substrate of reality: neurobiology is relevant to the life-world (*Lebenswelt*), but can never fully represent it. As Merleau-Ponty argued:

> if we want to subject science itself to rigorous scrutiny and arrive at a precise assessment of its meaning and scope, we must begin by reawakening the basic experience of the world, of which science is the second-order expression.
>
> (1962: viii–ix)

From this phenomenological perspective, science can only provide an incomplete, and inevitably reduced, account of the mind and of consciousness. But in sharp contrast, for Changeux, neurobiological activity represents the direct correspondence to our social, emotional and philosophical lives (Collier, 1994). Neuronal activity is frequently represented by Changeux as the biological replica of our thought and he repeatedly expresses a neurobiologist's desire to collapse the mind and the brain. In consequence, for Changeux to reach an interdisciplinary meeting ground with Ricoeur, he would have to accept that his science deals with substrates rather than with the full complexity of life. In other words, Changeux would need to accept a reduced and diminished role for neurobiology which can only explain biological processes that relate to, but cannot define, life. Given the ascendancy of the life sciences, it is perhaps not surprising that Changeux resists this role. The result is that his conversation with Ricoeur predominantly has the character of an earnest endeavour between different disciplinary positions, rather than a meaningful exchange. On the one hand, Changeux and Ricoeur attempt an 'open' conversation drawing on their respective disciplinary traditions, and this conversation appears to have occasioned mutual learning. On the other, the question remains as to whether this learning represents more than the kind of 'magpie' behaviour noted above where participants import occasional 'nuggets' from other disciplines and then 'translate' them into something more acceptable within the confines of their own 'camp'.

In general, discord prevails between Ricoeur and Changeux because of sharp separations in their view of knowledge and science. For instance, for Ricoeur, 'the idea of the unity of science is problematic' whereas Changeux confesses that he is 'much attached to it' (Changeux and Ricoeur, 2000: 242). Similarly, Changeux's Darwinian evolutionism justifies his naturalism through his assertion that evolutionary processes have led to human morality and ethic (Dupré, 2001). He states that 'evolutionism . . . offers us a human being who possesses not only a moral sense but also the predispositions of moral evaluation necessary to ethical deliberation' (Changeux and Ricoeur, 2000: 190). Yet for Ricoeur, such Darwinian naturalism represents a *post-hoc* rationalisation of our morality. *Contra* Changeux, Ricoeur argues that that people were first moralistic and then searched for the bases of their morality, varying their argument according to their social context. As Ricoeur asserts:

> Thus it was that the apology for competition and the struggle for life won the approval of Darwin himself during a period of unrestrained capitalism in the last [nineteenth] century: and it is because we are now concerned, at the end our own horrible [twentieth] century, to make sympathy prevail over aggression that we notice and emphasize signs of sympathy and sociability, for example among chimpanzees. It is therefore owing to a sort of *trompe l'oeil* effect – the forgetting of our own moral questioning – that we are now able to set compassion on the side of nature or against it. Apart from our moral questioning, however, nature does not move in any direction.
>
> (Changeux and Ricoeur, 2000: 192–193)

Such difficulties of obtaining consensus are apparent throughout Changeux and Ricoeur's interchange, even though both authors appear aware of the limitations of maintaining their disciplinary allegiance. For instance, Ricoeur talks of the need for 'zones of engagement' between disciplines, and the need for 'interdisciplinary collaboration' as a means to move beyond 'the hegemonic tendency of every scientific discipline to redefine the aims of adjacent fields in its own terms'

(Changeux and Ricoeur, 2000: 158). Yet in spite of this awareness, Ricoeur exhibits many of the usual 'hegemonic tendencies'. In particular, in redefining neurological research as working on 'substrates' of life, rather than life itself, Ricoeur reclassifies its argument according to the 'hegemony' of phenomenology. As noted above, this redefinition is unlikely to prove attractive to many neuroscientists precisely because it is written according to disciplinary assumptions that are at variance with those still dominant within many areas of life science. In effect, it proves very difficult for either Ricoeur or Changeux to move beyond the 'hegemonic' predilections of their disciplines.

Such observations may seem surprising to social scientists who believe that we are moving toward a dissolution of difference between the natural and social realm, especially where life scientists espouse a more complex philosophical orientation (Benton, 1991). Social scientists may be impressed that some biologists are 'alert to a debt to William James' or are sympathetic to 'many of the things Bergson says' (Connolly, 2002: 32, commenting on Damasio, 2000). Similarly, life scientists may perceive a greater ease of concourse with social scientists where the latter no longer reduce the biological to a language game. Yet the conversation between Changeux and Ricoeur illustrates the difficulties of obtaining consensus through interdisciplinary dialogue. Although both writers share Spinozist sympathies, their interplay cannot be said to result in a meaningful meeting of minds. It is not that 'Ricoeur deploys parallelism to protect thinking from technique' (Connolly, 2002: 204) but that both Changeux and Ricoeur hold ontological and epistemological differences that prove difficult to dispel.

It is interesting to note that Changeux contradicts the stereotype of scientists as ill-informed in relation to philosophy, social theory and the social sciences. For instance, he evinces some detailed knowledge of writers such as Spinoza and Bourdieu, and a working familiarity with philosophical influences upon ethics such as Aristotle, Bentham, Mill, and Kant, as well as more recent contributions such as that of Hans Jonas (1985). In addition, he believes that 'fruitful links can . . . be established with anthropology and sociology' (Changeux and Ricoeur, 2000: 160). In sum, Changeux appears as a representative of Benton's (1991) more holistically inclined biologists. In consequence, following Benton (1991), Changeux might seem like exactly the kind of life scientist with whom sociologists could make a meaningful alliance. However such an alliance is only likely to prove fruitful to sociologists who adopt a strongly naturalistic perspective (Benton, 1993) and who can tolerate a philosophy that still entertains reductionist proclivities. Others are likely to experience difficulties similar to those of Ricoeur, given Changeux's tendency to prioritise the biological and reduce the social to the level of the neuron. The problem is that Changeux resists agreeing with a statement that would still be happily endorsed by many sociologists of either a constructionist or realist persuasion, namely Ricoeur's assertion that 'mental experience implies the corporeal, but in a sense that is *irreducible* to the objective bodies studied by the natural sciences' (Changeux and

Ricoeur, 2000: 15, added emphasis). Furthermore, there are other problems with Changeux's 'neuronal theory of knowledge' (Changeux and Ricoeur, 2000: 110; cf. Changeux, 1985). In particular, Changeux's model of human sociality and learning is effectively that of a stereotype of scientific endeavour. For instance, the human child is described as proceeding 'by trial and error, trying to spot, to define, to frame, to categorize ... the objects and phenomena of the reality that surrounds him' (Changeux and Ricoeur, 2000: 113). It seems we are all little scientists who *rationally* engage with the world around us. And for all that Changeux explores widely across the psychological terrain, and to a lesser extent that of sociology and philosophy, his default position appears to be most strongly informed by experimental physiology and animal research. For instance, he asserts that 'we are now able to distinguish specific groups of neurons involved in motivation from those involved in the perception of reward' (Changeux and Ricoeur, 2000: 121). Yet most sociologists would need to question whether this mechanical image of human beings is sufficient, particularly as it remains strongly informed by experimental animal research – such as the reduced world of lever-pressing rats (see Chapter 8).

To some extent, the divide between Changeux and Ricoeur mirrors their different interpretations of Spinoza. As Changeux notes, there have 'been many reappropriations of Spinoza' (Changeux and Ricoeur, 2000: 24) and both writers proceed to appropriate Spinoza to their own ends. Ricoeur stays faithful to the notion that, although Spinoza underlined a unity of substance, it was the nevertheless the case that 'minds and bodies – as finite modes under irreducibly different attributes – remain distinct' (Lloyd, 1996: 49). Ricoeur's Spinozism means that, in relation to consciousness and neurology, there are 'two distinct discourses – one concerning the body and the brain, the other what I call the mental' (Changeux and Ricoeur, 2000: 14). In consequence, Ricoeur does not see 'a way of passing from one order of discourse to the other: either I speak of neurons and so forth ... or I speak of thoughts, actions and feelings that I connect with my body' (Changeux and Ricoeur, 2000: 15). In other words, Ricoeur suggests that, following Spinoza, we are left with these two different languages concerning the body and thought. We can 'speak both languages, without, however being able to merge them' (Changeux and Ricoeur, 2000: 20) even though 'the two discourses continually intersect at a great many points' since 'it is the same person who is "mental" *and* "corporeal" ' (Changeux and Ricoeur, 2000: 28, original emphasis). Following from this interpretation of Spinoza, it seems that we are faced with 'two systems [that] are *parallel but incommensurable* expressions of a single totality' (Scruton, 2002: 66, added emphasis).

In marked contrast to this position, Changeux advocates a more literal reading of Spinoza's unity of substance. He suggests that, as 'anticipated by Spinoza' we need 'to *unify* the anatomical and the behavioral, to link the neuronal description with that which is perceived or experienced' (Changeux and Ricoeur, 2000: 17). As evidence, Changeux cites argument from Spinoza that can appear supportive of a literal unity such as Spinoza's comment that 'men's judgement is a function of the disposition of the brain' (Spinoza, 1982: 62, cited in Changeux and Ricoeur, 2000: 201). This view reflects Changeux's naturalist view of biology as a replica of thought and his prioritisation of biological accounts of human thought and behaviour. In sum, Changeux and Ricoeur arrive at contradictory readings of Spinoza in line with their pre-existent disciplinary commitments.

The interchange between Ricoeur and Changeux therefore appears symbolic of many of the difficulties of realising interdisciplinary ambition. To achieve a rapprochement, either Changeux would need to accept a reduced role for his neurobiology which accepts that is an insufficient explanation of the life-world, or Ricoeur would have to sign up to a far more biologistic, and reductionist, account of ourselves. It is not surprising that neither author is willing to entertain such a compromise 'too far'. Throughout their conversation, Changeux stays faithful to the dominant biological motifs of Darwinian evolutionism, scientific reason, and the possibility of realising a naturalistic basis for human ethics. In contrast, Ricoeur sees scientific knowledge as partial, naturalistic ethics as post-hoc rationalisation, and ethics as the drive to human goodness that might be informed as much by the pre-Enlightenment traditions of religion as those of reason and science. Central to Ricoeur's position is the need to study a world *beyond* that which is 'already scientifically organized' (Changeux and Ricoeur, 2000: 117). These are fairly fundamental differences, and in spite of their mutual sympathy for interdisciplinary endeavour, their conversation appears unable to transcend their initial disciplinary allegiance.

It might of course still be argued that these differences do not prevent fruitful academic interchange. For instance, Nowotny *et al.* (2001) use Peter Gallison's (1997) concept of 'trading zones' to suggest that productive interchange can take place between academic fields in spite of differences in orientation. Gallison studied the collaboration between different sub-cultures of physicists, namely theoreticians, experimentalists and engineers, and argued that fruitful 'trading' occurred between these three 'tribes' in spite of their differing academic allegiances. Based on Gallison (1997), Nowotny *et al.* argue that 'communication is possible (*laying Kuhn's incommensurability thesis to rest*)' (2001: 146, added emphasis). Yet it is doubtful as to whether the difficulties of ontological and epistemological conflict, or incommensurability, can be so easily swept aside, especially when *one is comparing between social and natural science rather than within natural science*. The exchange between Ricoeur and Changeux attests to the continuing difficulties that can arise given different disciplinary allegiances and ontological commitments. For social scientists to sign up to Changeux's ontology, they would need to embrace what many might see as a rather reductionist account that places biology centre stage in accounting for human life. 'Trading' can take place but this may be limited by the sociological suspicion that surrounds knowledge reliant on reductionism or biologism (see Chapter 8). Furthermore, it is difficult to see how the normative desires of Nowotny *et al.* could be effected in this context. According to Nowotny *et al.* 'Mode-2 knowledge production transcends disciplinary boundaries' (2001: 89) through processes of *reinstitutionalisation* that corrodes traditional disciplinary boundaries. Yet Changeux and Ricoeur struggle to transcend their disciplinary attachments because of differences in cognitive orientation rather than institutional commitment (Whitley, 1982). In spite of their clearly stated desire for 'zones of engagement' that may transcend disciplinary hegemony (Changeux and Ricoeur, 2000: 158), the ability of Changeux and Ricoeur to engage in productive 'trading' is continually hampered by marked differences in their view of social and biological life. These differences mean that any sense of transcendence appears difficult, if not impossible, to realise.

Conclusion

As noted above, Paul Ricoeur declares that 'in the last analysis we are dealing with *two* discourses of the body', one that is concerned with biology and the 'neuronal system', the other with our 'mental experience' and the socio-psychological terrain which it implies (Changeux and Ricoeur, 2000: 29, added emphasis). In so doing, Ricoeur follows interpretations of Spinoza which suggest that the latter 'combined ontological monism with conceptual dualism' (Scruton, 2002: 61). Or as Ricoeur puts it, while there is no ontoogical divide between the natural and the social, there remains a 'semantic dualism' (Ricoeur in Changeux and Ricoeur, 2000: 27).

Is Ricoeur right? Or do differences between the natural and the social reflect a question of scale? In other words, do difficulties arise because the macroscopic cannot be easily reduced to the heterogeneity of the microscopic, whether we are concerned with the natural or the social arena (Dupré, 1996)? If so, one implication is that we need an interdisciplinary engagement that matches natural to social complexity. Yet such 'complexity projects' may also be problematic (see Chapter 8). In particular, they may not address a traditional concern of sociologists, namely that the social is on a different plane to the physiological and neurological. Social analysis involves assessing the relations between thousands, if not millions, of individual human brains and bodies. In consequence, although neuroscience may inform our understanding of, say, the neurological correlates of varying shades of emotion, it cannot adequately explain such matters as the historical sociology of emotion (Elias, 1994; Stearn, 1994; Newton, 1998), or the shifting form of social institutions, or processes of globalisation, or the 'larger . . . cultural world' (Connolly, 2002: 88). It remains difficult to relate such macro-social issues to brain imaging studies that show which areas of the brain 'light up' (however complex the latter neurology). In sum, there are differences in form as well as scale between the natural and the social. As a result, allying natural with social complexity may not provide the resolution between the social and the natural that some writers seem to expect.

From the perspective of the arguments advanced in the present book, bridging 'the old divide' necessitates addressing 'stubborn' differences in our perception of the social and the natural domain. In particular, due to our remarkable technolinguistic plasticity, we do not tend to see the temporality of natural and social process in equivalent terms, and as argued above, these differences in perception may condition our epistemological orientation (see Chapters 4–6). Put bluntly, natural scientists may have difficulty in applying temporal assumptions, such as those of conditional regularity and replicability, to the social arena, especially as they move from the more biologically informed provinces of psychology (such as that of perception and cognition) toward meso and macro social issues. To put this another way, although the metaphor of flux can be applied equally to the natural and the social terrain, that of 'longevity of process', or of 'dynamic stability', still fits more easily within the domain of nature (see Chapter 4). As a consequence, assumptions of conditional regularity and replicability appear easier to entertain in natural science.

Does this mean that there are clear differences in kind (Hacking, 1999) and a semantic dualism between discourses of the natural and the social (Changeux and Ricoeur, 2000)? Possibly, but we should still fight shy of resurrecting dualisms between nature and society or 'brain' and 'mind'. What may be more appropriate to say is that perceived differences in natural and social temporality make it difficult to apply uniform modes of inquiry across these domains. If nothing else, the argument of this book indicates that it is mistaken to allow anti-dualist desire to favour singular accounts of nature and society, whether ontological or epistemological. In addition, it suggests that those who repeatedly stress the literal unity of 'mind' and 'body' may have missed the point. For instance, Paul Churchland (1995) goes to considerable lengths to hammer home the point that mental experience is correlated with neurological and proprioceptive phenomena. Yet such exhortation appears unnecessary given that many writers accept that we are governed by a unity of substance and that the social and the biological are utterly interwoven. They might even agree that mental 'phenomena are paradigmatically physical' (Churchland, 1995: 198) or learn from a 'neural theory of language' which notes that language has 'physiological correlates' (Feldman, 2006: 331). Yet such acknowledgement does not mean that we can explain the mind and the body in the same terms. As Peter Jedlička argues, 'one should be careful to jump to the conclusion that mental events are *nothing but* neural states' (2005: 172, original emphasis). The psychology of the mind remains embedded in the social (Mead, 1934), and as argued above, the social arena appears to be characterised by a different temporality to that of the natural sphere, as well as differences in scale and form (see p. 158). This means that we cannot collapse our understanding of the mind and brain in the manner which philosophers such as Churchland, or neuroscientists such as Changeux and Damasio, appear to desire. In sum, it will remain difficult to treat them in equivalent terms, or arrive at a singular discourse or an omniscient survey of the biosocial field.

If we accept the notion of difference, we are left with the question of what programme we should pursue. As argued above, forms of parallelism can appear attractive. Following Spinoza (1996), we can maintain an anti-dualist allegiance to a unity of substance. At the same time, following Hampshire (1971), we can also assert that it is difficult, if not impossible, to collapse *our understanding* of the natural and the social domain – and we need not, therefore, be chained to a normative desire for symmetry (see Chapter 2). However there may be a 'downside' to parallelist orientations. In particular, 'parallelists' can exhibit a tendency to default to their primary disciplinary base so that, say, social theorists favour the social and neurologists, the biological. Just as actor-network theorists perversely privileged the natural terrain (see Chapter 2), so parallelists may have to fight against their own one-sided tendencies.[8]

In addition, from the perspective of this book, Hampshire's neo-Spinozist parallelism is relevant, but not sufficient. In other words, parallelism is not just a consequence of the need to 'switch from considering reality under one heading to considering things under the other' (Hampshire, 1996: viii). The problem is that, in moving from 'one heading to the other', we are not only moving from the neurological to the macro-social, but also between different kinds of perceived temporality. In consequence, epistemological assumptions, such as those of conditional regularity, cannot be equally applied to both domains. Given that these differences are likely to condition epistemological orientation, the move from one heading to the other may involve considerable epistemological 'dislocation'. On the one hand, it is possible to imagine a greater epistemological accord than that observed in the conversation between Changeux and Ricoeur (2000). On the other, any journey between the social and the biological must still navigate across micro–macro issues as well as perceived differences in temporality, and such navigation is difficult to undertake if one remains enchanted by singular theories or overarching epistemologies.

In sum, the perspective advanced in this book is consonant with a parallelism that stresses differing temporalities and the consequent likelihood of differing epistemologies. If this is the case, parallel adventures may require consider-able sophistication and a level of interdisciplinary engagement that can grapple with marked shifts in epistemological framework. What this also suggests is that existing unitary ambitions are apt to be misguided, whether they derive from a desire to equate the regularities of physics with those of economics, or quantum physics to the fluidity of social life, or natural to social processes of emergence, or the complexity of nature to that of society.

What I have tried to argue in this book is that, instead of pursuing forlorn dreams that tend towards unity, we should acknowledge that perceived differ-ences may occur within a natural–social terrain that remains nothing if not intimately intertwined. Rather than repressing the perception of difference, we need to find ways that address it whilst resisting a return to ontological dualism.

NOTES

1 RECOVERING NATURE

1 We do of course share bodily aspects of language with other animals. As David Abram asserts, 'If language is always in its depths, physically and sensorially resonant, then it can never be definitively separated from evident expressiveness of bird-song, or the evocative howl of a wolf late at night' (1997: 80). Yet at the same time, as will be argued in Chapter 5, human beings are remarkable in the range and organisation of their symbolisation, and in its intergenerational communication.

2 Mead Cain (1993) suggests that fertility is higher in patriarchal societies since it is likely to deliver more surviving sons in situations where a premium is placed upon them. This occurs because, *ceteris paribus*, 5 per cent more boys will be born in the first place (Heer, 1975). In this way, what is already a complex social and biological process, namely the sex ratio, may itself be further interrelated with social issues such as patriarchy.

3 Publishing in this area has been remarkable with numerous books and book series dedicated to the social, epistemological and ethical implications of genomics. For example, MIT press has so far published at least 13 books dedicated to bioethics.

3 BEYOND ANTI-DUALISM?

1   Foucault carved numerous turns of phrase into ice sculptures, which had, for a moment, sharp contours. Then he walked away from them, insouciant, and let them melt, for he no longer needed them. His less-gifted readers put the half-melted shapes in the freezer and, without thinking, reproduced these figures as if they still glistened in the midnight sun and meant something.

(Hacking, 1998: 85)

Although the same comments might be said of the treatment of many a social thinker, they are particularly apt to the more formulaic renditions of Foucault.

2 As Collingwood puts it:

In the case of nature, this distinction between the outside and the inside of an event does not arise. The events of nature are mere events, not the acts of agents whose thought the scientist endeavours to trace. To the scientist, nature is always and merely a 'phenomenon', not in the sense of being defective in reality, but in the sense of being a spectacle presented to his intelligent observation; whereas the events of history are never mere phenomena, never mere spectacles for contemplation, but things which the historian looks, not at, but through, to discern the thought within them.

(Collingwood, 1946: 214)

3 Natural scientists might find Smith's position rather arrogant when he asserts that what differentiates the natural and social sciences is the latter's capacity for reflexivity. Seemingly, subjects such as psychology can be reflexive where they deal with social issues but not so where there deal with, say, physiological psychology (Smith, 2005: 17). Yet this position could be seen as erecting a new kind of dualism which relegates natural science to the non-reflexive, whilst implying the supremacy of literary, historical and constructionist thought.

4 As William Dray notes, 'Collingwood occasionally breaks out . . . far enough to admit that nature, as studied, for example, in geology or evolutionary biology, may have a quasi-history or a pseudo-history, since the object of such studies is a process which may exhibit development, or even novelty' (Dray, 1995: 36). Yet in general, Collingwood emphasised the static form of nature and its inaccessibility in terms of 're-enacting' its thoughts.

5 It is worth noting one other interesting facet of Hacking's argument. He effectively presents a theory of human exceptionalism since human beings are portrayed as possessing a distinct awareness and interactiveness (Catton and Dunlap, 1980). This is significant given the relevance of human exceptionalism to the politics of nature. Soper sums up this issue:

Unless human beings are differentiated from other organic and inorganic forms of being, they can be made no more liable for the effects of their occupancy of the ecosystem than can any other species, and it would make no more sense to call upon them to desist from destroying nature than to call upon cats to stop killing birds.

(1995: 160, cited in Murdoch, 2001: 127)

In this context, Hacking's project is relevant to questions of political engagement since it implies that human beings have a special responsibility for the care of the planet as a consequence of our 'language and culture and ability to reflect on our circumstances' (Murdoch, 2001: 127).

6 It is also easy to forget other aspects of our temporal integration with nature such as the way in which the 'tempo' of our bodies is closely connected with natural cycles. Women's reproductive cycles are linked to lunar cycles, while bodily processes such as body temperature and hormone secretion are interrelated with the circadian cycle of day and night (Adam, 1995).

7 On the one hand, Urry appears wary of simply importing post-Newtonian conceptions of time into social science. He stresses that he does not wish 'to imply that natural science models of time should be directly transplanted into social science' (Urry, 2000: 123). Yet he then devotes considerable space to drawing direct analogies between natural science temporal perspectives and those relevant to social processes. In consequence, Urry might be accused of ignoring his own caution.

8 Following Elias, this is because 'the relatively short time-span of a human life appears to serve people as their principal frame of reference' (Elias, 1991b: 30). As Elias emphasises, people tend to forget their 'social past' (Elias, 1992: 135) and it is consequently difficult for human beings to develop an intergenerational sense of time, never mind one that is inter-millennial or 'glacial'.

4 TIME

1 Elias notes that there is no such thing as 'timeless science' (1982: 27) and argues that science must be seen as *inextricably interwoven and interdependent* (1982: 62, original emphasis) with its historical and political development. He uses the development of quantum mechanics as one example:

> I find it difficult to imagine that anybody can hope to explain or to understand the transition from classical to quantum mechanics without reference to changes in technology that have occurred between the seventeenth and the twentieth centuries; these technological changes, in turn, cannot be understood and explained without reference to changes in the overall structure of societies where these technological and scientific changes have taken place; these changes of the overall structures of societies, again, can neither be understood nor explained without reference to the scientific changes.
>
> (1972: 130)

2 On the one hand, there were those who followed Darwin in arguing that evolutionary change is gradual, with species slowly evolving over millennia (Futuyma, 1983: 84–85). Examples exist of species which appear to exhibit gradual evolution such as the gradual increase in size of the protozoan, *Pseudocubus*, over two million years (Kellogg, 1975). Yet on the other hand, the problem with the Darwinian account of gradual evolution was the lack of continuity in the fossil record of many species, and the seemingly 'sudden' appearance of new species (who have no fossil intermediaries connecting them to their presumptive ancestors). The best-known explanation for this discontinuity was Eldredge and Gould's (1972) proposition that evolution is characterised by 'punctuated equilibria'. This thesis maintained that though the evolution of species may be 'punctuated' by 'rapid' genetic modification (within new 'founder' populations), or species extinction (as a result of, say, 'catastrophic' environmental change), it is nevertheless generally characterised by a stabile equilibrium that may last millions of years. Since such 'punctuations' are rapid, it is unlikely that they will be preserved in the fossil record. In describing these postulated changes as 'rapid' or 'sudden' however, it is critical to remember that the temporal yardstick is that of geological time, where 'rapid' can refer to evolutionary change in less than 100000 years. Following such argument, evolutionary change appears to be characterised by its 'frequency of stasis' (Mayr, 1997: 196).

3 The need to attend to these alternate images of evolution is reinforced by their incredible frequency. Dupré comments that

> It has been suggested that perhaps ten to the power of 24 viruses are produced on Earth every second. And these massive replication rates are tied to high mutation rates and almost unlimited mutation mechanisms. Viruses can thus evolve at rates that are far beyond even what is possible for cellular microbes . . . It is thus no surprise that viruses are the greatest producers and reservoir of genetic diversity on Earth.
>
> (2006b: 13)

4 On the one hand, credit in early English modernity was a source of liberation from a client economy and the feudal legacy of a 'nation conveniently divided into the two classes of "patricians" and "plebeians" ' (Brewer, 1982: 197). On the other, it

represented a continual threat for the emergent bourgeois since it entailed the 'spectre of debt' (Leyshon and Thrift, 1997: 17). Both personal circumstances and market volatility meant that being in credit generally implied continuing risk (Giddens, 1991). The consequences of continued indebtedness could be severe since it usually resulted in imprisonment, 'a hazardous and expensive experience' where 'fever was rampant' and many debtors 'found themselves even more heavily in debt because of the expenses incurred in gaol' (Brewer, 1982: 211). Jailed debtors 'were not rich merchants... but tradesmen, shopkeepers, small masters and retailers: the men who stood at the centre of the web of credit' (Brewer, 1982: 211).

5 Where physics and economics are similar is in their tendency toward abstract and rarefied models. Yet there is increasing criticism of the use of such models in economics. A variety of commentators inside and outside the discipline have noted the difficulty of making economic models work in 'real' situations. Even such 'pillars' of the discipline as Milton Friedman have argued that 'economics has become increasingly an arcane branch of mathematics rather than dealing with real economic problems' (1999: 137; cf. Blaug, 1999: 323), while other 'mainstays' such as Richard Lipsey have questioned the orthodox over-reliance on 'tightly specified models which are wide of the empirical mark' (2001: 188). In addition, there has been an increased questioning of economic orthodoxy, as reflected in book series such as Routledge's *Economics as Social Theory*. Existing critique includes work drawing on feminist argument (e.g. Folbre, 1994; Ferber and Nelson, 2003), literary analysis (e.g. Osteen and Woodmansee, 1999), ethical and moral proposition (e.g. Vanberg, 1994; O'Neill, 1998), historicism (e.g. Hodgson, 2001), critical realism (e.g. Lawson, 2003; Fleetwood, 1999), as well as a range of challenges to economic methodology (e.g. Backhouse, 1994; Boylan and O'Gorman, 1995; Fullbrook, 2002) and the orthodox construction of economic knowledge (e.g. Garnett, 1999; Cullenberg *et al.*, 2001).These studies utilise argument which questions key assumptions within economics, such as Alan Kirman's contention that there is 'a problem... in an essential feature of a centuries-long tradition in economics, that of treating individuals as acting independently of one another' (1989: 137). Tony Lawson argues that the summative effect of this critique is that the economics 'project is recognized as being in a state of disarray and unclear even as to its own rationale' (2003: 8–9).

6 For example, they continue to form a key element of standard physiology textbooks. As Birke observes:

> Control and regulation are key concepts in this physiology; *stability and constancy* are what result. One consequence of this conceptualisation is that lack of constancy is taken to indicate a failure or breakdown of the system. Fluctuations thus become constructed... as verging on the pathological.
>
> (1999: 89–90, added emphasis)

7 However this last argument does look a little like hyperbole. Though social pace may be rapidly accelerating, our 'just-in-time' industrialised culture *glorifies* rather than *denies* time. It is *the* precious resource (Adam, 1990). Rather than Castell's 'timeless time' (1996: 464), we have an intensification and glorification of time.

8 Thrift suggests that the 'cultural creation of speed itself depends on a depiction of certain places, things and people as slow-moving, most particularly those places, things and people connected with nature, the countryside and so on' (2001: 41). He contends that this contrast between 'fast' society and 'slow' nature is false because 'nature is actually very fast' as is reflected in the 'speed of light' and 'even that slow old thing, the human body' which 'works reasonably fast' (2001: 41). Yet the problem with this aspect of Thrift's argument is that it is one-sided. As argued above, physical and biological

reactions are fast but they also depend on processes that have extraordinary longevity. The speed of light is fast but remains constant over numerous millennia. Human cellular reactions are characterised by flux but also appear to rely on the dynamic constancy of the 'millennial processes' that seem to surround DNA. It is the latter constancy and longevity which influences the cultural perception of nature as slow in relation to the seeming speed of social life.

5 LANGUAGE AND TECHNOLOGY

1 This does not imply that Elias sees human social development as necessarily linear or progressive. As he notes, human societies can move from 'tribe to empire and from empire to feudal disintegration' (1991a: 31).

2 Central to his project is the desire to avoid 'the choice only between a wholesale reduction of the human condition to that of animals *or* to a mode of existence partly or wholly divorced from that of animals' (Elias, 1991a: 43, added emphasis).

3 As they are acellular, viruses cannot replicate through cell division. Instead they appear to rely on the biology of their 'host' for replication. In the 'lytic' cycle, the virus induces host cells to manufacture the proteins necessary for its reproduction. In the 'lysogenic' cycle, the viral genome integrates into the host DNA and replicates along with it.

4 In so doing, Elias also challenges the fears we observed in Chapter 2 in the writing of Rose, Kamin and Lewontin (1964; cf. Jenkins, 2002; Murphy, 1997). Following Elias, if we emphasise human plasticity, this does not mean that we have 'to deny biology and acknowledge only social construction' (Rose *et al.*, 1984: 10).

5 In full, Elias describes this process in the following terms:

> they compared the interval between the beginning and end of the flow of two speeches or, in other words, of two *non-repeatable social change-continua* which occurred one after another, with the interval between the beginning and end of the flow of sand in an hourglass – of a *repeatable change-continuum* which, according to our scheme of things, is *classified as 'physical' or 'natural'*. By saying that the Athenians 'timed' the speeches, one simply means that they rendered the intervals between their beginnings and their ends comparable by reference to the intervals between the beginnings and ends of inanimate processes which, *in contrast to the speeches, were repeatable and more reliable and controllable than sequences of human actions.*
>
> (1992: 102–103, added emphasis)

6 It is important to note of course that such regularities are conditional (see Chapter 4). As Cartwright (1999) observes, Galileo's experiments in mechanics operated under certain sets of conditions. For instance, Galileo had challenged the Aristotelian view that heavy objects fall faster to the ground than lighter ones by demonstrating that two balls of differing weights hit the ground at the same time. However Cartwright questions this relationship by drawing on Otto Neurath's argument that it does not hold when one is observing the descent of light objects, such as that of 'a thousand dollar bill' (Neurath, 1987: 13) on a windy day. In other words, regularities are often conditional and it remains the case that 'the theory is true in its domain, not that its domain is universal' (Cartwright, 1999: 27). Yet as Cartwright also acknowledges, within its domain, 'mechanics is a powerful and precise tool for prediction' (1999: 27).

7 In *The Symbol Theory* Elias notes that 'it has become quite usual to count tool-making among the distinguishing characteristics of human beings' (1991a: 35). Yet this passage does not reflect their general tenor of Elias's argument which focuses almost exclusively on language and symbolisation.

6 TEMPORALITY AND REALISM

1 In his 'game models', Elias (1970) did consider the conditions under which people's intentions may be more realisable. Nevertheless, his overall thesis stresses the unplanned and unpredictable nature of social outcomes.

2 Elias particularly highlights one social regularity, namely that between interdependency complexity and self-restraint. Although Elias (1996) resisted the implication that there is anything inevitable about the civilizing process, he nevertheless argued that lengthening interdependencies have occasioned greater self-restraint 'from the earliest period of the history of the Occident to the present' (Elias, 1994: 445). He asserted that 'the *general direction* of the change in conduct, the "trend" of the movement of civilization, is *everywhere* the same . . . *always* . . . towards a more or less automatic self-control' (Elias, 1994: 458, added emphasis). While there is no uniform process, there is nevertheless a clear direction.

> *Regardless*, therefore, of how much the tendencies may criss-cross, advance and recede, relax or tighten *on a small scale*, the direction of the main movement – as far as is visible up to now – is the *same* for all kinds of behaviour'.
>
> (1994: 154, added emphasis)

In other words, Elias posited this relationship as a social regularity that would occur across time and space. As 'the social fabric grows more intricate, the sociogenetic apparatus of individual self-control also becomes more differentiated, more all-round and more stable' (1994: 447), leading to a 'a strictly regulated super-ego' (1994: 154).

3 This argument applies even if one focuses, as Aronson *et al.*, suggest, on laws as 'invariant relations between properties' rather than in terms of how each law 'corresponds to the facts' (1994: 142). The problem is that the relation between social properties may well change so that putative social laws are no longer invariant.

4 In addition, as Bryan Turner and Chris Rojek observe, 'the round of daily activities – sleeping, eating, talking and cleaning the house – *may* remain relatively normal and stable despite considerable macro dislocation' (2001: 77, original emphasis).

5 As Anna Green and Kathleen Troup also observe, successive generations of *Annales* school historians have struggled to develop an adequate 'metanarrative for historical change' (1999: 93).

6 It has also been recently argued that afforestation is only likely to be effective in carbon containment within a very narrow band of the tropics (Jha, 2006).

7 Archer argues that the inherited nature of social structures has been insufficiently emphasised:

> No-one would seriously deny this in its common sense form, e.g. those whose activities generated the relations constitutive of industrialism, imperialism, political parties, a state educational system or a national health service, were quite different people from those who later had to live in a society made up of these structures amongst others . . . Since it seems unlikely that anyone would seriously deny this lay insight, why has it failed to be taken seriously in social theorizing?
>
> (1995: 72)

7 GENOMICS

1 Then at the premier French genomics laboratory, the Centre d'Etude du Polymorphisme Humain (now the Fondation Jean Dausset – CEPH).

2 The Oxford Future of Humanity Institute forms part of the new James Martin 21st Century School at Oxford. The latter aims 'to foster new thinking that will tackle the pressing issues facing the world today' (including environmental degradation, genomics, global inequality and food shortages, population growth and warfare – see http://www.21school.ox.ac.uk/research/). This new school has hosted debates about genomics and bioethics, as in the recent conference, *Tomorrow's People; The Challenges of Technology for Life Extension and Enhancement*, held at the Said Business School in March 2006 (http://www.martininstitute.ox.ac.uk/jmi/forum2006/).

3 Companies such as Affymetrix can supply microarray technology which uses silicon chips that are etched to receive multiple samples of DNA which can then be rapidly screened using automated information technology.

4 At its most fervent, it suggests that our body is 'our foe' and regards the 'future perfect body' as something that 'will not be permitted to falter' (Elshtain, 2005: 163).

5 There are a number of life scientists who appear to take eugenic thinking for granted. For example, James Watson was instrumental in funding research into the ethical implications of genomics (Kevles, 1995) and he has declared that he is 'certainly . . . very conscious of eugenics' (Watson, 2000: 78). Yet 'Mr DNA if anyone was' (Kevles, 1992: 26) also argues that:

> the question we're going to have to face is, what is going to be the least unpleasant? Using abortion to get rid of nasty genes from families? Or developing *germline* procedures with which . . . you can go in and *get rid* of a bad gene.
>
> (Watson, 2000: 79, added emphasis)

What is remarkable about this quotation is the way in which Watson assumes that getting 'rid of nasty genes' is common sense even though this desire represents a eugenic will to permanently 'purify' the human race (cf. Nelkin and Lindee, 1999).

6 In a later commentary, Habermas (2003: 86–87) notes that his concern is contested by those who argue that it will be possible to allow redesigned children to choose whether to 'activate' their 'new genetic modules'. For instance, Stock suggests that bioengineers could 'include a mechanism for selectively switching off the expression . . . of the genetic module . . . An injection could provide the chemical signal that would trigger the shut-off' (2002: 67). Yet even if Stock's gene dreams could be fulfilled, Habermas still strongly objects to any interference with the human germline.

7 In the UK these include the Human Genetics Commission, the Gene Therapy Advisory Committee, the Genetics and Insurance Committee, the Human Fertilisation and Embryology Authority, the Committee on the Safety of Medicines, the UK Xenotransplantation Interim Regulatory Authority, the UK Foresight Programme, the Medicines Control Agency, the National Institute for Clinical Excellence, the Food Standards Agency, the Agriculture and Environment Biotechnology Commission, amongst others. In addition, there are non-governmental advisory bodies such as the Nuffield Council on Bioethics, the Medical Research Council and The Wellcome Trust. For an overview of the regulatory and advisory bodies in the UK, see http://www.hgc.gov.uk/about_regulatory.htm.

8 An illustration of these conjoint interests is found in Catherine Waldby and Robert Mitchell's (2006) study of the use of embryonic stem cells. On the one hand, they document the commercial incentive to commodify the 'harvesting' of stem cells. As they observe, 'tissue donors are effectively open sources of biological material, which can be disentangled in ways that favour the rights and profits of biotechnology companies' (Waldby and Mitchell, 2006: 76). On the other, they note that institutions such as the UK Stem Cell Bank apply a range of conditions which are designed to insure public

sector access and which, to some extent, dissipate commercial advantage (Waldby and Mitchell, 2006: 80–81; cf. Kent et al., 2006).

8 TRANSGRESSION

1 Hosted jointly be the London School of Economics BIOS centre and the University of Nottingham Institute for the Study of Genetics, Biorisks and Society. See: http://www.lse.ac.uk/collections/BIOS/neuroscience_identity_society.htm.

2 Kramer later ignores this wise caution by concluding that 'the parallels between a rat's response to electrical currents and to psychic stress make it tempting to combine the two models conceptually' (1993: 117).

3 The work of Grosz and Wilson also reminds us of the distance that can still exist between feminist and social science sympathy, and contemporary life science. For instance, in a chapter on what might be termed 'gut psychology', Wilson draws out the 'neuropsychological profile' of the enteric nervous system (ENS) that contains bodily tissue from the 'esophagus to the anus' (2004: 41, 34). In portraying the gut as an autonomous system that is psychologically responsive, Wilson's primary references are historical, especially the work of Freud. Using such references, she suggests that the gut forms 'differentiated networks for mood, affect regulation, and attachment along with the networks for sensation and motility' (2004: 41). In so doing, Wilson is aware that her 'gut psychology' is antithetical to many contemporary life scientists. As an example of the latter, she quotes Wilhelmsen's argument that 'there is no evidence that emotions can "pile up" somewhere in the body and that psychological conflicts, if unresolved, are converted to somatic symptoms or diseases' (Wilhelmsen, 2000, cited in Wilson, 2004: 42). In effect, Wilson illustrates the distance between her post-psychoanalytic position and that of many contemporary life scientists who are opposed to neo-Freudian accounts of the psychosomatic.

4 In consequence, those drawing on Freund need to be aware of critique of Hochschild such as that of Wouters (1989) or Barbalet (1998).

5 Though the implicit reference is as much that of Elias as Freud, the dualistic notion of some outmoded, now 'uncivilised', fight/flight instinct is still clearly implied.

6 Elsewhere Wilkinson has described Robert Sapolsky's studies of baboons in detail (Wilkinson, 1996). Wilkinson notes that there are constraints on the ability to draw parallels between baboon and human society because 'social hierarchy is negotiated in such different ways among humans compared to other primates' (1996: 196). Yet Wilkinson still implies that baboon studies are of direct relevance to human society because they illustrate the 'common association of stress with lower social status', an argument which is conveniently supportive of Wilkinson's thesis that income inequality, rather than income per se, is a key determinant of human ill-health, and that this process works through psychosocial concerns such as social capital.

7 However I do not accept Williams' contention that Elias 'reproduces this division' between humans and animals (Williams, 2003b: 556) – see Chapter 5.

8 This is illustrated by the common experience of back pain. If I experience back pain, it may be through a complex of bad posture, dealing with physical loads, and work or other 'demands', rather than any one of these. Furthermore, my back pain may have been 'learnt' over a very lengthy period (e.g. bad posture since childhood). Back pain may also be seen over the very 'longue durée' as the consequence of a quadruped animal which has not quite evolved to become an easily functioning 'upright' biped. The form and intensity of back pain that I experience will be influenced by all of the above as well as all the complex interrelations between posture and physiology.

9 This is not to deny that physiological measures provide useful medical information as in the case of strong hormonal deficiency. Yet in stress and emotion research, the

concern is with establishing whether an individual is showing elevated hormonal levels (beyond their baseline state) rather than a marked deficiency or excess. In this context, the problem is that elevated levels may occur because of the influence of a large array of extraneous variables.

9 NEUROLOGICAL ADVENTURES

1 For instance, we are told that if someone sees a spectacular view of the sea, the initial reaction is bodily, biological, and thereby, 'emotional' in Damasio's terms. *Following* this emotional bodily response, there is an 'internal construction' by the mind, the province of 'feeling': *The sight of a spectacular seascape is an emotionally competent object. The body state that results from beholding that seascape x is the actual object at the origin x, which is then perceived in the feeling state* (Damasio, 2003: 91, original emphasis).

2 The explanation for this causation relies on a simple evolutionary argument. As Damasio notes:

> It is legitimate to ask at this point why emotions precede feelings. My answer is simple: we have emotions first and feelings after because evolution came up with emotions first and feelings later. Emotions are built from simple reactions that easily promote the survival of an organism and thus could easily prevail in evolution.
>
> (2003: 30)

Yet one can question this mechanist developmentalism. For instance, emotions are almost equivalent to neurochemistry in Damasio's account. It therefore follows that if emotions preceded feelings in an evolutionary timescape, we once had a neurochemical response without a cognitive appraisal/mapping of our neurochemistry. Yet why did our forebears 'fight or flee', say, the woolly mammoth without feeling anything and without appraising that said mammoth represented danger. In other words, can one logically separate emotion from feeling, or assume a predominant causal direction between them?

3 For instance, Nowotny *et al.* draw on Karin Knorr Cetina's (1996, 1999) comparison between the context of experimental high energy physics and molecular biology. They note the 'essential differences' between these two fields, especially in regard to what they see as the 'communitarian' orientation of particle physics and the individualistic regime of molecular biology' (Nowotny *et al.*, 2001: 98). Whereas work in high-energy physics is about the meeting of 'collectives of physicists, matched with collectives of instruments', molecular biology is based on 'individual, bodily, lab-bench science' (Knorr Cetina, 1999: 4, cited in Nowotny *et al.*, 2001: 97).

4 For example, particle physics is portrayed as rather ineffective due to its segregation and relative isolation:

> once [particle physicists] had lost their powerful status... which had been prolonged by the security concerns of the Cold War era, they apparently had few other resources left that could now usefully be employed in the new game over local politics, national funding patterns and the general demand for greater accountabilty.
>
> (Nowotny *et al.*, 2001: 127)

5 Nowotny and her colleagues might counter such argument by noting that their concern with local context predominantly arises because it provides a nexus for inter-disciplinary research. As Nowotny argues, 'the first attribute of Mode-2 is the fact that contemporary research is increasingly carried out in the *context of application*'

(Nowotny, 2001: 2, added emphasis). In other words, transdisciplinary research often takes place in response to particular local research needs, and it is this very context which stimulates researchers to work beyond their 'insular' disciplinary concerns. Nevertheless, it still remains difficult to see how a single normative template can be applied across contexts which are likely to vary considerably from one setting to another.

6 Ricoeur asserts that 'if I had to claim a philosophical ancestor it would be Spinoza' (Changeux and Ricoeur, 2000: 20), while Changeux states that Spinoza is 'an essential point of reference' (Changeux and Ricoeur, 2000: 201).

7 In spite of his seeming anti-naturalistic argument, Ricoeur does acknowledge the force of the 'naturalistic element in ethics' (Changeux and Ricoeur, 2000: 218) and displays naturalistic sympathies such as when he states that 'I am, by my very *biological nature*... disposed to display not only cruelty, but also sympathy, towards others' (Changeux and Ricoeur, 2000: 218, added emphasis). This naturalistic sympathy complements Changeux's more thorough-going naturalism and, combined with Ricoeur's willingness to overlook some of the desocialised and biologistic aspects of Changeux's thesis (such as the latter's argument that violence inhibition is one of the 'intrinsic and innate properties of the human brain'; Changeux and Ricoeur, 2000: 218), allows for a small measure of correspondence in their joint deliberations over ethics and morality.

8 To which the present author also pleads, *mea maxima culpa.*

BIBLIOGRAPHY

Abbott, Andrew (2001) *Chaos of Disciplines*. Chicago: University of Chicago.

Abbott, L. F. and Nelson, Sacha B. (2000) Synaptic plasticity: taming the beast. *Nature Neuroscience* (supplement), 3: 1178–1183.

Abram, David (1997) *The Spell of the Sensuous: Perception and Language in a More-Than-Human World*. Vintage Books (Random House).

Acheson, Sir D. (chair) (1998) *Independent Inquiry into Inequalities in Health*. London: The Stationery Office.

Adam, Barbara (1988) Social versus natural time: A traditional distinction re-examined. In Michael Young and Tom Schuller (eds), *The Rhythms of Society*. London: Routledge, pp. 198–226.

Adam, Barbara (1990) *Time & Social Theory*. Cambridge: Polity.

Adam, Barbara (1995) *Timewatch: The Social Analysis of Time*. Cambridge: Polity.

Adam, Barbara (1996) Beyond the present: Nature, technology and the democratic ideal. *Time & Society*, 5 (3): 319–338.

Adam, Barbara (1998) *Timescapes of Modernity: The Environment and Invisible Hazards*. London: Routledge.

Agamben, Giorgio (1998) *Homo sacer: Sovereign Power and Bare Life*. Stanford: Stanford University Press.

Albrecht, Andreas and Magueijo, Joao (1999) A time varying speed of light as a solution to cosmological puzzles. *Physical Review D.*59 (043516): 1–13.

Alexander, Samuel O. M. (1921) *Spinoza and Time, etc.* (Fourth "Arthur Davis Memorial Lecture"). London: Allen & Unwin.

Allen, Garland E. (1999) Modern biological determinism; the Violence Initiative, the Human Genome Project, and the new eugenics. In Michael Fortun and Everett Mendelsohn (eds), *The Practices of Human Genetics*. Dordrecht: Kluwer Academic Publishers.

Allen, Laura, Hines, Melissa, Shryne, James and Gorski, Roger (1989) Two sexually dimorphic cell groups in the human brain. *Journal of Neuroscience*, 9: 497–506.

Angell, Marci (2004) *The Truth About the Drug Companies: How They Deceive Us and What to do About it*. New York: Random House.

Anthias, Floya (2001) The material and the symbolic in theorizing social stratification: issues of gender, ethnicity and class. *British Journal of Sociology*, 52 (3): 367–390.

Appadurai, Arjun (1996) *Modernity at Large: Cultural Dimensions of Globalization*. Minneapolis: University of Minnesota Press.

Archer, Margaret S. (1988) *Culture and Agency: The Place of Culture in Social Theory*. Cambridge: Cambridge University Press.

BIBLIOGRAPHY

Archer, Margaret S. (1995) *Realist Social Theory: The Morphogenetic Approach*. Cambridge: Cambridge University Press.

Archer, Margaret S. (1996) Social integration and system integration: Developing the distinction. *Sociology*, 30 (4): 679–699.

Archer, Margaret (1998) Introduction: Realism in the social sciences. In Margaret Archer, Roy Bhaskar, Collier, Andrew, Lawson, Tony and Norrie, Alan (eds), *Critical Realism: Essential Readings*. London: Routledge.

Archer, Margaret, Bhaskar, Roy, Collier, Andrew, Lawson, Tony and Norrie, Alan (1998) *Critical Realism: Essential Readings*. London: Routledge.

Armstrong, D. (1987) Theoretical tensions in biopsychosocial medicine. *Social Science and Medicine*, 25 (11): 1213–1218.

Aronson, Jerrold L., Harré, Rom and Cornell Way, Eileen (1994) *Realism Rescued: How Scientific Progress is Possible*. London: Duckworth.

Arendt, Hannah (1970) *On Violence*. San Diego: Harcourt Brace.

Arroba, T. and James, K. (1987) *Pressure at Work*. London: McGraw-Hill.

Ayman, P. and Goldshine, A. D. (1940) Blood pressure determinations by patients with essential hypertension: 1 the differences between clinic and home readings before treatment. *American Journal of Medical Science*, 200: 465–474.

Bachelard, Gaston (1983) *Water and Dreams*. Dallas: The Pegasus Foundation.

Backhouse, R. E. (ed.) (1994) *New Directions in Economic Methodology*. London: Routledge.

Badagliacco, Joanna M. and Ruiz, Carey D. (2006) Impoverished Appalachia and Kentucky genomes: What is at stake? How do feminists reply? *New Genetics and Society*, 25 (2): 209–226.

Baillie, Harold W. (2005) Aristotle and genetic engineering: The uncertainty of excellence. In Harold W. Baillie and Timothy K. Casey (eds), *Is Human Nature Obsolete? Genetics, Bioengineering and the Future of the Human Condition*. Cambridge, MA: MIT Press, pp. 209–232.

Banerjee, S. B. (2003) Who sustains whose development? Sustainable development and the reinvention of nature. *Organization Studies*, 24 (1): 143–180.

Barbalet, Jack T. (1998) *Emotion, Social Theory and Social Structure: A Macrosociological Approach*. Cambridge: Cambridge University Press.

Barnes, Barry (2001) On 'the construction of social reality'. *Revue Internationale de Philosophie*, 55 (216): 263–267.

Barnes, Barry, Bloor, David and Henry, John (1996) *Scientific Knowledge: A Sociological Analysis*. London: Athlone.

Baum, A. and Grunberg, N. (1997) Measurement of stress hormones. In S. Cohen, R. C. Kessler and L. Underwood Gordon (eds), *Measuring Stress: A Guide for Health and Social Scientists*. New York: Oxford, pp. 175–192.

Bauman, Zygmunt (1989) *Modernity and the Holocaust*. Cambridge: Polity.

Bauman, Zygmunt (1992) *Mortality, Immortality and Other Life Strategies*. Cambridge: Polity.

Baverstock, Keith (2006) What kind of a thing is the genome? Paper presented to the Department of Sociology and Philosophy, University of Exeter, 4 July 2006.

Beck, Stefan and Niewöhner, Jörg (2006) Somatographic investigations across levels of complexity. *BioSocieties*, 1(2): 219–227.

Beck, Ulrich (1992) *Risk society*. London: Sage.

Beck, Ulrich (1995) *Ecological Politics in an Age of Risk*. Cambridge: Polity.

Bendelow, Gillian and Williams, Simon (1998) (eds) *Emotions in Social Life: Social Theories and Contemporary Issues*. London: Sage.

BIBLIOGRAPHY

Benoist, Jean Marie (1978) *The Structural Revolution*. New York: St Martin's Press

Benton, Ted (1981) Realism and social science: Some comments on Roy Bhaskar's 'The Possibility of Naturalism'. *Radical Philosophy, No.* 27: 13–21.

Benton, Ted (1991) Biology and social science: Why the return of the repressed should be given a (cautious) welcome. *Sociology*, 25 (1): 1–29.

Benton, Ted (1993) *Natural Relations? Animal Rights, Human Rights and the Environment*. London: Verso.

Benton, Ted (1994) 'Biology and social theory', In Ted Benton and Michael Redclift (eds), *Social Theory and the Environment*. London: Routledge.

Benton, Ted (2003) Ecology, health and society: A red-green perspective. In Simon Williams, Lynda Birke and Gillian Bendelow (eds), *Debating Biology: Sociological Reflections on Health, Medicine and Society*, London: Routledge, pp. 283–297.

Bergson, Henri (1911) *Matter and Memory*. London: Allen & Unwin.

Berman, Marshall (1982) *All That is Solid Melts into Air: The Experience of Modernity*. New York: Simon and Schuster.

Bermingham, Ann and Brewer, John (eds) (1995) *The Consumption of Culture, 1600–1800: Image, Object, Text*. London: Routledge.

Bernstein, Richard J. (1979) *The Restructuring of Social and Political Theory*. London: Methuen.

Bhaskar, Roy (1978) *A Realist Theory of Science, 2nd edn*. Brighton: Harvester.

Bhaskar, Roy (1989a) *The Possibility of Naturalism, 2nd edn*. Hemel Hempstead: Harvester Wheatsheaf.

Bhaskar, Roy (1989b) *Reclaiming Reality: A Critical Introduction to Contemporary Philosophy*. London: Verso.

Bird, R. J. (1997) Chaos and social reality: An emergent perspective. In Raymond A. Eve, Sara Horsfall and Mary E. Lee (eds), *Chaos, Complexity and Sociology: Myths. Models and Theories*. Thousand Oaks, Calif.: Sage.

Birke, Lynda (1986) *Women, Feminism and Biology*. Brighton: Wheatsheaf.

Birke, Lynda (1999) *Feminism and the Biological Body*. Edinburgh: Edinburgh University Press.

Birke, Lynda (2003) Shaping biology: feminism and the idea of the 'biological'. In Simon Williams, Lynda Birke and Gillian Bendelow (eds), *Debating Biology: Sociological Reflections on Health, Medicine and Society*, London: Routledge, pp. 39–52.

Blaug, Mark (1999) Conversation with Mark Blaug. In B. Snowdon and H. R. Vane (eds), *Conversations with Leading Economists: Interpreting Modern Macroeconomics*, Northampton, MA: Edward Elgar, pp. 314–333.

Blaxter, Mildred (2003) Biology, social class and inequalities in health: Their synthesis in 'health capital'. In Simon Williams, Lynda Birke and Gillian Bendelow (eds), *Debating Biology: Sociological Reflections on Health, Medicine and Society*, London: Routledge, pp. 69–83.

Bloor, David (1976) *Knowledge and Social Imagery*. London: Routledge and Kegan Paul.

Bloor, David (1999) Anti-Latour. *Studies in History and Philosophy of Science*, 30 (1): 81–112.

Bohm, David (1980) *Wholeness and the Implicate Order*. London: Routledge and Kegan Paul.

Bourdieu, Pierre (1989) *Distinction: A Social Critique Of The Judgement of Taste*. London: Routledge.

Bourdieu, Pierre (1990) *The Logic of Practice*. Cambridge: Polity.

Boylan, Thomas A. and O'Gorman, Paschal F. (1995) *Beyond Rhetoric and Realism in Economics: Towards a Reformulation of Economic Methodology.* London: Routledge.

Braudel, Fernand (1972) *The Mediterranean and the Mediterranean World in the Age of Philip II, Volume I.* London: Collins.

Braudel, Fernand (1985) *Civilisation and Capitalism, 15th to 18th Century, volume 3: The Perspective of the World.* London: Fontana.

Braudel, Fernand, (1993) *A History of Civilizations.* Harmondsworth: Penguin.

Breggin, Peter R. and Breggin, Ginger Ross (1994) *Talking back to Prozac: What Doctors Aren't Telling You about Today's Most Controversial Drug.* New York: St Martin's Press.

Brewer, John (1982) Commercialization and politics. In Neil McKendrick, John Brewer and J. H. Plumb (eds), *The Birth of A Consumer Society: The Commercialization of Eighteenth Century England.* London: Europa Publications, pp. 197–262.

Briner, R. and Reynolds, S. (1999) The costs, benefits, and limitations of organizational level stress interventions. *Journal of Organizational Behavior,* 20 (5): 647–664.

Brown, Nik (2003) Hope against hype – accountability in biopasts, presents and futures. *Science Studies,* 16: 3–21.

Brown, Nik and Webster, Andrew (2004) *New Medical Technologies and Society: Reordering Life.* Cambridge: Polity.

Buchanan, Allen E., Brock, Dan W., Daniels, Norman and Wikler, Daniel (2000) *From Chance to Choice: Genetics and Justice.* Cambridge: Cambridge University Press.

Burch, William R. (1971) *Daydreams and Nightmares: A Sociological Essay on the American Environment.* New York: Harper & Row.

Burkitt, Ian (1997) Social relations and emotions. *Sociology,* 31 (1): 37–55.

Burkitt, Ian (1999) *Bodies of Thought; Embodiment, Identity and Modernity.* London: Sage.

Burman, Marshall (1982) *All that is Solid Melts into Air: The Experience of Modernity.* New York: Simon and Schuster.

Burningham, Kate and Cooper, Geoff (1999) Being constructive: social constructionism and the environment, *Sociology,* 33 (2): 297–316.

Bury, Michael R. (1986) Social constructionism and the development of medical sociology. *Sociology of Health and Illness,* 8: 137–169.

Bury, Michael R. (1995) The body in question. *Medical Sociology News,* 21 (1): 36–48.

Bury, Michael R. (1997) *Health and Illness in a Changing Society.* London: Routledge.

Bury, Michael R. and Wadsworth, M. (2003) The 'biological clock'? Ageing, health and the body across the lifecourse. In Simon J. Williams, Lynda Birke and Gillian A. Bendelow (eds), *Debating Biology: Sociological Reflections on Health, Medicine and Society.* London: Routledge.

Burrell, Gibson and Morgan, Gareth (1979) *Sociological Paradigms and Organisational Analysis: Elements of the Sociology of Corporate Life.* London: Heinemann Educational.

Buttel, Frederick H. (1978) Environmental sociology: a new paradigm? *American Sociologist,* 13: 252–256.

Buttel, Frederick H. (1996) Environmental and resource sociology: Theoretical issues and opportunities for synthesis. *Rural Sociology,* 61: 56–76.

Butler, Judith (1993) *Bodies That Matter: On the Discursive Limits of Sex.* New York: Routledge.

Byrne, David (1998) *Complexity Theory and the Social Sciences.* London: Routledge.

Cain, Mead T. (1993) Patriarchal structures and demographic change. In N. Federici, K. Oppenheim Mason and S. Sogner (eds), *Women's Position and Demographic Change.* Oxford: Clarendon Press.

Callon, Michel (1986) Some elements of a sociology of translation: domestication of the scallops and the fishermen of St Brieuc Bay. In John Law (ed.), *Power, Action and Belief.* London: Routledge and Kegan Paul.

Callon, Michel (1991) Techno-economic networks and irreversibility. In John Law (ed.), *A Sociology of Monsters? Essays on Power, Technology and Domination, Sociological Review Monograph 38.* London: Routledge.

Callon, Michel and Latour, Bruno (1992) Don't throw the baby out with the Bath School!: A reply to Collins and Yearley. In Andrew Pickering (ed.), *Science as Practice and Culture.* Chicago: University of Chicago Press.

Canguilhem, Georges (1994) *A vital rationalist: Selected writings from Georges Canguilhem,* Francois Delaporte (ed.). New York: Zone.

Cannon, Walter B. (1914) The interrelations of emotion as suggested by recent physiological researches. *American Journal of Psychology,* 25: 256–282.

Cannon, Walter B. (1932) *The Wisdom of the Body.* London: Kegan Paul, Trench and Trübner.

Capra, Fritjof (1975) *The Tao of Physics.* London: Fontana.

Capra, Fritjof (1983) *The Turning Point: Science, Society and the Rising Culture.* London: Fontana.

Capron, Alexander Morgan (1990) The impact of the report. *Splicing life. Human Gene Therapy,* 1 (1): 69–71.

Carroll, D., Davey Smith, G. and Bennett, P. (1996) Some observations on health and socio-economic status. *Journal of Health Psychology,* 1 (1): 23–39.

Cartwright, Nancy (1999) *The Dappled World: A Study of the Boundaries of Science.* Cambridge: Cambridge University Press.

Castells, Manuel (1996) *The Rise of the Network Society.* Oxford: Blackwell.

Castells, Manuel (1997) *The Information Age: Economy Society and Culture, Volume 2: The Power of Identity.* Oxford: Blackwell.

Castells, Manuel (1999) *The Information Age: Economy Society and Culture, Volume 3: End of Millennium.* Oxford: Blackwell.

Catton, William R. and Dunlap, Riley E. (1978) Environmental sociology: a new paradigm. *American Sociologist,* 13: 41–49.

Catton, William R. and Dunlap, Riley E. (1980) A new ecological paradigm for post-exuberant sociology. *American Behavioral Scientist,* 24 (1): 15–47.

Changeux, Jean-Pierre (1985) *Neuronal Man: The Biology of Mind.* London: Pantheon.

Changeux, Jean-Pierre and Ricoeur, Paul (2000) *What Makes Us Think? A Neuroscientist and a Philosopher Argue About Ethics, Human Nature, and the Brain.* Princeton: Princeton University Press.

Churchland, Paul M. (1995) *The Engine of Reason, the Seat of the Soul: A Philosophical Journey in the Brain.* Cambridge, MA: MIT Press.

Clutton-Brock, Tim H. and Iason, G. R. 1986. Sex ratio variation in mammals. *Quarterly Review of Biology,* 61 (3): 339–374.

Coburn, David (2000) Income inequality, social cohesion and the health status of populations: the role of neoliberalism. *Social Science and Medicine,* 51: 135–146.

Cohen, Daniel (1993) *Les genes de l'espoir [Genes of hope]: A la découverte du genome humain*. Paris: Robert Laffont.

Cohen, S. and Manuck, S. B. (1995) Stress, reactivity and disease. *Psychosomatic Medicine*, 57: 423–426.

Collier, Andrew (1994) *Critical Realism: An Introduction to Roy Bhaskar's Philosophy*. London: Verso.

Collingwood, Robin George (1946) *The Idea of History*. Oxford: Clarendon Press.

Collins, Harry M. (1992) *Changing Order: Replication and Induction in Scientific Practice*. London: Sage.

Collins, Harry M. (1996) Theory dopes: A critique of Murphy. *Sociology*, 30 (2): 367–373.

Connolly, William E. (2002) *Neuropolitics: Thinking, Culture, Speed*. Minneapolis: University of Minnesota Press.

Conrad, Peter (1992) Medicalization and social control. *Annual Review of Sociology*, 18: 209–232.

Conrad, Peter and Gabe, Jonathan (1999) Introduction: Sociological perspectives on the new genetics: an overview. *Sociology of Health and Illness*, 21 (5): 505–516.

Cook-Deegan, Robert M. (1990) Human gene therapy and congress. *Human Gene Therapy*, 1: 163–170.

Cook-Deegan, Robert M. (1994) *The Gene Wars: Science, Politics and the Human Genome*. New York: W. W. Norton.

Cooper, Melinda (2006) Resuscitations: stem cells and the crisis of old age. *Body & Society*, 12(1): 1–23.

Corea, Gina (1985) *The Mother Machine: Reproductive Technologies from Artificial Insemination to Artificial Wombs*. New York: Harper.

Cremante, Simona (2006) *Leonardo da Vinci: The Complete Works*, co-ordination and introduction by Carlo Pedretti. London: David & Charles.

Croce, Benedetto (1921) *Theory & History of Historiography*. London: George G. Harrap.

Crombie, A. C. (1994) *Styles of Scientific Thinking in the European Tradition*, 3 vols. London: Duckworth.

Crossley, Nick (1997) Corporeality and communicative action: embodying the renewal of critical theory. *Body and Society*, 3(1): 17–46.

Cullenberg, S., Amariglio, J. and Ruccio, D. (2001) *Postmodernism, Economics and Knowledge*. London: Routledge.

Damasio, Antonio (1995) *Descartes' Error: Emotion, Reason and the Human Brain*. London: Picador.

Damasio, Antonio (2000) *The Feeling of What Happens: Body, Emotion and the Making of Consciousness*. London: Vintage.

Damasio, Antonio (2001) Fundamental feelings. *Nature*, 413 (25 October): 781.

Damasio, Antonio (2003) *Looking for Spinoza: Joy, Sorrow and the Feeling Brain*. London: Heinemann.

Davey, Basiro, Halliday, Tim and Hirst, Mark (2001) *Human Biology and Health: An Evolutionary Approach, 3rd edn*. Buckingham: Open University Press.

Davis, Colin (1996) *Levinas: An Introduction*. Cambridge: Polity.

Decety, Jean and Keenan, Julian Paul (2006) Social neuroscience: a new journal. *Social Neuroscience*, 1 (1): 1–5.

Degler, Carl N. (1991) *In Search of Human Nature*. Oxford: Oxford University Press.

Deleuze Gilles and Guattari, Félix (1988) *A Thousand Plateaus: Capitalism and Schizophrenia*. London: Athlone Press.

Dickens, Peter (1992) *Society and Nature: Towards a Green Social Theory.* Hemel Hempstead: Harvester.

Dickens, Peter (1996) *Reconstructing Nature: Alienation, Emancipation and the Division of Labour.* London: Routledge.

Dickens, Peter (2000) *Social Darwinism: Linking Evolutionary Thought to Social Theory.* Buckingham: Open University Press.

Dickens, Peter (2001) Linking the social and natural sciences: is capital modifying human biology in its own image? *Sociology,* 35 (1): 93–110.

Dijck, José Van (1998) *Imagenation: Popular images of genetics.* New York: New York University Press.

Dray, William H. (1995) *History as Re-Enactment: R.G. Collingwood's Idea of History.* Oxford: Oxford University Press.

Dryzek, John S. (1997) *The Politics of the Earth: Environmental Discourses.* Oxford: Oxford University Press.

Dupré, John (1996) Metaphysical disorder and scientific disunity. In Peter Galison and David J. Stump (eds), *The Disunity of Science: Boundaries, Contexts, and Power.* Stanford: Stanford University Press, pp. 101–117.

Dupré, John (2000) The social construction of what? *The Journal of Philosophy,* 97 (12): 673–676.

Dupré, John (2001) *Human Nature and the Limits of Science.* Oxford: Oxford University Press.

Dupré, John (2002) Is 'natural kind' a natural kind term? *Monist,* 85 (1): 29–49.

Dupré, John (2006a) The Constituents of Life: Spinoza Lecture 1, University of Amsterdam. Paper delivered at an *Egenis* seminar (ESRC Centre for Genomics in Society), University of Exeter, 28 November 2006.

Dupré, John (2006b) The Constituents of Life: Spinoza Lecture 2, University of Amsterdam. Paper delivered at an *Egenis* seminar (ESRC Centre for Genomics in Society), University of Exeter, 5 December 2006.

Duster, Troy (1990) *Backdoor to Eugenics.* London: Routledge.

Ehrlich, Paul R. (2000) *Human Natures: Genes, Cultures, and the Human Prospect.* Washington, DC: Island Press.

Eldredge, Niles and Gould, Stephen Jay (1972) Punctuated equilibria: an alternative to phyletic gradualism. In Thoman J. M. Schopf (ed.), *Models in Paleobiology.* San Francisco: Freeman.

Elias, Norbert (1970) *What is Sociology?* New York: Columbia University Press.

Elias, Norbert (1972) Theory of science and history of science: Comments on a recent discussion. *Economy and Society,* 1 (2): 117–133.

Elias, Norbert (1974) The sciences: towards a theory. In Richard Whitley (ed.), *Social Processes of Scientific Development.* London; Routledge and Kegan Paul.

Elias, Norbert (1975/2005) Lessen van Elias (lessons of Elias). Video recording of an interview with Elias, 23 April 1975. From *Norbert Elias, Portret van Een Socioloog (Portrait of a Sociologist)*, Abram de Swaan en Paul van den Bos. dviezen: prof. J. Goudsblom. © VPRO. Online. Available at http://www.vpro.nl/programma/beschaving/afleveringen/22058443/items/2214935 (accessed 14 December 2006).

Elias, Norbert (1982) Scientific establishments. In Norbert Elias, Herminio Martins and Richard Whitley (eds), *Scientific Establishments and Hierarchies.* Dordrecht, Holland: D. Reidel Publishing.

Elias, Norbert (1983) *The Court Society.* Oxford: Blackwell.

Elias, Norbert (1985) *The Loneliness of Dying.* Oxford: Blackwell.

Elias, Norbert (1987a) On human beings and their emotions: a process-sociological essay. *Theory, Culture and Society*, 4(2–3): 339–361.

Elias, Norbert (1987b) *Involvement and Detachment*. Oxford: Blackwell.

Elias, Norbert (1991a) *The Symbol Theory*. London: Sage.

Elias, Norbert (1991b) *The Society of Individuals*. Oxford: Blackwell.

Elias, Norbert (1992) *Time: An Essay*. Oxford: Blackwell.

Elias, Norbert (1994) *The Civilizing Process*. Oxford: Blackwell.

Elias, Norbert (1996) *The Germans*. Oxford: Blackwell.

Elixir Pharmaceuticals (2005) Nature publication reports key links between mechanisms of aging and metabolic disorders. Online. Available at http://www.elixirpharm.com/company/pr/2005-07-06-nature.pdf (last accessed 22 November 2006).

Elshtain, Jean Bethke (2005) The body and the quest for control. In Harold W. Baillie and Timothy K. Casey (eds), *Is Human Nature Obsolete? Genetics, Bioengineering and the Future of the Human Condition*. Cambridge, MA: MIT Press, pp. 155–176.

Elstad, Jon Ivar (1998) The psycho-social perspective on social inequalities in health. *Sociology of Health and Illness*, 20 (5): 598–618.

Ernst and Young (2003) *Beyond borders: The global biotechnology report.*

Evans, P., Clow, A. and Hucklebridge, F. (1997) Stress and the immune system. *The Psychologist*, 10 (7): 303–307.

Eve, Raymond A. (1997) Afterword: So where are we now? A final word. In Raymond A. Eve, Horsfall, Sara and Lee, Mary E. (eds), *Chaos, Complexity and Sociology: Myths. Models and Theories*. Thousand Oaks, Calif.: Sage.

Faraday, Michael (1860/1962) *The Chemical History of the Candle*, edited by William Crookes. New York: Collier.

Fearnside, Philip M., Lashof, Daniel A. and Moura-Costa, Pedro (2000) *Mitigation and Adaption Strategies for Global Change*, 5 (3): 239–270.

Feldman, Jerome A. (2006) *From Molecules to Metaphor: A Neural Theory of Language*. Cambridge, MA: MIT Press.

Ferber, M. A. and Nelson, J. A. (eds) (2003) *Feminist Economics Today. Beyond Economic Man*. Chicago: University of Chicago Press.

Filon, Dvora, Faerman, Marina, Smith, Patricia and Oppenheim, Ariella (1995) Sequence analysis reveals a β-thalassaemia mutation in the DNA of skeletal remains from the archaeological site of Akhziv, Israel. *Nature Genetics*, 9: 365–368.

Fleetwood, Steve (ed.) (1999) *Critical Realism in Economics: Development and Debate*. London: Routledge.

Fletcher, B. and Jones, F. (1993) A refutation of Karasek's demand-discretion model of occupational stress with a range of dependent measures. *Journal of Organizational Behaviour*, 14 (4): 319–331.

Fogle, Thomas (1995) Information metaphors and the Human Genome Project. *Perspectives in Biology and Medicine*, 38 (4): 535–547.

Folbre, N. (1994) *Who Pays for the Kids? Gender and the Structures of Constraint*. New York: Routledge.

Fortun, Mike (1997) Projecting speed genomics In Michael Fortun and Everett Mendelsohn (eds), *The Practices of Human Genetics (Sociology of the Sciences, vol. XXI)*. Dordrecht: Kluwer, pp. 25–48.

Fortun, Mike (2003) To speculate – on genomics. Occasional paper, School for Social Science, Institute for Advanced Study. http://www.ss.ias.edu/home/papers.html (note although this is the web link cited by Wilson, 2004, it is no longer active. At the time of writing (22 November 2006), Michael Fortun appears to be based at the Department of Science and Technology Studies, Sage 5408, Rensselaer Polytechnic Institute, 110 8th Street, Troy, NY 12180, USA).

Fortun, Mike (2005) For an ethics of promising, or: a few kind words about James Watson. *New Genetics and Society*, 24 (2): 157–173.

Forum (2006) *Tomorrow's People: The Challenges of Technologies for Life Extension and Enhancement.* Conference organised by the James Martin Institute for Science and Civilization at the University of Oxford, Said Business School, 14–17 March 2006. Conference webcast available at http://www.martininstitute.ox.ac.uk/JMI/Forum2006/Forum+2006+Webcast.htm (last accessed 22 November 2006).

Foucault, Michel (1977) *Discipline and Punish.* New York: Vintage Books.

Foucault, Michel (1979) *The History of Sexuality, Volume 1.* London: Allen Lane.

Frankenhaeuser, Marianne (1989) A biopsychosocial approach to work life stresses. *International Journal of Health Services*, 19: 747–758.

Franklin, Adrian (2002) *Nature and Social Theory.* London: Sage.

Franklin, Sarah (2000) Life itself: global nature and the genetic imaginary. In Sarah Franklin, Celia Lury and Jackie Stacey (eds), *Global nature, global culture.* London: Sage, pp. 188–227.

Franklin, Sarah (2001) Culturing biology: Cell lines for the second millennium. *Health*, 5 (3): 335–354.

Franklin, Sarah and McKinnon, Susan (eds) (2001) *Relative Values: Reconfiguring Kinship Studies.* Durham and London: Duke University Press.

Franklin, Sarah, Lury, Celia and Stacey, Jackie (2000) In Sarah Franklin, Celia Lury and Jackie Stacey (eds), *Global Nature, Global Culture.* London: Sage, pp 1–16.

Freund, P. E. S. (1988) Bringing society into the body. *Theory and Society*, 17: 839–864.

Freund, P. E. S. (1990) The expressive body: a common ground for the sociology of emotions and health and illness. *Sociology of Health and Illness*, 12 (4): 452–477.

Freund, P. E. S. (1998) Social performances and their discontents: the biopsychosocial aspects of dramaturgical stress. In G. Bendelow and S. J. Williams (eds), *Emotions in Social Life.* London: Routledge, pp. 268–294.

Freund, P. E. S. and McGuire, M. B. (1991) *Health, Illness and the Social Body: A Critical Sociology.* Englewood Cliffs, New Jersey: Prentice Hall.

Friedman, Milton (1999) Conversation with Milton Friedman. In B. Snowdon and H. R. Vane (eds), *Conversations with Leading Economists: Interpreting Modern Macroeconomics*, Northampton, MA: Edward Elgar, pp. 124–144.

Fujimura, Joan H. (1999) The practices of producing meaning in bioinformatics. In Michael Fortun and Everett Mendelsohn (eds), *The Practices of Human Genetics (Sociology of the Sciences, Volume XXI).* Dordrecht: Kluwer, pp. 49–88.

Fujimura, Joan H. (2003) Future imaginaries: genome scientists as sociocultural entrepreneurs. In Alan Goodman, Deborah Heath and Susan Lindee (eds), *Genetic nature/culture.* Berkeley: University of California Press, pp. 176–199.

Fukuyama, Francis (1993) *The End of History and the Last Man.* Harmondsworth: Penguin.

Fukuyama, Francis (2002) *Our Posthuman Future: Consequences of the Biotechnology Revolution.* New York: Farrar, Straus and Giroux.

Fullbrook, E. (ed.) (2002) *Intersubjectivity in Economics: Agents and Structures.* London: Routledge.

Fuller, Steve (2000) The coming biological challenge to social theory and practice. In John Eldridge, John MacInnes, Sue Scott, Chris Warhurst and Anne Witz (eds), *For Sociology: Legacies and Prospects.* Durham: British Sociological Association, pp. 174–190.

Fuller, Steve (2003) *Interdisciplinarity. The Loss of the Heroic Vision in the Market-place of Ideas.* Online. Available at http://www.interdisciplines.org/ interdisciplin-arity/papers/3/version/original (last accessed 22 November 2006).

Furedi, Frank (2005) *Culture of Fear: Risk-taking and the Morality of Low Expectation.* New York: Continuum International Publishing Group – Academi.

Futuyma, Douglas J. (1983) *Science on Trial: The Case for Evolution.* New York: Pantheon Books.

Gadamer, Hans Georg (1986) *Hermeneutik 1: Wahrheit und Methode – Grundzüge einer philosophischen Hermeneutik.* Tübingen: J. C. B. Mohr.

Galison, Peter (1997) *Image and Logic: A Material Culture of Microphysics.* Chicago: University of Chicago Press.

Galison, Peter and David J. Stump (eds) (1996) *The Disunity of Science: Boundaries, Contexts, and Power.* Stanford: Stanford University Press.

Garnett, R. F. (ed.) (1999) *What Do Economists Know? New Economics of Knowledge.* London: Routledge.

Garreau, Joel (2006) Radical evolution: Heaven or hell? Paper presented at Forum 2006, *Tomorrow's People: The Challenges of Technologies for Life Extension and Enhancement.* Conference organised by the James Martin Institute for Science and Civilization at the University of Oxford, Said Business School, 14–17 March 2006. Conference webcast available at http://www.martininstitute.ox.ac.uk/JMI/Forum2006/Forum+2006+Webcast.htm (last accessed 22 November 2006).

Gee, H. (2000) Futurology: what next? *The Guardian,* 26 June, p. 14.

Gems, David (2003) Is more life always better? The new biology of aging and the meaning of life, *Hastings Center Report* 33 (4): 31–39.

Geron Corporation (1997) *Annual report.* Menlo Park, CA.

Geron Corporation (2003) Form 10-Q for Geron Corporation, *Quarterly Report,* 12 November: 1.

Gibbons, Michael, Limoges, Camille, Nowotny, Helga, Schwartzman, Simon, Scott, Peter and Trow, Martin (1994) *The New Production of Knowledge.* London: Sage.

Giddens, Anthony (1984) *The Constitution of Society: Outline of the Theory of Structuration.* Cambridge: Polity.

Giddens, Anthony (1991) *Modernity and Self-Identity: Self and Society in the Late Modern Age.* Cambridge: Polity.

Gimlin, Debra (2006) The absent body project: cosmetic surgery as a response to bodily dys-appearance. *Sociology,* 40 (4): 699–716.

Glasner, Peter and Harry Rothman (2004) *Splicing Life? The New Genetics and Society.* Aldershot: Ashgate.

Goffman, Erving (1971) *Relations in Public.* Harmondsworth: Penguin.

Goldblatt, David (1996) *Social Theory and the Environment.* Cambridge: Polity.

Goodkind, Daniel (1996) On substituting sex preference strategies in East Asia: does prenatal sex selection reduce postnatal discrimination. *Population and Development Review,* 22: 111–125.

Goodkind, Daniel (1999) Should prenatal sex selection be restricted? Ethical questions and their implications for research and policy. *Population Studies Journal of Demography,* 58 (1): 49–61.

Goodman, Alan H. and Leatherman, Thomas L. (1998) Traversing the chasm between biology and culture: An introduction. In Alan H. Goodman and Thomas L. Leatherman (eds), *Building a New Biocultural Synthesis: Political-Economic Perspectives on Human Biology*. Ann Arbor, Michigan: University of Michigan Press, pp. 3–41.

Gordon, Jon W. (1999) Genetic enhancement in humans. *Science*, 283 (5410): 2023–2024.

Gottweis, Herbet (2005) Governing genomics in the 21st century: between risk and uncertainty. *New Genetics and Society*, 24 (2): 175–193.

Goudsblom, Johan (1992) *Fire and Civilization*. London: Allen Lane.

Grace, Eric S. (1997) *Biotechnology Unzipped: Promises & Realities*. Washington, DC: Joseph Henry Press.

Grant, Valerie (1998) *Maternal Personality, Evolution and the Sex Ratio*. London: Routledge.

Gray, Barbara (1999) The development of global environmental regimes: organizing in the absence of authority. In David L. Cooperrider and Jane E. Dutton (eds), *Organizational Dimensions of Global Change: No Limits to Cooperation*. Thousand Oaks, Calif.: Sage.

Green, Anna and Troup, Kathleen (1999) *The Houses of History: A Critical Reader in Twentieth-century History and Theory*. Manchester: Manchester University Press.

Grosz, Elizabeth (1994) *Volatile Bodies: Toward a Corporeal Feminism*. Indianapolis: Indiana University Press.

Guattari, Felix (1992) Regimes, pathways, subjects. In Jonathan Crary and Sanford Kwinter (eds), *Incorporations*. New York: Zone, pp. 16–37.

Habermas, Jürgen (2003) *The Future of Human Nature*. Oxford: Polity.

Hacking, Ian (1975) *Why does Language Matter to Philosophy?* Cambridge: Cambridge University Press.

Hacking, Ian (1995) *Rewriting the Soul: Multiple Personality and the Science of Memory*. Princeton: Princeton University Press.

Hacking, Ian (1996) The disunities of science. In Peter Galison and David J. Stump (eds), *The Disunity of Science: Boundaries, Contexts, and Power*. Stanford: Stanford University Press, pp. 37–74.

Hacking, Ian (1998) *Mad Travellers: Reflections on the Reality of Transient Mental Illnesses*. Charlottesville: University Press of Virginia.

Hacking, Ian (1999) *The Social Construction of What?* London: Harvard University Press.

Hacking, Ian (2002) Between Michel Foucault and Erving Goffman: Between discourse in the abstract and face-to-face interaction. *Economy and Society*, 33 (3): 277–302.

Haddock, Adrian (2004) Rethinking the 'strong programme' in the sociology of knowledge. *Studies in History and Philosophy of Science*, 35: 19–40.

Halley, Janet (1994) Sexual orientation and the politics of biology: A critique of the argument from immutability. *Stanford Law Review*, 46: 503–568.

Hampshire, Stuart (1971) *Freedom of Mind, and Other Essays by Stuart Hampshire*. Princeton, New Jersey: Princeton University Press.

Hampshire, Stuart (1996) Introduction. In Benedict de Spinoza, *Ethics*, edited and translated by Edwin Curley. Harmondsworh: Penguin.

Hampshire, Stuart (2005) *Spinoza and Spinozism*. Oxford: Clarendon Press.

Hanlon, Gerard (1998) Professionalism as enterprise; service class politics and the redefinition of professionalism. *Sociology*, 32 (1): 43–63.

Harrington, Anne, Rose, Nikolas and Singh, Ilina (2006) Editors' introduction. *BioSocieties*, 1: 1–5.

Hayles, N. Katherine (1999) *How We Became Posthuman: Virtual Bodies in Cybernetics, Literature and Informatics*. Chicago: University of Chicago Press.

Hedgecoe, Adam (2004) *The Politics of Personalised Medicine: Pharmacognetics in the Clinic*. Cambridge: Cambridge University Press.

Heer, David M. (1975) *Society and Population, 2nd edn*. Englewood Cliffs, New Jersey: Prentice-Hall.

Hendry, Chris (2002) Science, industry and the laity: towards a knowledgeable society for biotechnology. *New Genetics and Society*, 21 (2): 177–198.

Henn, Wolfram (2000) Consumerism in prenatal diagnosis: a challenge for ethical guidelines. *Journal of Medical Ethics*, 26 (6): 444–446.

Hochschild, Arlie R. (1983) *The Managed Heart: Commercialization and Human Feeling*, Berkeley: University of California Press.

Hodgson, G. M. (2001) *How Economics Forgot History: The Problem of Historical Specificity in Social Science*. London: Routledge.

Holden, Constance (1993) Failing to cross the biology-culture gap. *Science*, 262: 1641–1642.

Holzenberger Martin, Dupont, Joëlle, Ducos, Bertrand, Leneuve, Patricia, Géloën, Alain, Even, Patrick C., Pascale, Cervera and Le Bouc, Yves (2003) IGF-1 receptor regulates lifespan and resistance to oxidative stress in mice. *Nature*, 421 (6919): 182–187.

Hoppit, Julian (1986) The use and abuse of credit in eighteenth-century England, in Neil McKendrick and R. B.Outhwaite (eds), *Business Life and Public Policy: Essays in Honor of D.C.Coleman*. Cambridge: Cambridge University Press, pp. 64–78.

Horigan, Stephen (1988) *Nature and Culture in Western Discourses*. London: Routledge.

Houghton, John T. (2004) *Global Warming: The Complete Briefing*. Cambridge: Cambridge University Press.

Houghton, John T., Y. Ding, D. J. Griggs, M. Noguer, P. J. van der Linden and D. Xiaosu (2001) *Contribution of Working Group I to the Third Assessment Report of the Intergovernmental Panel on Climate Change (IPCC)*. Cambridge: Cambridge University Press.

House of Commons Select Committee on International Development: Minutes of Evidence (1999) First Supplementary memorandum from Womankind Worldwide: The Declining Sex Ratio in India.

House of Commons Environmental Audit Committee (2003) *Budget 2003 and Aviation: Nineth Report of Session 2002–2003*, HC 672. Norwich: The Stationery Office.

Howell, Signe (1996) Nature in culture or culture in nature? Chewong ideas of 'humans' and other species. In Phillipe Descola and Gisli Palsson (eds), *Nature and Society: Anthropological Perspectives*. London: Routledge, pp. 127–144.

Howson, Alexandra and Inglis, David (2001) The body in sociology: tensions inside and outside sociological thought. *The Sociological Review*, 49 (3): 297–317.

Hughes, James (2004) *Citizen Cyborg: Why Democratic Societies must Respond to the Redesigned Human of the Future*. Cambridge, MA: Westview Press.

Huxley, Alduous (1932) *Brave New World*. London: Chatto.

Ingham, Geoffrey (1999) Capitalism, money and banking: a critique of recent historical sociology. *British Journal of Sociology*, 50 (1): 76–96.

Illich, Ivan (1975) *Medical Nemesis*. London: Calder and Boyars.

Ilyenkov, Evald V. (1977) *Dialetical Logic: Essays in its History and Theory*, trans, H. Campbell Creighton. Moscow: Progress Publishers.

Irwin, Alan (2001) *Sociology and the Environment: A Critical Introduction to Society, Nature and Knowledge*. Cambridge: Polity.

Jablonka, Eva and Lamb, Marion J. (1999) *Epigenetic Inheritance and Evolution: The Lamarckian Dimension*. Oxford: Oxford University Press.

Jacob, François (1976) *The Logic of Life: A History of Heredity*. New York: Vintage Books.

Jacob, Pierre (2003) *A Philosopher's Reflections on his Interactions with a Neuroscientist*. Online. Available at http://www.interdisciplines.org/interdisciplinarity/papers/4/version/original (last accessed 22 November 2006).

Jacob, Pierre and Jeannerod, Marc (2003) *Ways of Seeing: The Scope and Limits of Visual Cognition*. Oxford: Oxford University Press.

Jasanoff, Sheila (2005a) *Designs on Nature: Science and Democracy in Europe and the United States*. Princeton: Princeton University Press.

Jasanoff, Sheila (2005b) In the democracies of DNA: ontological uncertainty and political order in three states. *New Genetics and Society*, 24 (2): 139–155.

Jedlička, Peter (2005) Neuroethics, reductionism and dualism. *Trends in Cognitive Sciences*, 9 (4): 172.

Jenkins, Richard (2002) *Foundations of Sociology: Towards a Better Understanding of the Human World*. Basingstoke: Palgrave Macmillan.

Jha, Alok (2006) Planting trees to save planet is pointless, say ecologists. *The Guardian*, 15 December 2006.

Jonas, Hans (1985). *The Imperative of Responsibility: In Search of an Ethic for the Technological Age*. Chicago: University of Chicago Press.

Kaplan, Jonathan Michael (2000) *The Limits and Lies of Human Genetic research: Dangers for Social Policy*. New York: Routledge.

Karasek, R. and Theorell, T. (1990) *Healthy Work: Stress, Productivity and the Reconstruction of Working Life*, New York: Basic Books.

Karasek, R., Gardell, B. and Lindell, J. (1987) Work and non-work correlates of illness and behaviour in male and female Swedish white-collar workers. *Journal of Occupational Behaviour*, 8: 187–207.

Kass, Leon (2003) *Beyond Therapy: Biotechnology and the Pursuit of Happiness. A report of the President's Council on Bioethics*. New York: Dana Press.

Keller, Evelyn Fox (1991) Language and ideology in evolutionary theory: reading cultural norms into natural law. In James J. Sheehan and Morton Sosna (eds), *The Boundaries of Humanity: Humans, Animals, Machines*. Berkeley: University of California Press.

Keller, Evelyn Fox (1995) *Refiguring life: Metaphors of twentieth century biology*. New York: Columbia University Press.

Keller, Evelyn Fox (2000) *The Century of the Gene*. Cambridge, MA: Harvard University Press.

Keller, Evelyn Fox (2006) What's in a word? Genes, heritable traits and heritability. Paper delivered at the University of Exeter, 13 December 2006.

Kellert, Stephen H. (1993) *In the Wake of Chaos: Unpredictable Order in Dynamical Systems*. London: University of Chicago Press.

Kellogg, Davida E. (1975) *Paleobiology*, 1: 359.

Kelly, Michael P. and Field, David (1994) Comments on the rejection of the bio-medical model in sociological discourse. *Medical Sociology News*, 19 (2): 34–37.

Kelly, Michael P. and Field, David (1996) Medical sociology, chronic illness and the body. *Sociology of Health and Illness*, 18 (2): 241–257.

Kendall, Tim (2006) Can we rely on the evidence base? Case studies from NICE guidelines in mental health. Paper presented to the ESRC *Neuroscience, Identity and Society* seminar, 'Exploring the Meaning of Neurogenetic Reductionism in Science, Culture and the Clinic', University of Nottingham, 19 October 2006. See: http://www. neuroscienceandsociety.org/ (last accessed 22 November 2006).

Kennedy, A. L. (2004) Paradise. *The Independent on Sunday*, 22 August 2004: 24–25.

Kent, Julie, Faulkner, Alex, Geesink, Ingrid and Fitzpatrick, David (2006) Culturing cells, reproducing and regulating the self. *Body & Society*, 12(2): 1–23.

Kenyon Cynthia, Chang, Jean, Gensch, Erin, Rudner, Adam and Tabtiang, Ramon (1993) A C-Elegans mutant that lives twice as long as wild-type. *Nature*, 366 (6454): 461–464.

Kerr, Anne and Cunningham-Burley, Sarah (2000) On ambivalence and risk: Reflexive modernity and the new human genetics. *Sociology*, 34 (2): 283–304.

Kevles, Daniel J. (1992) Out of eugenics: the historical politics of the human genome. In Daniel J, Kevles and Leroy Hood (eds), *The Code of Codes: Scientific and Social Issues in the Human Genome Project*. Cambridge, MA: Harvard University Press.

Kevles, Daniel J. (1995) *In the Name of Eugenics: Genetics and the Uses of Human Heredity*. Cambridge, MA: Harvard University Press.

King, Tony (1999) Against structure: a critique of morphogenetic social theory. *The Sociological Review*, 47 (2): 199–227.

Kingsland, James (2003) I want to live forever (interview with Cynthia Kenyon). *New Scientist*, 180 (2417): 46–50.

Kirman, A. (1989) The intrinsic limit of modern economic theory: the emperor has no clothes. *The Economic Journal*, 99: 126–139.

Knorr Cetina, Karin D. (1996) The care of the self and blind variation: the disunity of two leading sciences. In Peter Galison and David J. Stump (eds), *The Disunity of Science: Boundaries, Contexts, and Power*. Stanford: Stanford University Press, pp. 287–310.

Knorr-Cetina, Karin D. and Mulkay, Michael (eds) (1983) *Science Observed: Perspectives on the Social Study of Science*, London: Sage.

Knorr Cetina, Karin D. (1999) *Epistemic Cultures: How the Sciences Make Knowledge*. London: Harvard University Press.

Koshland, Daniel Jr. (2000) Ethics and safety. In Gregory Stock and John Campbell (eds), *Engineering the Human Germline: An Exploration of the Science and Ethics of Altering the Genes We Pass to Our Children*. Oxford: Oxford University Press, pp. 25–30.

Kramer, Peter (1993) *Listening to Prozac*. New York: Penguin.

Krantz, D. S. and Falconer, J. J. (1997) Measurement of cardiovascular responses. In S. Cohen, R. C. Kessler and L. Underwood Gordon (eds), *Measuring Stress: A Guide for Health and Social Scientists*, New York: Oxford, pp. 193–212.

Kuhn, Thomas S. (1962) *The Structure of Scientific Revolutions*. Chicago: University of Chicago Press.

Kusum (1993) The use of pre-natal diagnosis techniques for sex selection: the Indian scence. *Bioethics*, 7 (2–3): 149–165.

Laclau, Ernesto (1990) *New Reflections on the Revolution of our Time*, London: Verso.

Lash, Scott and Urry, John (1994) *Economies of Sign and Space*. London: Sage.

Latour, Bruno (1987) *Science in Action*. Cambridge: Cambridge University Press.

Latour, Bruno (1988) *The Pasteurization of France*, trans. by Alan Sheridan and John Law. Cambridge, MA: Harvard University Press.

Latour, Bruno (1991) Technology is society made durable. In John Law (ed.), *A Sociology of Monsters? Essays on Power, Technology and Domination* (Sociological Review Monograph 38). London: Routledge.

Latour, Bruno (1999a) For David Bloor . . . and beyond: A reply to David Bloor's 'Anti-Latour'. *Studies in History and Philosophy of Science*, 30 (1): 113–129.

Latour, Bruno (1999b) On recalling ANT. In John Law and John Hassard (eds), *Actor Network Theory and After*. Oxford: Blackwell/The Sociological Review, pp. 15–25.

Law, John (1994) *Organizing Modernity*. Oxford: Blackwell.

Lawson, Tony (1997) *Economics and Reality*. London: Routledge.

Lawson, Tony (2003) *Reorienting Economics*. London: Routledge.

Leather, Suzi (2004) Presentation given at the University of Exeter *Shaping the Future* lecture series, 27 May 2004.

La Bruyère (1890) *The Morals and Manners of the Seventeenth Century, Being the Characters of La Bruyère*, translated by Helen Stott. London: David Stott.

Lazarus, R. S. and Folkman, S. (1984) *Stress, Appraisal and Coping*, Springer: New York.

Le Breton, David (2004) Genetic fundamentalism or the cult of the gene. *Body & Society*, 10 (4): 1–20.

Le Page, Michael (2006) Better than sex. *New Scientist Podcast*, 20 October 2006.

Leder, Drew (1984) Medicine and paradigms of embodiment. *The Journal of Medicine and Philosophy*, 9: 29–43.

Leder, Drew (1990) *The Absent Body*. Chicago: University of Chicago Press.

LeVay, Simon (1991) A difference in hypothalamic structure between heterosexual and homosexual men. *Science*, 253 (5023): 1034–1037.

Levi, L. (1974) Stress, disease and psychosocial stimuli. In A. McLean (ed.), *Occupational Stress*, Springfield, IL: C. C. Thomas.

Levinas, Emmanuel (1994a) *Totality and Infinity: An Essay on Exteriority*, trans. by Alphonso Lingis. Pittsburgh : Duquesne University Press.

Levinas, Emmanuel (1994b) *Beyond the Verse: Talmudic Readings and Lectures*, trans. by Gary D. Mole. London: Athlone Press.

Lewontin, Richard C. (1991) *Biology as Ideology: The Doctrine of DNA*. New York: Harper Perennial.

Leyshon, Andrew and Thrift, Nigel (1997) *Money/Space*. London: Routledge and Kegan Paul.

Li, Shu-Chen (2003) Biocultural orchestration of developmental plasticity across levels: The interplay of biology and culture in shaping the mind and behaviour across the life span. *Psychological Bulletin*, 129 (2): 171–194.

Lipsey, Richard G. (2001) Successes and failures in the transformation of economics. *Journal of Economic Methodology*, 8 (2): 169–201.

Lloyd, Genevieve (1996) *Spinoza and the Ethics*. London: Routledge.

Locker, David (2003) Social determinants of health and disease. In Graham Scambler (ed.), *Sociology as Applied to Medicine, fifth edn*. Edinburgh: Saunders.

Lomborg, Bjørn (2001) *The Skeptical Environmentalist: Measuring the Real State of the World*. Cambridge: Cambridge University Press.

Lovallo, W. R. (1997) *Stress and Health: Biological and Psychological Interactions*, Thousand Oaks, Calif.: Sage.

Lovejoy, Derek (1999) Objectivity, causality and ideology in modern physics. *Science and Society*, 63 (4): 433–458.

Luke, Timothy W. (1998) 'Moving at the speed of life?' A cultural kinematics of telematic times and corporate values. In Scott Lash, Andrew Quick and Richard Roberts (eds), *Time and Value*. Oxford: Blackwell.

Lupton, Deborah (1995) *The Imperative of Health*. London: Sage.

Lutz Catherine A. (1988) *Unnatural emotions: everyday sentiments on a Micronesian atoll and their challenge to western theory*. Chicago: University of Chicago Press.

Lynch, Michael (1993) *Scientific Practice and Ordinary Action: Ethnomethodology and Social Studies of Science*. Cambridge: Cambridge University Press.

Lynch, Michael (2001) The contingencies of social construction. *Economy and Society*, 30 (2): 240–254.

Lyon, Margot (1996) C. Wright Mills meets Prozac: the relevance of 'social emotion' to the sociology of health and illness. In Veronica James and Jonathan Gabe (eds), *Health and the Sociology of Emotions*. Oxford: Blackwell.

MacCormack, Carol (1980) Nature, culture and gender: a critique. In Carol MacCormack and Marilyn Strathern (eds), *Nature, Culture and Gender*. Cambridge: Cambridge University Press.

Macnaghten, Phil and Urry, John (1995) Towards a sociology of nature, *Sociology*, 29: 203–20.

Macnaghten, Phil and Urry, John (1998) *Contesting Natures*, London: Sage.

McGee, Glenn (2000) Parental choices. In Gregory Stock and John Campbell (eds), *Engineering the Human Germline: An Exploration of the Science and Ethics of Altering the Genes We Pass to Our Children*. Oxford: Oxford University Press, pp. 99–101.

McGuigan, Jim (1999) *Modernity and Postmodern Culture*. Buckingham: Open University Press.

McLennan, J. J. (1886) *Studies in Ancient History, Comprising a Reprint of Primitive Marriage*. London: Macmillan.

McNay, Lois (1992) *Foucault and Feminism*. Cambridge: Polity.

Macey, Samuel L. (1994) William Hogarth, 1697–1764. In Samual L. Macey (ed.), *Encyclopedia of Time*. New York: Garland Publishing.

Macy, Joanna (1993) *World as Lover, World as Self*. London: Rider.

Mariotte, Edme (1668) *Nouvelle Découverte Touchant la Veüe* (Extrait d'une lettre de Mariotte á M. Pecquet. Réponse de M. Pecquet à la lettre de Mariotte). Paris.

Marshall, Peter (1992) *Nature's Web: An Exploration of Ecological Thinking*. London: Simon and Schuster.

Martin, Paul (1999) Genes as drugs: The social shaping of gene therapy and the reconstruction of genetic disease. In Peter Conrad and Jonathan Gabe (eds), *Sociological Perspectives on the New Genetics*. Oxford: Blackwell, pp. 15–35.

Marx, Karl (1861–1863) *Marx's Economic Manuscripts of 1861–1863 Part 3 Relative Surplus Value*. Division of Labour and Mechanical Workshop. Tool and Machinery. Available online from: http://www.marxists.org/archive/marx/works/1861/economic/ch35.htm (last accessed 22 November 2006).

Marx, Karl (1973) *Grundrisse*. Harmondsworth: Penguin.

Matheson, Carl and Kirchhoff, Evan (1997). Chaos and literature. *Philosophy and Literature*, 21: 28–45.

Mathews, Freya (1991) *The Ecological Self*. London: Routledge.

Mayr, Ernst (1997) *This is Biology: The Science of the Living World*. Cambridge, MA: The Belknap Press of Harvard University Press.

Mead, George Herbert (1934) *Mind, Self, and Society: From the Standpoint of a Social Behaviorist*. Chicago: University of Chicago Press.

Mellor, Phillip A. and Shilling, Chris (1993) Modernity, self-identity and the sequestration of death. *Sociology*, 27 (3): 411–431.

Meltzoff, A. and Moore, M. (1983) Newborn infants imitate adult facial gestures. *Childhood Development*, 54: 702–709.

Mennell, Stephen (1989) *Norbert Elias: An Introduction*. Oxford: Blackwell.

Merleau-Ponty, Maurice (1962) *Phenomenology of Perception*. London: Routledge and Kegan Paul.

Merleau-Ponty, Maurice (1968) *The Visible and the Invisible*. Evanston, Ill.: Northwestern University Press.

Meyer, John M. (1999) Interpreting nature and politics in the history of western thought: The environmentalist challenge. *Environmental Politics*, 8 (2): 1–23.

Michael, Mike (2000) *Reconnecting Culture, Nature and Technology: From Society to Heterogeneity*. London: Routledge.

Mills, C. Wright (1959) *The Sociological Imagination*. Oxford: Oxford University Press.

Misner, Charles W., Thorne, Kip Stephen and Wheeler, John Archibald (1973) *Gravitation*. San Francisco: Freeman.

Mol, Annemarie and Law, John (1994) Regions, networks and fluids: Anaemia and social topology. *Social Studies of Science*, 24: 641–671.

Moncrieff, Joanna (2006) Drug company advertising. Paper presented at the Institute of Psychiatry, Kings College, London, and Royal Institution Lecture Series, *From bad to worse: The worst ideas on the mind*, Kings College, 18 July 2006.

Monod, Jacques (1972) *Chance and Necessity*. Glasgow: Collins.

Moore, George Edward (1903) *Principia Ethica*. Cambridge: Cambridge University Press.

Muldrew, Craig (1993) Interpreting the market: the ethics of credit and community relations in early modern England. *Social History* 18: 163–183.

Muldrew, Craig (1998) *The Economy of Obligation: The Culture of Credit and Social Relations in Early Modern England*. Basingstoke: Macmillan.

Murakumi, Jessica (2002) Gender and depression: explaining the different rates of depression between men and women. *Perspectives in Psychology*, Spring 2002: 27–34.

Murdoch, Jonathan (2001) Ecologising sociology: actor-network theory, co-construction and the problem of human exemptionalism, *Sociology*, 35 (1): 111–133.

Murphy, Raymond (1994a) *Rationality and Nature: A Sociological Inquiry into a Changing Relationship*, Boulder, Colorado: Westview Press.

Murphy, Raymond (1994b) The sociological construction of science without nature, *Sociology*, 28 (4): 957–974.

Murphy, Raymond (1997) *Sociology and Nature: Social Action in Context*. Colarado: Westview Press.

Needham, Joseph (1956) *Science and Civilisation in China. Volume 2, History of Scientific Thought*, by Joseph Needham with the research assistance of Wang Ling. Cambridge: Cambridge University Press.

Nelkin, Dorothy and Andrews, L. (1999) DNA identification and surveillance creep. In Peter Conrad and Jonathan Gabe (eds), *Sociological Perspectives on the New Genetics*. Oxford: Blackwell.

Nelkin, Dorothy and Lindee, Susan M. (1995) *The DNA Mystique: The Gene as a Cultural Icon*. New York: W.H. Freeman.

Nelkin, Dorothy and Lindee, Susan M. (1999) Good genes and bad genes: DNA in popular culture. In Michael Fortun and Everett Mendelsohn (eds), *The Practices of Human Genetics (Sociology of the Sciences, Volume XXI)*. Dordrecht: Kluwer, pp. 155–168.

Nerlich, Brigitte and Hellsten, Iina (2004) Genomics: shifts in metaphorical landscape between 2000 and 2003. *New Genetics and Society*, 23 (3): 255–268.

Neuhaus, Richard John (1988) The return of eugenics. *Commentary*, April 1988: 1–28.

Neurath, Otto (1987) United science and psychology. In B. McGuiness (ed.), *Unified Science*. Dordrecht: Reidel.

Newton, Tim (1989) Occupational stress and coping with stress: A critique. *Human Relations*, 42: 441–461.

Newton, Tim (1995) *'Managing' Stress: Emotion and Power at Work.* London: Sage.

Newton, Tim (1998) An historical sociology of emotion? In Gillian Bendelow and Simon Williams (eds), *Emotions in Social Life: Social Theories and Contemporary Issues.* London: Sage, pp. 60–80.

Newton, Tim (1999) Power, subjectivity and British industrial and organizational sociology: The relevance of the work of Norbert Elias, *Sociology*, 33 (2): 411–440.

Newton, Tim (2002) Creating the new ecological order? *Academy of Management Review*, 27 (4): 523–540.

Newton, Tim (2003a) Truly embodied sociology: Marrying the social and the biological? *The Sociological Review*, 51 (1): 20–42.

Newton, Tim (2003b) Credit and civilization, *British Journal of Sociology*, 54 (3): 347–371.

Newton, Tim (2003c) Crossing the great divide: time, nature and the social. *Sociology*, 37 (3): 433–457.

Newton, Tim (2004) From freemasons to the employee: organization, history and subjectivity. *Organization Studies*, 2004, 25 (8): 1363–1387.

Newton, Tim (2005) Practical idealism: An Oxymoron? *Journal of Managment Studies*, 42 (4): 869–884.

Nietzsche, Friedrich (1968) *The Will to Power*, trans. by Walter Kaufmann and R. J. Hollingdale. New York: Random House.

Nowotny, Helga (1994) *Time: The Modern and Postmodern Experience.* Cambridge: Polity.

Nowotny, Helga (2001) *The Potential of Transdisciplinarity.* Online. Available at http://www.interdisciplines.org/interdisciplinarity/papers/5/language/en (last accessed 22 November 2006).

Nowotny, Helga, Peter Scott and Michael Gibbons (2001) *Re-thinking Science: Knowledge and the Public in an Age of Uncertainty.* Cambridge: Polity.

Nuñez, Rafael (1999) Reclaiming mind, body and cognition. In Rafael Nuñez and Walter J. Freeman (eds), *Reclaiming Cognition: The Primacy of Action, Intention and Emotion.* Exeter: Imprint Academic.

Obrist, P. A. (1981) *Cardiovascular Physiology: A Perspective*, New York: Plenum.

Odell, Peter R. (2004) *Why Carbon Fuels Will Dominate the 21st Century's Global Energy Economy.* Brentwood: Multi-Science Publishing.

O'Neill, J. (1998) *The Market: Ethics, Knowledge, and Politics.* New York: Routledge.

Orne, Martin Theodore (1962), On the social psychology of the psychological experiment: With particular reference to demand characteristics and their implications. *American Psychologist*, 17: 776–783.

Osteen. M. and Woodmansee, M. (eds) (1999) *The New Economic Criticism.* New York: Routledge.

Outhwaite, William (1987) *New Philosophies of Social Science: Realism, Hermeneutics and Critical Theory.* Basingstoke: Macmillan Education.

Pagán, Sylvia (2004) Just add a chromosome. *New Scientist*, 182 (2452): 10.

Parisi, Luciana (2004) *Abstract Sex: Philosophy, Bio-technology and the Mutations of Desire.* London: Continuum.

Paul, Diane B. (2005) Genetic engineering and eugenics: the uses of history. In Harold W. Baillie and Timothy K. Casey (eds), *Is Human Nature Obsolete? Genetics, Bioengineering and the Future of the Human Condition*. Cambridge, MA: MIT Press, pp. 123–151.

Peng, X. H. and Huang, J. (1999) Chinese traditional medicine and abnormal sex ratio at birth in China. *Journal of Biosocial Science*, 31 (4): 487–503.

Pennebaker, J. W. (1984) Accuracy of symptom perception. In A. Baum *et al.* (eds) *Handbook of Psychology and Health*, New Jersey: Erlbaum.

Perls, Thomas and Dellara, Terry (2003) Genetics of exceptional longevity. *Experimental Gerontology*, 38 (7): 725–730.

Petersen, Alan (1998) The new genetics and the politics of public health. *Critical Public Health*, 8 (1): 59–71.

Petersen, Alan and Bunton, Robin (2002) *The New Genetics and Public Health*. London: Routledge.

Pickering, Andrew (1983) *Constructing Quarks*. Edinburgh: Edinburgh University Press.

Pickering, Andrew (ed.) (1992) *Science as Practice and Culture*. Chicago: University of Chicago Press.

Pinker, Steven (2003) Human nature and its future. Presentation to the President's Council on Bioethics, 6 March 2003, Washington DC. Transcript available at: http://bioethicsprint.bioethics.gov/transcripts/march03/session3.html.

Plumwood, Val (1993) *Feminism and the Mastery of Nature*. London: Routledge.

Poldrack, Russell A. (2000) Imaging brain plasticity: conceptual and methodological issue – A theoretical review. *NeuroImage* 12: 1–13.

Pollock, K. (1988) On the nature of social stress: production of a modern mythology. *Social Science and Medicine*, 26 (3): 381–392.

Prigogine, Ilya (1997) *The End of Certainty: Time, Chaos and the New Laws of Nature*. New York: Free Press.

Rabinow, Paul (1992) Artificiality and enlightenment: from sociobiology to biosociality. In Jonathan Crary and Sanford Kwinter (eds), *Incorporations*. New York: Zone, pp. 234–252.

Rabinow, Paul (1999) *French DNA: Trouble in Purgatory*. Chicago, IL: University of Chicago Press.

Rabinow, Paul (2005) Life sciences: Discontents and consolations. In Harold W. Baillie and Timothy K. Casey (eds), *Is Human Nature Obsolete? Genetics, Bioengineering and the Future of the Human Condition*. Cambridge, MA: MIT Press, pp. 99–121.

Rabinow, Paul and Rose, Nikolas (2006) Biopower today. *BioSocieties*, 1 (2): 195–217.

Raichle, Marcus (2003) Social neuroscience: a role for brain imaging. *Political Psychology*, 24 (4): 759–764.

Ramachandran, Vilayanur S. and Blakeslee, Sandra (1998) *Phantoms in the Brain: Human Nature and the Architecture of the Mind*. London: Fourth Estate.

Rao, Mahendra S. and Mark P. Mattson (2001) Stem cells and aging: Expanding the possibilities, *Mechanisms of Ageing and Development* 122 (7): 713–34.

Rasnick, David (2003) The biotechnology bubble machine. *Nature Biotechnology*, 21 (April): 355–356.

Reenen, John Van (2002) Economic issues for the UK biotechnology sector. *New Genetics and Society*, 21 (2): 109–130.

Rose, Nikolas (2001) The politics of life itself. *Theory, Culture and Society*, 18 (6): 1–30.

Rose, Nikolas (2005) Will biomedicine transform society? The political, economic, social and personal impact of medical advances in the twenty first century. Clifford Barclay Lecture, London School of Economics, 2 February 2005.

Rose, Steven (1997) *Lifelines: Biology, Freedom and Determinism.* Harmondsworth: Penguin.

Rose, Steven (2001) The Biology of the Future and the Future of Biology. *Perspectives in Biology and Medicine,* 44 (4): 473–484.

Rose, Steven, Kamin, Leon J. and Lewontin, Richard C. (1984) *Not in Our Genes.* Harmondsworth: Penguin.

Ruane, Joseph (2003) Structure and conjuncture in the contemporary transition: theorising change and continuity. Paper presented to the Historical Sociology stream of the European Sociological Association Conference, Murcia, September 2003 (Joseph Ruane, University College, Cork: j.ruane@ucc.ie).

Sagoff, Mark (2005) Nature and human nature. In Harold W. Baillie and Timothy K. Casey (eds), *Is Human Nature Obsolete? Genetics, Bioengineering and the Future of the Human Condition.* Cambridge, MA: MIT Press, pp. 67–98.

Salter, Brian, Cooper, Melinda and Dickins, Amanda (2006) China and the global stem cell bioeconomy: an emerging political strategy? *Future Medicine,* 1 (5): 671–683.

Sahlins, Marshall D. (1972) *Stone Age Economics,* Chicago: Aldine-Atherton.

Sapolsky, R. M. (1982) The endocrine stress response and social status in the wild baboon. *Hormones and Behavior,* 1: 279–292.

Sapolsky, R. M. (1992) Endocrinology alfresco: Psychoendocrine studies of wild baboons. *Recent Progress in Hormone Research,* 48: 437–468.

Sayer, Andrew (1984) *Method in Social Science: A Realist Approach.* London: Hutchinson.

Sayer, Andrew (1997) Essentialism, social constructionism, and beyond. *Sociological Review,* 45 (3): 453–487.

Sayer, Andrew (1999) Long live postdisciplinary studies! Sociology and the curse of disciplinaryparochialism/imperialism. Paper presented to the British Sociological Association Conference, April 1999, Glasgow, UK.

Schneider, David M. (1972) What is kinship all about? In Priscilla Reining (ed.), *Kinship Studies in the Morgan Centennial Year.* Washington, DC.: The Anthropological Society of Washington, pp. 32–63.

Schneider, David M. (1984) *A Critique of the Study of Kinship.* Ann Arbor: University of Michigan Press.

Schroeder, D. H. and Costa, P. T., (1984) Influence of life event stress on physical illness: Substantive effects or methodological flaws? *Journal of Personality and Social Psychology,* 46: 853–863.

Schwartz, G. E. (1982) Testing the biopsychosocial model: The ultimate challenge facing behavioral medicine? *Journal of Consulting and Clinical Psychology,* 50 (6): 1040–1053.

Scruton, Roger (2002) *Spinoza: A Very Short Introduction.* Oxford: Oxford University Press.

Shakespeare, Tom (1998) Choices and rights: eugenics, genetics and disability equality. *Disability and Society,* 13 (5): 665–681.

Shaw, Mary, Dorling, Daniel and Mitchell, Richard (2002) *Health, Place and Society.* Harlow: Prentice Hall.

Shaw, Mary, Dorling, Daniel, Gordon, David and Davey Smith, George (1999) *The Widening Gap: Health Inequalities and Policy in Britain.* Bristol: The Policy Press.

Shelley, Mary Wollstonecaft (1831) *Frankenstein.* London: Colburn & Bentley.

Shilling, Chris (1993/2003) *The Body and Social Theory, 1st/2nd edn.* London: Sage.

Sibeon, Roger (1999) Anti-reductionist sociology. *Sociology,* 33 (2): 317–334.

Simmel, Georg (1990) *The Philosophy of Money, 2nd edn.* London: Routledge.

Silver, Lee M. (1997) *Remaking Eden: How Genetic Engineering and Cloning will Transform the American Family.* New York: Avon Books.

Slater, Don and Tonkiss, Fran (2001) *Market Society: Markets and Modern Social Theory.* Cambridge: Polity.

Slimp, Jefferson, Hart, Benjamin and Goy, Robert (1978) Heterosexual, autosexual and social behavior of adult male rhesus monkeys with medial preoptic-anterior hypothalamus lesions. *Brain Research,* 142: 105–122.

Smith, Dennis (2000) *Norbert Elias and Modern Social Theory.* London: Sage.

Smith, Roger (2005) Does reflexivity separate the human sciences from the natural sciences? *History of the Human Sciences,* 18 (4): 1–25.

Soper, Kate (1995) *What is Nature? Culture, Politics and the Non-Human.* Oxford: Blackwell.

Sorokin, Pitirim A. and Merton, Robert K. (1937) Social time: A methodological and functional analysis, *American Journal of Sociology,* 42 (5): 615–629.

Spector, Malcolm and Kitsuse, John I. (1987) *Constructing Social Problems.* New York: Aldine de Gruyter.

Spinoza, Baruch/Benedict de (1982) *The Ethics and Selected Letters,* edited by Seymour Feldman and translated by Samuel Shirley. Indianapolis: Hackett.

Spinoza, Baruch/Benedict de (1996) *Ethics,* edited and translated by Edwin Curley with an Introduction by Stuart Hampshire. Harmondsworth: Penguin.

Stafford, Barbara (1991) *Body Criticism: Imaging the Unseen in Enlightenment Art and Medicine.* Cambridge, MA: MIT Press.

Stearn, P. N. (1994) *American Cool: Constructing a Twentieth-Century Emotional Style.* New York: New York University Press.

Steinberg, Deborah Lynn (1997) *Bodies in Glass: Genetics, Eugenics, Embryo Ethics.* Manchester: Manchester University Press.

Stephen, E. H. (2000) Demographic implications of reproductive technologies. *Population Research and Policy Review,* 19 (4): 301–315.

Stock, Gregory (2002) *Re-designing Humans: Our Inevitable Genetic Future.* Boston: Houghton Mifflin.

Strathern, Marilyn (1980) No nature, no culture: the Hagen case. In Carol MacCormack and Marilyn Strathern (eds), *Nature, Culture and Gender.* Cambridge: Cambridge University Press.

Strathern, Marilyn (1992) *After Nature: English Kinship in the Late Twentieth Century.* Cambridge: Cambridge University Press.

Strohman, Richard (2000) Genetic determinism as a failing paradigm in biology and medicine: implications for health and wellness. In Margaret Schneider Jammer and Daniel Stokols (eds), *Promoting Human Wellness: New Frontiers for Research, Practice and Policy.* Berkeley, CA: University of California Press, pp. 99–130.

Stump, David J. (1996a) Afterword: New directions in the philosophy of science studies. In Peter Galison and David J. Stump (eds), *The Disunity of Science: Boundaries, Contexts, and Power.* Stanford: Stanford University Press, pp. 443–450.

Stump, David J. (1996b) From epistemology and metaphysics to concrete connections. In Peter Galison and David J. Stump (eds), *The Disunity of Science: Boundaries, Contexts, and Power.* Stanford: Stanford University Press, pp. 255–286.

Sudha, S. and Rajan, S. Irudaya (1999) Female demographic disadvantage in India, 1981–1991: Sex selective abortions and female infanticide. *Development and Change,* 30 (3): 585–618.

Sullivan, Terry (2004) 'Genes – just how causally important are they?' Paper delivered at an *Egenis* seminar (ESRC Centre for Genomics in Society), University of Exeter, 8 June 2004.

Sutton, Philip W. (2004) *Nature, Environment and Society*. Basingstoke: Palgrave Macmillan.

Taussig, Michael (1980) Reification and the consciousness of the patient. *Social Science and Medicine*, 14B: 3–13.

Taussig, Karen-Sue, Rapp, Rayna and Heath, Deborah (2003) Flexible eugenics: Technologies of the self in the age of genetics. In Alan Goodman, Deborah Heath and Susan Lindee (eds), *Genetic Nature/Culture*. Berkeley: University of California Press, pp. 58–76.

Terry, Jennifer (2000) 'Unnatural acts' in nature: The scientific fascination with queer animals. *GLQ: A Journal of Lesbian and Gay Studies*, 6 (2): 151–193.

Thomas, Sandy (2000) Thoughts on the ethics of germline engineering. In Gregory Stock and John Campbell (eds), *Engineering the Human Germline: An Exploration of the Science and Ethics of Altering the Genes we Pass to our Children*. Oxford: Oxford University Press, pp. 101–104.

Thrift, Nigel (1999) The place of complexity. *Theory, Culture and Society*, 16 (3): 31–69.

Thrift, Nigel (2001) Still life in nearly present time: the object of nature. In Phil Macnaghten and John Urry (eds), *Bodies of Nature*. London: Sage, pp. 35–57.

Townsend, P and Davidson, N. (1980) *Inequalities in Health: The Black Report*. Harmondsworth: Penguin.

Travis, John (2003) Old worms, new aging genes. *Science News*, 164 (5): 75–78.

Tucker, Robert C. (ed.) (1978) *The Marx-Engels reader, 2nd edn*. New York: Norton.

Turner, Bryan S. (1991) Recent developments in the theory of the body. In Mike Featherstone, Mike Hepworth and Bryan S. Turner (eds), *The Body: Social Process and Cultural Theory*. London: Sage.

Turner, Bryan S. (2003) Biology, vulnerability and politics. In Simon Williams, Lynda Birke and Gillian Bendelow (eds), *Debating Biology: Sociological Reflections on Health, Medicine and Society*. London: Routledge, pp. 271–283.

Turner, Bryan S. and Rojek, Chris (2001) *Society and Culture: Principles of Scarcity and Solidarity*. London: Sage.

Urry, John (2000) *Sociology Beyond Societies: Mobilities for the Twenty-First Century*. London: Routledge.

Vanberg, V. J. (1994) *Rules and Choice in Economics*. London: Routledge.

Viner, R. (1999) Putting stress into life: Hans Selye and the making of stress theory. *Social Studies of Science*, 29 (3): 391–410.

Virilio, Paul (1986) *Speed and Politics*. New York: Semiotext(e).

Virilio, Paul (1991) *The Lost Dimension*. New York: Semiotext(e).

Wadman, Meredith (19 February 2001) So you want a girl? A new technology lets parents order up the sex of their child. It's poised to become big business–and a big ethical dilemma. *Fortune*, 143 (4): 174–175. Website address: http://money.cnn.com/magazines/fortune/fortune_archive/2001/02/19/296875/index.htm.

Wagner, Andreas (1999) Causality in complex systems. *Biology and Philosophy*, 14 (1): 83–101.

Waldby, Catherine (2001) Code unknown: histories of the gene. *Social Studies of Science*, 31 (5): 779–791.

Waldby, Catherine and Mitchell, Robert (2006) *Tissue Economics: Blood, Organs and Cell Lines in Late Capitalism*. Durham: Duke University Press.

Wall, T. D., Jackson, P. R., Mullarkey, S. and Parker, S. K. (1996) The demands-control model of job strain: A more specific test. *Journal of Occupational and Organizational Psychology*, 69: 153–166.

War on Want (2006) *Fashion Victims: The True Cost of Cheap Clothes at Primark, Asda and Tesco*. London: War on Want. Online. Available at http://www.waronwant.org/Fashion+Victims+13593.twl (accessed 11 December 2006).

Warr, P. B. (1990) Decision latitude, job demands and employee well-being. *Work and Stress*, 4 (4): 285–294.

Washburn, Sherwood L. (1960) Tools and human evolution. *Scientific American*, 203 (3): 63–75.

Watson, James (2000) Contribution to 'A Panel Discussion'. In Gregory Stock and J. Campbell (eds), *Engineering the Human Germline: An Exploration of the Science and Ethics of Altering the Genes We pass to Our Children*. Oxford: Oxford University Press, pp. 73–95.

Webster, Andrew (2005) Social science and a post-genomic future: alternative readings of genomic agency. *New Genetics and Society*, 24 (2): 227–238.

Wertz, Dorothy C. and Fletcher, John C. (1998) Ethical and social issues in prenatal sex selection: a survey of geneticists in 37 nations. *Social Science and Medicine*, 46 (2): 255–273.

West, Stuart A. and Sheldon, Ben C. (2002) Constraints in the evolution of sex ratio adjustment. *Science*, 295: 1685–1688.

Wetherell, Margaret and Potter, Jonathan (1992) *Mapping the Language of Racism; Discourse and the Legitimation of Exploitation*. Hemel Hempstead: Harvester Wheatsheaf.

Whitehead, M. (1988) *The Health Divide*. Harmondsworth: Penguin.

Whitley, Richard (1982) The establishment and structure of the sciences as reputational organizations. In Norbert Elias, Herminio Martins, and Richard Whitley (eds), *Scientific Establishments and Hierarchies*. Dordrecht: Reidel, pp. 313–357.

Whitley, Richard (2000) *The Intellectual and Social Organization of the Sciences, 2nd edn.* New York: Oxford University Press.

Wilhelmsen, Ingvard (2000) Brain-gut axis as an example of the bio-psycho-social model. *Gut*, 47 (IV): 5–7.

Wilkinson, Richard G. (1996) *Unhealthy Societies: The Afflictions of Inequality*. London: Routledge.

Wilkinson, Richard G. (1997a) Socio-economic determinants of health. Health inequalities: relative or absolute material standards? *British Medical Journal*, 314: 591.

Wilkinson, Richard G. (1997b) Comment: income inequality and social cohesion. *American Journal of Public Health*, 89 (9): 1504–1506.

Wilkinson, Richard G. (2000a) *Mind the Gap: Hierarchies, Health and Human Evolution*, London: Weidenfeld and Nicolson.

Wilkinson, Richard G. (2000b) Deeper than 'neoliberalism': a reply to David Coburn, *Social Science and Medicine*, 51: 997–1000.

Williams, Simon (1996) The vicissitudes of embodiment across the chronic illness trajectory. *Body and Society*, 2 (2): 23–47.

Williams, Simon (1998) 'Capitalising' on emotions? Rethinking the inequalities in health debate. *Sociology*, 32 (1): 121–139.

Williams, Simon (1999) Is anybody there? Critical realism, chronic illness, and the disability debate. *Sociology of Health and Illness*, 21 (6): 797–819.

Williams, Simon (2001) *Emotions and Social Theory*. London: Sage.

Williams, Simon (2003a) *Medicine and the Body*. London: Sage.

Williams, Simon (2003b) Marrying the social and the biological? A rejoinder to Newton. *The Sociological Review*, 51 (4): 550–561.

Williams, Simon and Bendelow, Gillian (1998) *The Lived Body: Sociological Themes, Embodied Issues*. London: Routledge.

Williams, Simon and Bendelow, Gillian (2003) Childhood bodies: Constructionism and beyond. In Simon Williams, Lynda Birke and Gillian Bendelow (eds), *Debating Biology: Sociological Reflections on Health, Medicine and Society*, London: Routledge, pp. 133–144.

Willmott, Hugh (2000) Death. So what? Sociology, sequestration and emancipation. *The Sociological Review*, 48 (4): 649–665.

Wilson, Elizabeth A. (2004) *Psychosomatic: Feminism and the Neurological Body*. Durham: Duke University Press.

Winner, Langdon (2005) Resistance is futile: the Posthuman condition and its advocates. In Harold W. Baillie and Timothy K. Casey (eds), *Is Human Nature Obsolete? Genetics, Bioengineering and the Future of the Human Condition*. Cambridge, MA: MIT Press, pp. 385–411.

Winter, Stefan F. (2000) Our societal obligation for keeping human nature untouched In Gregory Stock and John Campbell (eds), *Engineering the Human Germline: An Exploration of the Science and Ethics of Altering the Genes we Pass to our Children*. Oxford: Oxford University Press. pp. 113–116.

Woolgar, Steve (1983) Irony in the social study of science. In Karin D. Knorr-Cetina and Michael Mulkay (eds), *Science Observed: Perspectives on the Social Study of Science*. London: Sage, pp. 239–266.

World Transhumanist Association (WTA) (2006) http://transhumanism.org/index.php/WTA/declaration/.

Wouters, Cas (1989) The sociology of emotions and flight attendants: Hochschild's. *Managed Heart. Theory, Culture and Society*, 6: 95–123.

Wray, K. Brad (2005) Does science have a moving target? *American Philosophical Quarterly*, 42 (1): 47–58.

Wyndham, John (1960) (pseudonym of John Benyon Harris) *Trouble with Lichen*. London: Michael Joseph.

Yanagisako, Sylvia J. and Delaney, Carol (1995) *Naturalizing Power: Essays in Feminist Cultural Analysis*. New York: Routledge.

Yearley, Steven (1996) *Sociology, Environmentalism, Globalization: Reinventing the Globe*. London: Sage.

Žižek, Slavoj (2004) *Organs Without Bodies: On Deleuze and Consequences*. New York: Routledge.

Zola, Irving K. (1972) Medicine as an institution of social control. *Sociological Review*, 20: 487–503.

AUTHOR INDEX

SUBJECT INDEX